CLASSIC
ROCK
STARS

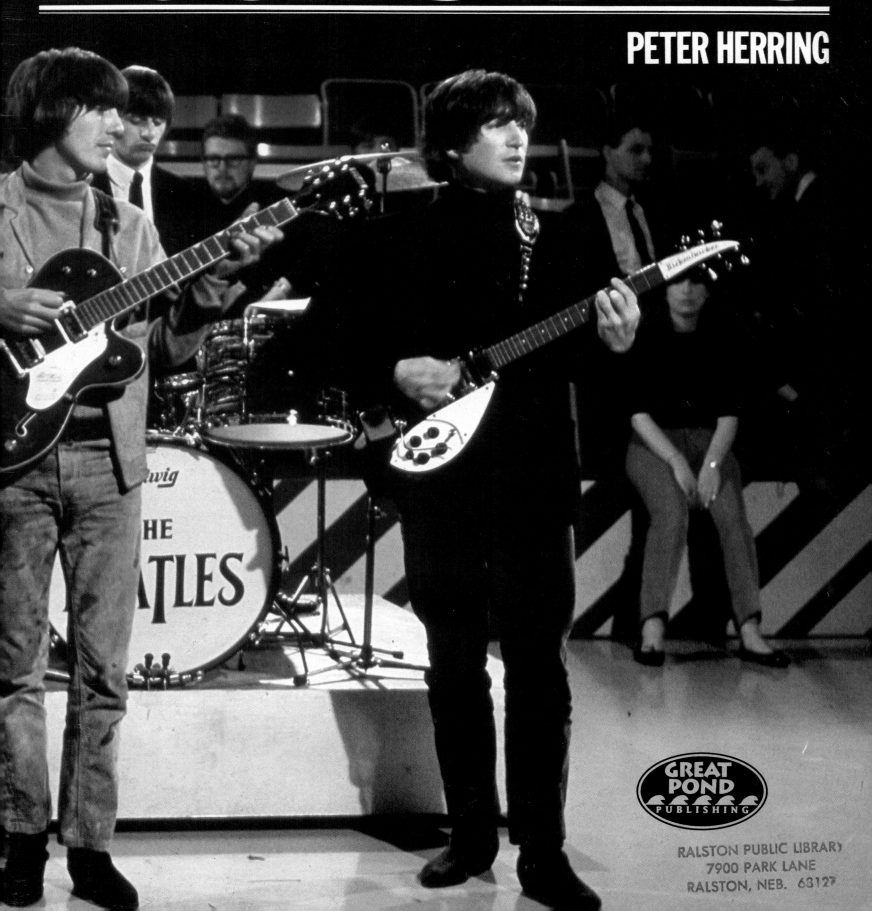

CLASSIC
ROCK STARS

PETER HERRING

GREAT POND PUBLISHING

CONTENTS

SUPERSTARS

SUPERGROUPS

OFF BEAT

This edition published in 1992 by NDM Publications, Inc. Great Pond Publishing, Ltd. is an imprint of NDM Publications, Inc.
30 Inwood Road
Rocky Hill, CT 06067

Produced by Brompton Books Corp.
15 Sherwood Place
Greenwich, CT 06830

Copyright © 1984 Brompton Books Corp.

ISBN 1-56657-000-0

Printed in Hong Kong
Reprinted 1992

BLACK MAGIC

ROOTS

GREAT BRITISH

SUPERSTARS

ELVIS PRESLEY

The arithmetic speaks for itself: by the time of Elvis' death in 1977, over 480 million copies of his records had been sold. He still accounts for the largest number of gold record awards (38) and in terms of No 1 hits is equalled only by The Beatles. Figures alone, however, do not convey the full extent of Presley's influence. Elvis Aaron Presley was rock's biggest single preformer, its undisputed king. In the early fifties the new music of rock and roll needed a dynamic, youthful figurehead but Presley never anticipated himself as that person. In summer 1953 he became a truck driver. A year later, he was becoming a celebrity in his own town. He had also become determined to use his talents to full effect: an effect, however, that he never seemed quite to comprehend.

So if Presley himself didn't see his own potential, then who did? Credit for that must go to Sam Phillips whose Sun Records studio in Memphis was set up mainly to record the music of local negro musicians. The Presley family had moved to Memphis in 1948, from East Tupelo, Mississippi, where Elvis was born on 8 January 1935. It was an intensely religious family and no doubt the boy's first singing experience came in church. He would have heard the gospel music of the local black population too, and, listening to the radio in the cab of his father's truck, their brand of rhythm and blues.

Indirectly, his devotion to his parents gave him his break. He went to the Sun studio to make a private recording as a birthday present for his mother – the Inkspots' *My Happiness*. A secretary (Marion Keisler) noted the performance and his name, but nothing happened for a year. Then Phillips called him in for some sessions with guitarist, Scotty Moore and bassist, Bill Black. At first they worked, unproductively, on country material, then Phillips suggested a stab at some blues numbers by singer/songwriter Arthur 'Big Boy' Crudup. Legend has it that they jammed *That's Alright Mama* during a break between sessions; Phillips heard it and told them to record it. For years, Sam Phillips had searched for a 'white boy who could sing like a negro,' convinced that such a combination just had to succeed. Little did he know just how successful.

Radio made the record a local hit, and Presley made his professional debut to an enthusiastic audience at Overton Park, Memphis, on 30 July 1954. The energy, fiery aggression

Above: The suggestive swivel of the hips that brought criticism, notoriety and a nickname that became known the world over.
Left: An ecstatic welcome from his hometown audience in Tupelo as Elvis plays the state fair in late summer 1956.
Opposite: The truck-driver's son became the King of Rock and Roll – and seemed as surprised as anyone by his success.
Previous pages: Jimi Hendrix on stage.

and sense of rhythm of the nineteen-year old were impressive. Backed by the accomplished Moore and Black, he toured the Southern states as *The Hillbilly Cat* and two further singles became regional successes. During this period he was seen by country-music promoter-cum-carnival barker, self-styled 'Colonel' Tom Parker, who was destined to have the greatest influence of anyone on Presley's future career.

Dewey Phillips (Presley's manager prior to Tom Parker) engineered Presley's first appearance on radio in the show *Louisana Hayride* in March 1955, and in July a version of *Baby, Let's Play House* made the American charts in a small way. Minor hits in the country charts followed.

By now, major record companies had noticed Presley and there was considerable competition for him. Eventually Atlantic bowed out as the stakes grew higher and left the field to RCA. In 1955 they paid Sam Phillips $20,000 for the contract, Hill and Range $15,000 for the publishing rights, and $5000 to Presley as an advance – then a staggering sum for a relative unknown.

The first session for RCA took place in Nashville, where Moore and Black were augmented

ELVIS PRESLEY

by Chet Atkins (guitar), D J Fontana (drums) and Floyd Crammer (piano). After his coast-to-coast TV appearance on *Jackie Gleason's Stage Show*, hosted by Tommy and Jimmy Dorsey, in early 1956, the success of *Heartbreak Hotel* was phenomenal: No 1 in the USA (for seven weeks) and No 2 in Britain. It was also the beginning of controversy over Presley's stage act. Parker capitalized on criticism of the gyrating hip movements as suggestive and liable to corrupt young innocents. But Presley was exactly what those 'young innocents' wanted: this was music the like of which they'd never heard before, and it was for *them*. Presley had single-handedly created a generation gap.

The hits just kept coming, and the following gathered momentum. *Don't Be Cruel, Hound Dog, All Shook Up, Blue Suede Shoes* and the like added up to six gold discs and seventeen US chart entries within a year. At $25,000, RCA had got themselves a bargain!

The business was still unsure how to treat Presley – they couldn't ignore him, but he was unlike anything they'd seen before; even Bill Haley hadn't had this sort of impact. National TV, of course, was the showcase any aspiring performer needed and Presley duly made appearances on programs such as *The Ed Sullivan Show*.

The first phase of his development was drawing to a close. Toward the end of the year, he returned triumphantly to Sun Studios, where Phillips was furthering the careers of Johnny Cash, Carl Perkins and Jerry Lee Lewis. With the last two, Presley made some impromptu recordings which remained stored away for nearly 25 years. When finally released, they showed the corrupting sex symbol and his friends to have put together a selection of sentimental religious numbers, which no one could object to.

The next obvious step was into films. The first was due to be a Western, titled *The Reno Brothers*. After hearing Elvis sing the main theme, *Love Me Tender*, on TV, the promoters wisely amended it to that. *Loving You* followed in 1957, together with the best of all his movies, *Jailhouse Rock* (1957) and *King Creole* (1958). Both, of course, produced singles that have become rock classics. The dance sequence over the title track of *Jailhouse Rock* is one of the best things Elvis ever commited to celluloid.

John Lennon once said, 'Elvis died the day he went into the army,' and, although Parker had ensured plenty of material was in the can to cover the two-year absence, there is a lot of truth in that remark. The Elvis that re-emerged in 1960 was an unobjectionable family entertainer. The look was tamed, the music was tamed, the out-and-out rock numbers were tempered by sugary ballads and simpering love-songs. The raw, biting sound of *Hound Dog* was replaced by lush orchestration and big production and, although some of the songs were among his best – *It's Now or Never, Are You Lonesome Tonight* – some were dire. The former number was to become the biggest single hit of his career, selling over ten million copies worldwide and spending eight weeks at No 1 in the UK charts.

He surrounded himself with the 'Memphis Mafia,' a group of associates who served to insulate him from the outside world right up to his death. On 12 May 1960 Presley gave his last American TV show for eight years, Frank Sinatra's *Welcome Home Elvis* for ABC. He received $125,000 for a six-minute spot. A

succession of largely forgetable films followed (although *Flaming Star* is an exception) and equally unmemorable soundtrack albums. However, he retained his knack for making best-selling singles, of which *(Marie's the Name of) His Latest Flame, Good Luck Charm, Return to Sender, Burning Love* and the Memphis-recorded, *Suspicious Minds*, are among the best.

It wasn't until 1968 that Parker decided absence wasn't making the heart grow fonder and, capitalizing on a revival of interest in fifties rock and roll, reintroduced Presley with a recorded TV special. It was greeted enthusiastically and seemed to fire Elvis as well, for the subsequent album, *From Elvis in Memphis*, is one of his finest. It includes one of the few 'social conscience' songs he ever recorded – *In the Ghetto*. It became a welcome, if unexpected, hit.

More live appearances followed, many on the lucrative Las Vegas cabaret circuit, but it was the fans from the fifties who were coming to see him and buying the albums. In 1973 he made another TV special, *Aloha from Hawaii*, which was beamed to 40 countries by satellite, and the sound track became the last major hit album of his career. Two fascinating documentaries were made about him, but then came an event which was to end abruptly any hope of a lasting comeback.

His six-year marriage to Priscilla Beaulieu came to an end in October 1973 and the effect on Presley was rapid and disastrous. His live performances deteriorated; so did his health. There were weight problems, rumors of over-indulgence in many things, and he required extensive hospital treatment five times in as many years. It was a grotesque figure that continued to take the stage in Las Vegas, and even the most loyal fans were forced to admit that his

Above: Elvis acknowledging the applause during a concert in the seventies.
Right: 'Go cat, go . . .' Elvis, electrifying on stage.

recordings had hit an all-time low. Yet, with bitter irony, he died with one of his best up-tempo numbers of recent years, *Way Down*, riding high in the American and British charts.

He collapsed at his Memphis mansion, Gracelands, and died at the Memphis Baptist Hospital on 16 August 1977. The verdict was heart failure brought on by unspecified contributory factors. He was 42.

Fans came to mourn in their thousands, shocked and disbelieving. Sales of his records rocketed: long-forgotten numbers became chart hits again. He even had a posthumous hit with Sinatra's swan-song, *My Way*. Just about anything with Elvis Presley stamped upon it would sell. It was just like the old days.

Despite being derivative, Presley was the first, the beginning, and his presence, if not his music, continued to dominate rock and roll for the next twenty years. He became the focus for teenagers everywhere, and many stuck with him through good and bad until his tragic end. But maybe for them, Elvis Presley has never died, and will never die.

RECOMMENDED RECORDINGS

Elvis Presley
Elvis
Loving You
King Creole
From Elvis in Memphis
Aloha from Hawaii
Elvis' Golden Records Vols 1, 2, 3, and 4
Worldwide 50 Gold Award Hits Vols 1, 2
The Elvis Presley Sun Collection

MICHAEL JACKSON

*P*opular music has produced its fair quota of child stars, most long-forgotten once adolescence arrived. Few have possessed the depth of talent, the staying power, or the personal maturity to progress further. Stevie Wonder, of course, was one exception, and his fellow black American, Michael Jackson has proved to be another.

With four of his brothers from Gary, Indiana, Michael started out as the dynamic nine-year-old lead singer of The Jackson Five, often being described as a diminutive James Brown! After five highly successful years in that role, during which the group gathered a vast teeny following, Michael embarked on a parallel solo career in 1971 which has subsequently eclipsed even the achievements of the Five; a succession of hit singles and high quality albums have earned him a reputed $40 million. His album Thriller sold 23 million copies. In 1984 he collected eight Grammy awards.

Comparisons with the career of Stevie Wonder are inevitable: not only are the two's vocal and production styles similar, but both were to be the last superstar acts to emerge from the Motown hit factory. It's awe-inspiring to consider just how much great talent has been nurtured under Motown's guidance; at its peak the company became the largest black-owned business in the United States. Its list of hit records remains unmatched in rock music, and the Motown magic continues with the enduring popularity of Diana Ross, Stevie Wonder, Marvin Gaye and, of course, the young pretender to the throne, Michael Jackson, even though all have now parted from the all-embracing influence of Motown's founder, Berry Gordy Jr.

It was Joe Jackson, one-time guitarist with soul group The Falcons, who encouraged each of his children to become proficient players of at least one musical instrument. The tradition ran in the family; their mother was a fine clarinetist.

There were nine children in all (six boys and three girls) and it was the second-eldest of the boys, thirteen-year-old Tito, who in 1966, encouraged his brothers to form a group. Michael, born in August 1958, became the energetic and exuberant lead singer. They gigged in the Chicago area, using mainly Temptations and Smokey Robinson material, and proceeded to win a number of local talent contests. Legend

has it that Diana Ross discovered the group at one of those concerts and urged Berry Gordy to sign them. True or not, he did spot their potential and their first single release early in 1970 confirmed the accuracy of his judgment. *I Want You Back*, with a scorching vocal from Michael and some of the tightest and toughest instrumental playing ever heard on a soul record, began a sequence of four million-selling American No 1 hit singles that year (and four British top-ten entries): *ABC, The Love You Save* and *I'll Be There* (which sold four million). They were immediately famous worldwide and they quickly earned a fanatical following among teenage audiences everywhere.

It led them to being seen, disparagingly, as black American's answer to the Osmonds, but from the start it was obvious that the Jackson Five had more going for them in terms of sheer talent and potential. Their stage act was superb and their colorful costumes and dance routines exciting. The Diana Ross connection continued

Above: Sweet sixteen, in 1974.
Right: Randy, Tito, Jackie, Michael and Marlon.
Overleaf, both: Michael, stunning on stage.

with the album *Diana Ross Presents the Jackson Five* and an appearance on her 1971 US TV spectacular. The same year saw American No 2 hits with *Mama's Pearl* and *Never Can Say Goodbye* (curiously, both failed to make the UK top twenty) and the start of Michael's solo career with *Got To Be There* (US No 4, UK No 5).

He bettered that in 1972 with *Rockin' Robin* (US No 2, UK No 3), the Bill Withers' classic, *Ain't No Sunshine* (UK No 8) and his first solo American No 1, *Ben*. This theme song from the film of the same name was a gentle ballad that contrasted strongly with the Jacksons' usual up-tempo style, and indicated for the first time how Michael's career would develop quite differently from his brothers. It could also be seen in his duet single with Diana Ross *Ease Down The Road*.

The Jackson Five, by now a group with an across-the-board, all-ages appeal (they had even hosted a cartoon series about their lives) had to settle for four lesser successes in 1972, and only one British chart entry, a No 7 with *Lookin' Through The Windows* (also the title of that year's album release). Their success rate after that was variable, although *Doctor My Eyes* gave them another UK No 9 in 1973 and *Dancing Machine* a US No 2 in 1974. Some of their album tracks, such as 1973's *Get It Together* and 1975's *Forever Came Today*, were outstanding, but the spotlight increasingly fell on Michael as a solo performer. He notched six high-selling albums with Motown between 1972-76, including *Ben* and *Got To Be There*, at which point the brothers were offered a multi-million-dollar contract by the Epic label and thus ended their association with Motown. Michael's last work for Motown was on their ambitious but unsuccessful 'black remake' of *The Wizard of Oz*. Although Michael (and Diana Ross) were praised for their parts in the movie, *The Wiz* has never recouped the $23 million which Motown invested in an effort to broaden the scope of the label's activities.

Also in 1976, 21-year-old Jermaine Jackson left the group after marrying Berry Gordy's daughter and later pursued as active, if less lucrative, a solo career as his younger brother, releasing four albums between 1980-82. Adding fourteen-year-old brother Randy to the line-up, the group renamed themselves The Jacksons, and undertook their first UK tour for five years in 1976. They enjoyed 1977 hits with *Enjoy Yourself* (US No 6) and a British No 1 with *Show You the Way To Go*.

Their first album on Epic, simply titled *The Jacksons* achieved gold status and they attained their highest album chart placing to date in 1978 with the excellent *Destiny*, a self-produced LP that employed some first-ranking session men. Capitalizing on the disco boom, *Shake Your Body (Down to the Ground)* became a dance favorite and hit single in 1979, reaching No 7 in the UK and No 4 in Britain.

It was during this period that Michael's personal popularity and success began to outstrip that of the group. *Don't Stop Till You Get Enough* gave him a US No 1 and UK No 3 and was followed by the sensational *Off The Wall* album. Produced by the great Quincy Jones, whom he'd met while working on *The Wiz*, the title track gave him another hit single (US No 10, UK No 7) while *Rock With You* went to the top in America. The beautiful Tom Bahler ballad, *She's Out Of My Life* made No 3 in Britain, but strangely only No 10 in the US. However, these fine songs gave him no less than three US top-ten entries there during one week in 1979.

Off The Wall also employed the songwriting skills of ex-Heatwave keyboardist Rod Temperton, Paul McCartney (*Girlfriend* – first of a number of collaborations with Michael) and Stevie Wonder (*I Can't Help It*). This faultless album was reputed to be the biggest-seller of all time in black music, and the Jacksons' 1981 LP, *Triumph*, couldn't match it. However, the group did score with two British top-ten entries, *Can You Feel It* making No 6 and *Walk Right Now*, No 7, and their dazzling stage act was well captured in a live album of their greatest hits from Motown days. Motown themselves successfully capitalized on Michael's burgeoning popularity by reissuing *One Day In Your Life* as a single: it made only No 55 in the US, but went to the top in Britain.

Then, in 1982, *The Girl Is Mine* gave him an unlikely duet hit with Paul McCartney (although the song was Michael's) reaching No 2 in the US and No 8 in the UK. It was actually one of the less memorable tracks from a new LP released in 1983, and was once again immaculately produced by Quincy Jones; *Thriller* was unquestionably one of the 'albums of the year.' As with *Off The Wall*, the credits were varied and the instrumental and production assistance read like a who's who of rock! Among the musicians, Eddie Van Halen contributed a distinctive guitar solo to *Beat It* which made No 1 in America (and No 3 in the UK). It was one of four Michael Jackson compositions on the album, of which he co-produced three, including the deeply felt story of romance-turned-sour, *Billie Jean*, which gave him a top placing both sides of the Atlantic. The title track, one of three new Rod Temperton songs, is one of the most dramatic things he has ever committed to vinyl, an eerie evocation of the world of the horror movie and 'thriller nights' on TV.

In 1984, he was nominated for an unprecedented twelve Grammys – and won

MICHAEL JACKSON

eight. The following year saw him join his brothers for a final Jacksons album (*Victory*) and tour.

The long-awaited follow-up to *Thriller* appeared in September 1987. Though not as big a seller in absolute terms, *Bad* topped the charts in 25 countries, with pre-orders breaking recording company records at 2.25 million. September also saw him start his world tour in Tokyo: seven months later, *Dirty Diana* became the fifth US No 1 from *Bad*.

After a best-selling book and video (*Moonwalk*) Michael released *Dangerous* in late 1991. It set yet more records, selling twice as quickly as its two predecessors, while the first single *Black or White* was a UK/US No. 1 with more hits to come. With an estimated annual income of over $100 million, the reclusive Jackson was making records in more ways than one.

RECOMMENDED RECORDINGS
(with The Jackson Five/The Jacksons)
ABC
Lookin' Through the Windows
Destiny
Triumph
Live
Greatest Hits (compilation)
20 Golden Greats (compilation)
(solo)
Ben
Got To Be There
Off The Wall
Thriller
Bad
Dangerous

Far right: In his video *Thriller*.
Right: Confident and compelling on stage.
Below: With Olivia Newton-John.

14

BRYAN ADAMS

One of rock's least likely superstars, Canada's Bryan Adams is so anonymous that a security man at the door of a concert in France once refused to let him in! Yet underneath the T-shirt and Levi's lies an honest rock'n'roller who survives in a video age by supplying traditional rock, hot and sweaty, to an audience that still prefers live music to wall-to-wall video clips.

Born in the small town of Kingston, Ontario, in November 1959, Adams's English mother and father emigrated before he was born. His father's job in the Canadian army took the family to Europe and the Middle East.

He bought his first guitar at the age of 12, but it was assumed that he would follow in his father's footsteps. His parents' divorce saw Adams turning increasingly to music, and in 1976, at the age of 16, he formed his first band. Originally playing lead guitar, he soon found himself center stage. 'No one else could sing,' he recalls. 'So it was left to me to learn pretty fast!'

Shack played the club circuit in Vancouver on Canada's West Coast where he bumped into Jim Vallance, drummer with Prism. The pair started writing songs together and soon attracted the interest of bands like Bachman Turner Overdrive, Loverboy and Kiss.

His first album appeared in 1980, but it was *You Want It, You Got It* with four successful singles in the USA, that made his name. *Cuts Like A Knife* shot into the American top ten in 1982, selling two million copies and yielding hits in the title track, *Straight From The Heart*, *This Time* and *The Best Was Yet To Come*.

Adams spent 283 days of 1983 on the road, and reaped the reward with *Reckless*. The single *Heaven* hit the US No 1 spot and sales of the album turned it five times platinum. Hit singles included *Run To You, Somebody* and *It's Only Love*, recorded with Tina Turner.

He appeared in Philadelphia in 1985 on the Live Aid bill and wrote Canada's Band Aid anthem *Tears Are Not Enough*. After releasing his *Into The Fire* album in 1987, Adams deferred work on his own projects to play with, write songs for and/or produce Joe Cocker, Belinda Carlisle and Mötley Crüe. Stage appearances included Roger Waters' all-star tribute to the people of East Germany – The Wall, live from Berlin – in 1990.

Everything I Do (I Do It For You), produced by Robert 'Mutt' Lange and taken from the soundtrack of the year's smash movie, *Robin Hood – Prince Of Thieves* announced Adams's return to recording in no uncertain terms. It stayed at No 1 in Britain for a record 16 weeks, while the follow-up album *Waking Up The Neighbours* was a success on both sides of the Atlantic. The single also topped the US charts and became the highest selling No 1 single in seven years.

Even if he never writes another *Everything I Do*, Adams's style of gutsy yet radio-friendly AOR is unlikely to go out of fashion. Co-writer Vallance is now freelancing (for Aerosmith and others), while Adams/Vallance songs have been covered by Joe Cocker, Bonnie Tyler, .38 Special and many others.

RECOMMENDED RECORDINGS
Cuts Like A Knife
Reckless
Waking Up The Neighbours

Top: Waking up the neighbors? Not what you expect from the boy next door.
Above: Bryan Adams, singer/songwriter of the highest order.
Right: No frills. Just great tunes, great lyrics and a whole load of passion.

BOB DYLAN

*S*ometime poet of protest and rebellion, mystic minstrel, country singer and lately born-again Christian, Dylan has never ceased to confound followers and critics alike with his abrupt changes of musical direction.

The best of his songs summed up the anger and the fears of his audience, and have lost little of their power in the ensuing twenty years; they are still painfully relevant. And the raw, rasping and insistent quality of that voice well-suited the bitter and ironic nature of his lyrics.

Dylan is no longer the towering, commanding personality of the early sixties. But he has never stood still, and certainly retains the capacity to surprise.

Robert Allen Zimmerman did not stumble into fame and fortune. He really worked at it. Born on 24 May 1941, in Duluth, Minnesota, his family were respectable middle-class Jewish shop-keepers – none of them descended from the Sioux Indian tribe as Dylan was to claim later. His childhood was unremarkable: he started playing the guitar and formed several groups with school friends. He went to the University of Minnesota in 1959 where he became known as Bob Dylan (probably taking the name from the Welsh poet, Dylan Thomas). He played around the local coffee houses in Minneapolis, just proficient on guitar and certainly no great shakes as a singer. He began to idolize the American folk singer, Woody Guthrie.

Determined to meet Guthrie, Dylan dropped out of university in 1961 and went to New York. He not only met Guthrie, but ingratiated himself into the circle of poets, folk singers and musicians that had grown up around the man. Dylan was soon playing the clubs in Greenwich Village, and gaining attention, including that of John Hammond of Columbia/CBS Records. Dylan duly signed for CBS and cut his first album in late 1961. It cost just $402 to make.

Released in March 1962 *Bob Dylan* contained mostly existing blues and folk material, but the interpretation of these traditional war-horses was sufficiently different and refreshing to arouse comment, but in CBS circles the project was known as 'Hammond's Folly.'

Left: One of the many faces of Bob Dylan: voice of protest, surrealist poet, now born-again Christian.

Above: Dylan in contemplative mood: which direction will his music take next? He's never lost the capacity to surprise.

However, the second album *The Freewheelin' Bob Dylan* firmly established the baby-face from Minnesota as the most powerful voice of the folk protest movement. Songs such as *A Hard Rain's Gonna Fall* were blunt, unequivocal antiwar statements. It was a calculated stance, and the sleeve picture of Dylan and girlfriend, Susie Rotolo, hustling along a snowbound street was all part of the image.

With *The Times They are A'changing*, the political gestures were becoming more sophisticated and the subjects more diverse, concern for the treatment of blacks in the USA but one of them. The title song gave Dylan his first British hit in 1965, but the burgeoning protest movement was largely disappointed with the follow-up, *Another Side of Bob Dylan*; the sentiments were more personal than global, the imagery less accessible.

The Newport Folk Festival of 1963 confirmed Dylan's status and acceptability to the folk purists. Two years later he stunned the self-same audience by appearing backed by the electrified and amplified Paul Butterfield Blues Band, and more-or-less created the folk-rock movement overnight. The first recorded fruit of this new stage in Dylan's development was the remarkable *Highway 61 Revisited* ('I'll never make another album as good as that,' he is reported to have said some years later). As well as the title track, it contained such definitive songs as *Ballad of a Thin Man, Desolation Row* and, arguably his finest of all, six minutes of *Like a Rolling Stone*. It was a radical departure for a record industry conditioned to three-minute sides for it to appear as a single. But it *was* played on radio and became a worldwide hit, although his concerts were still receiving mixed receptions from those convinced he had betrayed his 'folk roots.' It is true the broad human concerns of the early songs had been replaced by more complex themes, not least an element of selfishness and arrogance in personal relationships *(It Ain't Me, Babe, Don't Think Twice, It's Alright)*, but Dylan had always displayed the knack of guessing where his audience was heading – and getting there before them.

By *Blonde on Blonde*, the first double-album in rock history that wasn't a compilation of past hits, Dylan was writing eleven-minute songs for his newly wedded wife, Sara *(Sad-Eyed Lady of the Lowlands)*, and urging that 'everybody must get stoned,' a sentiment which got the song *Rainy Day Women Nos 12 and 35* banned on US radio. *Blonde on Blonde* remains one of the momentous inspirations in rock music.

On 29 July 1966, Bob Dylan broke his neck in a motor-cycle accident. Or did he? The truth has never been revealed, but accident or no, he may well have needed the chance to escape from the pressure and the pace of his existence.

Although he withdrew from public life, Dylan was not inactive. He joined with his immensely talented backing group, The Band, to make the legendary *Basement Tapes*. For many years, Dylan refused to release these recordings but, such was the quality of the material, it wasn't long before cover versions of some of the songs were around. When the double album eventually appeared, it was a revelation, not least for the outstanding contribution of the musicians in The Band.

Dylan's exile on record ended with one of his most poetic yet enigmatic collections, *John Wesley Harding*. The backings were simple and austere – guitar, bass and drums – and suited the spare, concentrated songs with their strange, vivid and, at times, haunting imagery. *I dreamed I saw St. Augustine, I am the Lonesome Hobo, I Pity the Poor Immigrant* and, of course, *All Along the Watchtower* (later immortalized by Jimi Hendrix) rank among his finest inspirations.

The final two songs on *John Wesley Harding* are odd men out, but their rambling, sing-a-long style presaged Dylan's next move: the quasi-Country music of *Nashville Skyline*. By his standards, it was uninspired, and the next two albums were similarly disappointing. Had he burned out? He rarely gave public performances, although he did reappear to play at the Woody Guthrie Memorial Concert, at the Isle of Wight Festival in 1969 and he also supported George Harrison's Concert for Bangla Desh. He recorded some new tracks for a 'greatest hits' compilation and even did some session work. His only other work of note during this period was the soundtrack for the film *Pat Garrett and Billy the Kid*, which produced one hit song for him – the wickedly catchy, *Knocking on Heaven's Door*.

Then in January and February 1974 he undertook a comeback tour in the USA with The Band and the resulting live album is quite magical. Dylan invests his old favorites with a new vitality and excitement. *Blowing in the Wind, Rolling Stone, Highway 61* and the rest are sung with such intensity and urgency, it sounds as though he had written them that very evening. Yet the concurrent studio album, *Planet Waves* was again uneven. The spark, sadly, seemed only to return when he parted from Sara, for *Blood on the Tracks* is a record of sadness, reflection, and not a little pain, and makes for compelling listening.

Returning to the road, Dylan put together a tour of the northeast USA, calling it *The Rolling Thunder Revue* and pulling in all manner of musicians for appearances – including his one-time close ally, Joan Baez. Coincidentally, he released *Desire* which, deservedly, has probably become his best-selling recording. Like *John Wesley Harding*, the arrangements were lean, and included no less than Emmylou Harris as background vocalist. It reached No 3 in the US and UK album charts.

Above: When Dylan went electric, he started the whole folk-rock movement.
Left: Portrait of the artist with top hat.
Below: A breath of air between sixties gigs.

His first concert appearances outside the USA for eleven years were also well-received. Australia, New Zealand, Europe and Japan were visited, the latter resulting in the *Bob Dylan at Budokan* live double album. An autumn 1978 North American tour was less critically successful, as was the studio album *Street Legal*.

Virtually all the songs on *Slow Train Coming* reflect Dylan's new-found Christianity. With Mark Knopfler of Dire Straits embellishing the guitar lines, the album sold surprisingly well, even if the disarming naivity lost Dylan some of his fans forever. Religious material dominated the San Francisco concerts of 1979 and, possibly showing a 'once bitten, twice shy' reaction, the next gospelizing recording, *Saved*, sold less well than its predecessor.

The eighties saw him stop preaching and link live with Tom Petty's Heartbreakers and the Grateful Dead, but he failed to hit top form until he joined forces in 1988 with Petty, George Harrison, Roy Orbison and Jeff Lynne in 'wrinkly supergroup' the Traveling Wilburys.

Although his melodic invention may sometimes have failed him, some of the versifying and rhyming have been agonizingly contrived, and some of his songs failed to stand the test of time, Bob Dylan's achievements as a rock songwriter can still only be compared to those of Lennon and McCartney. Dylan's music demanded to be noticed, *had* to be noticed, and every serious rock musician who has followed is indebted to him for that if nothing else.

RECOMMENDED RECORDINGS
The Freewheelin' Bob Dylan
The Times They are A-Changin'
Another Side of Bob Dylan
Bringing it all Back Home
Highway 61 Revisited
Blonde on Blonde
John Wesley Harding
Blood on the Tracks
Desire
Shot of Love
Biograph (*compilation*)
The Bootleg Series (*compilation*)

SIMON & GARFUNKEL

I t was an emotional reunion for the half-a-million New Yorkers gathered in Central Park one September evening in 1981 for a unique free concert. Two 39-year-olds took the stage with songs that ten, twelve years ago had meant so much to so many in that audience. Finely crafted, poetic, evocative songs of personal concerns and gentle, liberal-minded protest. As the recordings of the event demonstrate so well, Paul Simon's early songs have a lasting quality and appeal.

Paul Simon was born in October 1941 in Newark, New Jersey, into a Jewish/Hungarian family but moved to the middle-class area of Queens as a child. Arthur Garfunkel was born in Forest Hills in the November of the same year and the pair attended school together. They played at fraternity parties in the late fifties and, taking the names Tom (Graph) and Jerry (Landis) from the cat-and-mouse cartoon, made some recordings. *Hey! Schoolgirl* made No 59 in the US chart in 1957 and was followed by an appearance on the popular *American Bandstand* TV show. That had proved a useful jumping-off point for many aspiring pop acts of the era, but not this time. Art returned to Columbia University, and Paul to Queens College, where he met another ambitious songwriter, Carole Klein (later King) and they made some demonstration tapes. If nothing else, Paul learned how to make records and after spells in several semiprofessional groups, cut *The Lone Teen Ranger* using the Jerry Landis pseudonym. It made No 97 in 1962, but *Motorcycle* recorded as Tico and the Triumphs didn't register in the top 100 at all.

1964 was to be the key year. Paul had dropped out of law school and getting together once again with Garfunkel, he persuaded CBS/Columbia to let them record an album. Among them was the song *He was my Brother* which had been released under yet another alias – Paul Kane. CBS had Dylan's producer, Tom Wilson, work on *Wednesday Morning 3 a.m.* However, it had little initial impact: Garfunkel resumed his academic career while Simon tried his luck in Britain.

He enjoyed quite a following in the folk clubs, including Judith Piepe, who persuaded the UK management of CBS to record a solo Paul Simon album in May 1965; *The Paul Simon Songbook* contains many of the songs that were later so successful for the duo, including *I Am A Rock*. All the compositions were his own, the only accompaniment was his own acoustic guitar, and it was evident a great talent had been uncovered.

Things had also been happening in the US. A Boston disc jockey had been repeatedly playing a track from *Wednesday Morning 3 a.m., The Sound of Silence*. CBS were encouraged, but wanted something more commercial. Tom Wilson gave the track more of a folk-rock sound, adding electric guitar, bass and drums in the way he'd engineered Dylan's *Like A Rolling Stone*. The result was a US No 1 in 1966, while Paul was still in Britain. He hastily returned home and, reuniting with Art, took off on a tour of the American college circuit.

The follow-up album took the title of the hit single and included rerecordings of much of the *Songbook* material. One of the new tracks was the poignant *Homeward Bound*. It gave them a US No 5 and UK No 9, their breakthrough in the British singles charts.

1966 eventually registered four US hit singles, the others being *I Am a Rock*, (US No 3 and UK No 17) and *A Hazy Shade of Winter* (US No 13). Another successful album, *Parsley, Sage, Rose-mary and Thyme*, demonstrated the variety of Simon's songwriting with the cheery *59th Bridge Street Song (Feelin' Groovy)* contrasting sharply with the antiwar *7 o'clock News/Silent Night*. All the creative input came from Paul Simon, Art contributing solely, but importantly, the precise, pure, and highly appealing harmonies that characterized their sound.

However, Paul Simon has never been prolific and 1967 was to prove a lean year for the pair, with just one US top-twenty entry, *At The Zoo*, and no new albums. Although they retained their following among American college kids, a tour of Britain that year saw many less-than-full houses. But *Bookends* became a No 1 album in 1968 despite a side given over entirely to 'B' songs from already-issued singles. One of the new tracks brought them a second US No 1 and their highest placing yet in the UK (No 4). *Mrs Robinson* came about almost by accident while Paul was working on the score for Mike Nicholls' film *The Graduate*. Originally just a casual attempt to fit a lyric to some of the music, Nicholls heard the song and included part of it

Above: Answering questions from the press on their recent reunion tour, Art (left) and Paul (right).
Left: Performing on British television in the sixties. Their hit songs were all penned by Paul, his partner only contributing to the vocals.
Below: Just two college kids from New York City. In 1981, they came home to give a triumphant 'neighborhood concert' in Central Park.

in the movie. It earned a Grammy award for best record of the year, while the soundtrack itself collected the prize for Best Original Motion Picture Score.

Their huge following was firmly established, despite just one hit single in 1969, the touching tale of *The Boxer* (No 7 in the US, No 6 in the UK). Then in 1970, Simon took the lyric of a new song to Art Garfunkel. Working at the time on the film *Catch 22*, Art was at first reluctant to commit himself, but eventually he was persuaded and with *Bridge Over Troubled Water* the duo secured their biggest-ever success. The single reached No 1 worldwide, while the album of the same name has become the third highest seller of all time, over nine-million copies. It was the top-selling album of the seventies in Britain, and the zenith of their career as a duo.

Although 1970 produced further US hits with *Cecilia* (No 4) and *El Condor Pasa*, Paul was beginning to resent a little the ovations given his partner after every performance of *Bridge*. He realized that their partnership should end. The split was amicable; they played a final concert in Forest Hills in 1970 and thereafter concentrated on solo careers, apart from the very occasional live or studio reunion.

For Garfunkel, it meant a mixture of film work and recording mainly 'easy listening' material,

with success at both. He starred in Mike Nicholls' *Carnal Knowledge* (1971) and Nicholas Roeg's *Bad Timing* (1979) and his first solo album *Angel Clare* earned gold status. *Breakaway* (1975), produced by Richard Perry, was even more successful, with a UK No 1 in *I Only Have Eyes For You*. The album also included a duet with Paul Simon, *My Little Town* (also included on one of the latter's albums) which reached No 9 in the US.

Watermark (1977) included a recording with Simon and James Taylor: a version of the great Sam Cooke number, *(What A) Wonderful World*. His biggest solo success in the UK came in 1979 with a track from *Fate for Breakfast*, and the theme song from *Watership Down*. His voice was perfect for *Bright Eyes*, which became a UK No 1 and the best-selling single of 1979. *Since I don't Have You* produced another hit in this period, but 1981's album *Scissors Cut* went largely unnoticed.

Curiously, the songwriter of the two, Paul Simon, has made only one album more than Art Garfunkel since the split. He is very selective in his choice of subject matter, meticulous in his musical arrangements and careful in the choice of musicians to accompany him. He has shown great wit and pungency in his later songs. The lyrics are simpler, less self-consciously poetic, and he has turned away from the lavish, highly sugared productions of his earlier songs.

His first solo effort, *Paul Simon* (1972) typified this, and had some fine tracks: *Duncan; Mother And Child Reunion* (an American No 4 and UK No 5); and *Me and Julio Down By The Schoolyard* (No 22 and No 15, respectively). 1973's *There Goes Rhymin' Simon* was notable for the varied styles employed: gospel in *Love me Like a Rock* (a US No 2); hard rock in *Koda-*

Above: Reunited in concert, London 1982.
Left: Songs of gentle protest and teenage insecurities made them the most popular duo of the sixties.
Below: Paul solo, with new scope and ambition to his songs.

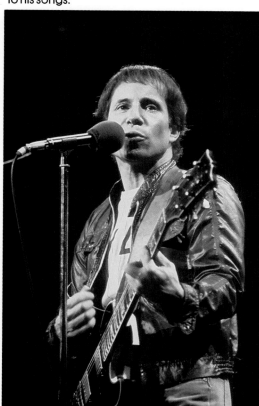

chrome, which made No 2 in the US. The 'B' side, the New Orleans-jazz flavored *Take Me To The Mardi Gras* was promoted as an 'A' in Britain and made No 7. Perhaps the finest track on the album was the subtly political *American Tune*, an indication of just how far his lyrical talent had matured.

The inevitable critical concentration on his words rather than his music irritated Simon a little, for he was developing considerable musical skills as well, shown to the full on the *Live Rhymin'* album resulting from a 1973 US/European tour. On it he was accompanied by both a gospel group and a South American band, Urubamba. He also came under the spell of reggae, as well as working with jazz violinist, Stephane Grappelli.

For the once-reticent Simon, *Still Crazy After All These Years* is a surprisingly honest assessment of his own failings, including his contribution to the breakdown of his marriage. From this 1975 album (which earned two Grammy awards to bring his total to 12), *50 Ways to Leave Your Lover* produced a US No 1.

What was to provide his last album for CBS, *Greatest Hits etc*, appeared in 1977, a mixture of new and old material; *Slip, Slidin' Away* made a US No 5. In 1978 he moved to Warner Brothers and worked on a film project, *One Trick Pony* (1980). Paul financed and starred in the film, but it was unsuccessful. Unlike Art, he was no actor, and the soundtrack album was below his best.

Simon turned his declining fortunes round by returning to ethnic idioms. He went to South Africa to cut the pioneering *Graceland* with local musicians, risking United Nations wrath. The album hit the transatlantic top three in 1986.

He followed up four years later with the South American-recorded *Rhythm Of The Saints*, reprising his new influences in the live *Concert In The Park*, recorded in 1991. While he risked the charge of cultural kleptomania, Simon's past record suggests his songwriting had as much to do with the success as the style in which those songs were performed.

RECOMMENDED RECORDINGS

(Simon and Garfunkel)
The Sounds of Silence
Parsley, Sage, Rosemary and Thyme
Bookends
Bridge over Troubled Water
Greatest Hits *(compilation)*
The Simon and Garfunkel Collection *(compilation)*
The Concert in Central Park *(live/double)*
(Paul Simon)
Paul Simon
There Goes Rhymin' Simon
Still Crazy After All These Years
Graceland
Rhythm Of The Saints
(Art Garfunkel)
Angel Clare
Breakaway
Watermark
Fate for Breakfast

BRUCE SPRINGSTEEN

*W*as it inevitable that many of the lean and hungry rock heroes of the sixties would become the lazy fat cats of the seventies? Critics searched for a new talent capable of challenging the self-satisfied rock establishment, and when they found it in Bruce Springsteen, their ridiculously high expectations almost suffocated it at birth. However, Springsteen was good enough to survive one of the most lavish, yet ill-conceived, hypes the record industry has ever seen, and its inevitable backlash. He is now just about the most exciting rock act around today.

Above: Bruce enjoys a solo from Clarence Clemons, whose sax playing was a distinctive feature of albums like *Born To Run*.

Right and over page: Playing flat out for as much as four hours, Springsteen has boundless energy when on stage.

Much of Springsteen's music is rooted in the streets of industrial New Jersey, the state where he was born in 1949. Like so many others, radio was his introduction to rock and roll: he listened avidly to the stars of the early sixties. He formed his first band at fourteen. By 1965, he was commuting to New York to play guitar at the Cafe Wha in Greenwich Village with a group called the Castiles. Playing at the Upstage Club in Asbury Park, New Jersey, he became lasting friends with many local musicians, but after a short spell at the Ocean County Community College decided to try his luck on the West Coast. He was soon back East, having failed an audition with a record company, and once again playing the clubs.

In 1971, he met Mike Appel who became his manager, producer and promoter. In his haste to sign, he didn't appreciate the long-term implications of the contract. Appell took him for an audition with John Hammond of CBS, the man who 'discovered' Bob Dylan. 'Let's see if that was luck, or whether you really have ears,' Appel is supposed to have said to Hammond. He signed Springsteen on the spot.

Given the Hammond connection, it is hardly surprising that the claim was soon put about 'Springsteen – the next Bob Dylan.' And just as inevitably, it backfired completely. His first album, *Greetings from Asbury Park, NJ*, released in January 1973, had many fine songs but was very loose and poorly put together. *Blinded by the Light, Spirit in the Night*, and *It's Hard to be a Saint in the City* were evidence that Springsteen was not just another Dylan copyist. There was an urgency and animation about his music which demanded attention, but he was clearly not the polished performer critics had been led to expect.

Springsteen's management committed another commercial error in sending Springsteen on tour in 1973 supporting Chicago. The poor reception – it was utterly the wrong audience – made him vow never to play supporting act again, unless it was to someone he personally approved.

At this time he was assembling an exceptional backing group – the E-Street Band – which included the superb Clarence Clemons (late of James Brown's Famous Flames) on saxophone. Together, they made the second LP, *The Wild, the Innocent and the E-Street Shuffle* which included the dramatic *Rosalita*, the song which was to become the overwhelming conclusion to most of his concerts.

Springsteen was now achieving cult status among critics and aficionados, chiefly in the northeast USA, where he toured in 1974. Good as the tour was, some of his dramatized narrative songs were becoming too deeply profound and too long. This was Springsteen, the gifted but still raw performer, trying to live up to the 'superstar' image being foisted upon him. When Jon Landau of *Rolling Stone* described Springsteen as 'the rock and roll future,' CBS seized upon it – and the repercussions almost finished Springsteen. CBS even subtly altered the emphasis to 'the future of rock and roll.'

The pressure on Springsteen as he produced his third album must have been overwhelming. CBS staged a publicity campaign of huge proportions in an effort to make him the most discussed rock performer around, and it worked. Luckily, *Born to Run*, issued in autumn 1975, was immediately recognizable as one of the great rock albums of the seventies. Due in no small part to the efforts of critic-turned-producer Jon

Landau, Springsteen had refined his songs and their delivery. His songs are powerful, dramatic poetry, put across with the total commitment that characterizes everything Springsteen does. The playing is intense and committed; a sharp, clean production that owes something to Phil Spector and early electric Dylan.

In the US, the album *Tenth Avenue Freeze Out* achieved a gold award. Although it crept into the lower reaches of the UK chart, sales of *Born to Run* were not helped by another massive publicity gaffe on Springsteen's first visit to London. The concerts at the Hammersmith Odeon were announced with the offensive slogan, 'Finally London is ready for Bruce Springsteen.' The audience reaction was predictably skeptical and the British press sharpened its pens with relish. Although he played well, Springsteen saw the experience as a disaster and determined to control his own career from then on.

But his contract with Mike Appel was inviolable. Appel obtained a court injunction preventing Springsteen from making any recordings until the case was settled. Although he toured in 1976 and 1977, he was unable to put down a note in the studio for three years. He didn't stop composing however.

Darkness on the Edge of Town, issued in 1978, reflects the frustration that Springsteen must have felt during his three-year enforced silence. It spawned only a moderate hit with *Prove It All Night,* but contained many other fine songs. Lengthy sell-out tours in 1978 were followed by a memorable set at the Musicians for Safe Energy 'No Nukes' benefit concert in 1979. Tours of the US and Europe accompanied the release of a double LP, *The River* in 1980. Springsteen said that he had put some 50 songs in the can for this album, but the final selection is once again characterized by the image of the motor car as a 'suicide machine.'

'Doing it is the goal,' says Springsteen. He sings and plays flat-out for anything up to four hours, maintaining an extraordinary feverish tension and communication with his audience.

Toward the end of his performance, he plays fast rockers and the adrenalin flows. His energy seems limitless. He is exceptional among the top live rock acts of today; he doesn't play at his fans, he plays for them and with them. It was no different with the mammoth 1985 tour, playing to full houses in arenas everywhere. The *Born in the USA* album, with not a bad track on it, brought him chart success with *Dancing in the Dark* and *I'm on Fire*, and to cap it all Bruce got married!

The marriage didn't last, and neither did his musical link with the E-Street Band, celebrated by the 1986 release of the box set *Live* 1975-85. 1987's *Tunnel Of Love* (a UK chart-topper) featured the band only intermittently and with the simultaneous 1992 release of *Human Touch* and *Lucky Town* Springsteen was officially a solo – apart, that was, from his new wife, backing singer Patti Scialfa!

RECOMMENDED RECORDINGS

The Wild, The Innocent and the E-Street Shuffle
Born to Run
Darkness on the Edge of Town
The River (*double*)
Nebraska
Born in The USA

GEORGE MICHAEL

The lifespan of most teenage heart-throbs is as brief as the average house-fly. Yet George Michael proved the exception to the rule, growing up and out of the teen audience that had thrilled to Wham!, the partnership with schoolfriend guitarist Andrew Ridgeley, to attract an older listenership. The key to the metamorphosis? His carefully crafted songs in a vein as traditional as his fashions were up-to-the-minute, plus a willingness of his American audience to accept him from the outset as a sensitive singer-songwriter.

Michael, born Georgios Panayioutou in 1963, was the driving force behind Wham!, an early-Eighties dance music act who scored three UK top-ten hits in 1983. Those songs, *Young Guns (Go For It)*, *Wham! Rap* and *Club Tropicana* mixed escapism with street-level philosophy: *Wham! Rap* concerned the importance of the unemployed to retain pride and self-belief.

A switch of labels to Epic in 1984 brought them US success to go with British chart domination: the uptempo *Wake Me Up Before You Go-Go* topped the charts on both sides of the Atlantic, but it was *Careless Whisper*, credited in the UK to Michael alone, that set the tone for things to come. A moody, sensitive ballad with acoustic guitars and exotic percussion it was America's top single of 1985. *Everything She Wants*, a double A-side with the seasonal *Last Christmas* in Britain, became their third US No 1 before Michael announced a split in 1986. Prior to this they appeared at Live Aid, became the first Western pop group to tour China and Michael was the youngest winner of the Ivor Novello songwriters' award.

Since Ridgeley had played little part in Wham!'s success as singer or songwriter, Michael's solo career merely carried on where *Careless Whisper* had left off. A second solo 45, *A Different Corner* had hit the top in 1986 along with the Wham!-credited *I'm Your Man* and *Edge Of Heaven*. He briefly replaced Ridgeley with Aretha Franklin for the single *I Knew You Were Waiting (For Me)* for a transatlantic No 1, then wrote, produced and played most of his 1987 debut album *Faith*. Selling 14 million copies worldwide, it was the biggest-selling album ever by a British solo artist in the US and spawned three more US No 1s in *Father Figure*, *One More Try* and *Monkey*.

Michael repeated the trick in 1990 with *Listen Without Prejudice Vol 1* (reaching No 2 in the US and No 1 in the UK), the title a suggestion to any of his UK audience who still associated him with Wham! (Former partner Ridgeley by this time had cut a flop solo album and enjoyed a brief, unbrilliant career as a racing driver.) Hit singles included *Praying For Time* (another US No 1), *Waiting For That Day* and *Freedom* (not the Wham! song). A 1991 duet for Aids charities, *Don't Let The Sun Go Down On Me* with Elton John topped the UK charts in late 1991, hitting the top Stateside early the following year. *Listen Without Prejudice Volume 2* was expected in 1992, prior to which he had toured playing a cover version set of classic soul songs. Clearly not lacking in confidence, George Michael – not yet in his thirties – has the music world at his feet.

RECOMMENDED RECORDINGS
The Final *(Wham! compilation)*
Faith
Listen Without Prejudice Vol 1

Far right: Gorgios giving his all. His vocal range and power mark him out as one of the great singers in modern rock.
Below right: George on stage exudes a magnetism which has won him a worldwide following.
Below: After immense success with Wham!, George's solo career has profited from his shift to a cooler image.

ERIC CLAPTON

Modest about his talents and an unwilling showman, it is hardly surprising Clapton appeared puzzled and embarrassed when the infamous 'Clapton is God' graffiti began to decorate the walls of London in the mid-sixties. He had developed a style of guitar playing that, although rooted in the blues, was fast, furious and very flash. He was unquestionably the most technically accomplished British guitarist of the period. With Cream, he attained the pinnacle of virtuosity; long improvisations displayed his fabulous skills and produced an awesome barrage of sound. Yet by the mid-seventies he was playing a relaxed, economical country-blues style. And he seemed to be enjoying it. Such a change did not come easily.

Clapton was born in the middle-class town of Ripley, England, on 30 March 1945. After being brought up by his grandparents he went to art college. He spent too much time absorbed in the music of Chuck Berry, Robert Johnson, Bill Broonzy, Skip James and the like and was asked to leave. He busked a little around the Surrey suburbs and on occasions stood in for Mick Jagger as lead singer of Blues Incorporated. He played with a couple of bands before becoming lead guitar with the Yardbirds in October 1963. The group soon took over as resident band at the famous Crawdaddy Club in Richmond, replacing the Rolling Stones. The Yardbirds produced some singles and a live album and made the top 50 with *Good Morning Little Schoolgirl* in November 1964. However, making unashamedly pop hits was not in Eric Clapton's plans, and although the group reached No 3 with *For Your Love*, he quit.

He did a short stint as a building site laborer, but a call from John Mayall soon had Clapton playing with his current Bluesbreakers line-up. As for many musicians, Mayall's influence was the catalyst Clapton needed. At the end of a fourteen-month stint with the band, Clapton was being acclaimed as the UK's finest blues guitarist. Together, Mayall, Clapton, John McVie and Hughie Flint produced but one album, but it was outstanding. Clapton's brief but brilliant solos on *Steppin' Out* and *Hide-away* were an appetizing taste of what was to follow.

He made several recordings outside the Bluesbreakers, including some with the aspiring

Jimmy Page which were later released on blues anthologies. On a session for the sampler LP *What's Shakin'*, he jammed with bass and harmonica player, Jack Bruce, of the Graham Bond Organisation. Also in Bond's line-up was Ginger Baker, a flamboyant drummer of extravagant talents, quite capable of simultaneously handling two drum kits and a battery of percussion! Clapton and Baker got together and suggested to Jack Bruce that they form a trio. The result was Cream. The original intention was simply to play blues in clubs and pubs, but at the debut performance at the 1966 Jazz and Blues Festival at Windsor, they ran out of material and had to improvise. It set the pattern of their concerts for the next two years. Audiences demanded, and got, marathon solos of breathtaking virtuosity: Bruce on harmonica in *Traintime*, Baker alone on stage to improvise fifteen minutes of drumming during *Toad*, and Clapton bringing audiences to their feet, cheering, with dazzling performances in *Steppin' Out, Spoonful, I'm So Glad* and many others.

Their studio albums couldn't capture the experience on record – at least not in the regimented days of 1967. They recorded much-abbreviated versions of their live numbers plus a series of self-composed pop numbers. *Fresh*

Cream was a good opener, but *Disraeli Gears* (a pun on the derailer gears on racing bicycles) outstripped it with songs of the lasting quality of *Strange Brew, Sunshine of Your Love* and *Tales of Brave Ulysses*.

After a series of British concerts Cream concentrated on the American scene and it was a concert in Bill Graham's Fillmore East, San Francisco, that finally captured the live Cream sound for posterity. The two live sides of the double album *Wheels of Fire* are uneven, but make for compelling listening. Clapton's furious solos on Robert Johnson's *Crossroads* are among his best, almost a kind of musical 'thank you' to his blues hero.

After five months in the US, Clapton seemed exhausted. He says that one night he stopped playing during one number to see if Baker and Bruce would notice. They didn't. That, and a scathingly hurtful review in *Rolling Stone* magazine, persuaded him that Cream had finally gone sour. The final UK concert in 1968 was a rapturous affair at the Albert Hall and the group's last album was appropriately called *Goodbye*. It ensured that Cream had at least finished at the top.

Soon Clapton and Baker had joined with Steve Winwood (ex-Traffic) and Rick Grech (ex-Family) in another supergroup of even greater

Above: Eric Clapton playing his brand of blues at a London concert.
Left: Cream, at the time of their formation in 1967, the first of the supergroups and stylesetters for the heavy metal bands of the seventies. Bassist, Jack Bruce (right) and drummer Ginger Baker (center) seen with Eric Clapton (left).
Right: The rare sight of Eric playing Spanish guitar, if an amplified one. In the seventies he rejected the style of virtuoso solos that fans from Cream days still expected, and tried a return to pure blues.

potential, Blind Faith. The pressures were too great. They had barely sufficient material (and much of it was less than perfect) when they made their debut before a crowd of 100,000 in London's Hyde Park. Although their first and only album was a chart-topper, it didn't come up to expectations, despite Clapton's magical *Presence of the Lord*.

It was Clapton who had requested Delaney and Bonnie Bramlett as the support act for Blind Faith's American tour. Clapton decided he would rather be playing with them than the monster he'd helped create. He toured with Delaney and Bonnie, and recorded an album with them and their friends, who included Leon Russell and Stephen Stills. Using Delaney and Bonnie's musicians his first solo album brought him an American hit with JJ Cale's *After Midnight*.

Seeking a kind of anonymity, he formed Derek and the Dominoes. As well as Derek (Eric), he took along Jim Gordon, Carl Radle and Bobby Whitlock from the Delaney and Bonnie line-up and fellow guitar virtuoso, Duane Allman.

He'd also fallen in love – with Patti, wife of his closest friend, George Harrison of the Beatles. When Patti decided to return to George, Clapton was heartbroken. He expressed the pain in one of the classic rock compositions, *Layla*.

It came at the end of the first Dominoes album, *Layla and Other Assorted Love Songs*, a collection of mainly easy-going optimistic numbers. Clapton and Allman play searing, blistering guitar, and the despair he felt writing and singing *Layla* is all too evident. By Clapton's

ERIC CLAPTON

Top: Clapton on stage, the finest white blues guitarist, but within two years he had become deeply dissatisfied with his role in the band.
Above: In serious vein at a concert.
Right: In concert during 1980, the year of *Just One Night*, the live double album that confirmed Clapton's return to form. He had married his love of many years, Patti, ex-wife of George Harrison, in '79.
Far right: A little sartorial self-promotion.

standards, the album was a relative failure, and the single only received its rightful acclaim upon rerelease and shortened from the full seven-minute version. Derek and the Dominoes did some more concerts and began another recording, but Clapton was broken and the band split after the tour. He became a recluse at his home in Surrey; he had lost Patti (although they eventually married in 1979), and the deaths of Duane Allman and Jimi Hendrix deeply affected him. He found solace in heroin.

He made a rare appearance in Harrison's 'Concert for Bangla Desh' and at a Leon Russell show at the Rainbow, London. In 1973, Pete Townshend, along with Steve Winwood, Ron Wood, and Jim Capaldi, organized a comeback concert. However, the subsequent live album shows a performer sadly below his best. It wasn't until the winter of 1973/74 that his addiction was cured.

One day, so the story goes, he simply felt fit enough to start again and went to see his manager, Robert Stigwood. With enough material for an album, Clapton flew to Florida and the result simply took the number of the house he stayed in, *461 Ocean Boulevard*. It was a good recording, the guitar fireworks were relegated to a supporting role, and he had himself a hit single with an easy-going version of Bob Marley's *I Shot the Sheriff*. It was his first single to reach No 1 in America.

Clapton was rejuvenated, but the style was laid-back, economical and deliberately understated, which disappointed those still expecting Cream-style solos. He became interested in country music, audible in the series of recordings that began in 1977 with *Slowhand*. *Slowhand* is an album of memorable songs superbly produced by Glyn Johns. It still offers great guitar work, but the solos are tighter, more subtle.

Prior to this, he had produced a live session (*E.C. Was Here* from the 1974/75 American tour) and two studio albums. During 1976 he toured England for the first time in five years and then followed the success of *Slowhand* in 1978 with *Backless*. Also in this period, *Lay Down Sally*, a joint composition with Marcy Levy, and his self-penned, *Wonderful Tonight* were hit singles in the US. Another US tour came in 1979, and in 1980 a live double recorded at the Budokan in Japan confirmed Clapton's rehabilitation. Recent albums, *Another Ticket* and *Money and Cigarettes* show him pushing on toward his goals without quite matching the inspiration of, say, *Slowhand*.

Eric Clapton inspired a generation of guitar-playing kids, acknowledged his debt to the great blues players by adapting their music for a wider audience without losing its essential character, and of course thrilled and excited audiences on stage and on record. He is master of the guitar, one of the few genuine virtuosos of rock music.

RECOMMENDED RECORDINGS

(with John Mayall)
Bluesbreakers

(with Cream)
Fresh Cream
Disraeli Gears
Wheels of Fire *(live/studio)*
Goodbye *(live/studio)*
Live Cream Vol 1
Live Cream Vol 2

(with Delaney and Bonnie and Friends)
Layla and Other Assorted Love Songs

(Solo)
461 Ocean Boulevard
E.C. Was Here
Slowhand
Backless
Just one Night *(live)*
History of Eric Clapton *(compilation)*

JIMI HENDRIX

Hendrix was arguably the most accomplished and gifted electric guitarist of the sixties, yet for much of the time he didn't so much play the instrument as physically assault it.

Even so, it seemed no guitars yet conceived could reproduce all the sounds that were spinning in his head. So in his frustration he first seduced them, then he smashed them, and, in a spectacular moment at the Monterey Festival in 1967, he set fire to them.

But the showmanship and overt sexuality of Hendrix' stage act formed just one aspect of his music. Despite the aggressive and violent stage aura, Hendrix was in truth a manipulable character who found it difficult to say no to anyone or anything. Evidence is the laughable, and eventually aborted, US tour of 1967 playing second string to — of all people — The Monkees.

James Marshall Hendrix came from a solidly middle-class black family in Seattle, Washington. His father played saxophone and an aunt rattled out stirring hymn tunes on the organ of the local baptist church. Hendrix senior was an avid collector of blues and R&B records and legend has it that the boy's first acoustic guitar arrived after his parents had seen him lying back on the sofa strumming a broomstick to a favorite tune. At the age of twelve he had graduated to the electric version and was soon playing with half-a-dozen local bands in Seattle, and up the coast, in Vancouver.

In 1959, James Hendrix dropped out of high school and joined the US Army. He was discharged when injured in a parachute drop. He went South, and joined a circuit of big-time black performers, playing backing guitar to Little Richard, Wilson Pickett, Sam Cooke and others. However revolutionary his own music, it is rooted here in the realms of BB King and Muddy Waters. The guitar-playing gimmicks that were later to astonish white audiences — behind the back, or behind the head, or even plucking the strings with his teeth — were all derived from the tricks of the old blues' players.

At this time, whatever aspirations he had for his own career were restrained by an unremarkable vocal talent — until he heard Dylan and noted that purity of voice was not a prerequisite for success. In 1965 he formed his first band, Jimmy James and the Blue Flames, and was soon playing the clubs in Greenwich Village — mainly blues and R&B material, but already injecting a taste of the effects from feedback, fuzz boxes and the like that were to become his trademark.

The breakthrough came, ironically, not in the USA but in Britain. At that time Chas Chandler was playing bass with The Animals and on an American tour he heard Hendrix and persuaded him to move across the Atlantic. Chandler quickly formed a 'power trio' with British musicians Mitch Mitchell (drums) and Noel Redding (bass); a threesome along the lines of the recently formed Cream, but with a more carefully-cultivated image.

The hair was frizzed extravagantly, the clothes colorful, and the posture of anarchy, decadence and outrage perpetuated. They called themselves the Jimi Hendrix Experience, and each performance was just that.

More importantly, Hendrix at last had his chance to produce previously unimagined sounds from a guitar. He stretched the instrument to its absolute limit, redefining the art of guitar playing — with indisputable mastery. Others attempted to exploit distortion, feedback and other effects, but none could control and harness them like Hendrix.

On their first UK tour in March 1967, The Experience played the thriving clubs and colleges circuit. Indeed, it is a measure of the group's rapid rise that only months before the celebrated Monterey performance, they were appearing in shabby, crowded rooms in London pubs. The repertoire was a mixture of blues standards, reworded pop numbers, and new material which gave full rein to Hendrix' musical and physical abilities.

A single release, *Hey Joe*, was moderately successful, and another, *Purple Haze*, more so. Both were included on the first album *Are You Experienced*, a stunning debut which has lost none of it's impact in the ensuing sixteen years. Although Hendrix spawned a generation of heavy metal guitarists, no one has been able to improve on, or even duplicate his original sounds. His playing was a combination of extraordinary talent, huge imagination, great ingenuity and a lot of experiment.

Above: Playing the guitar — or attacking it?
Top: Hendrix with drummer Mitch Mitchell.
Right: His style and sound were completely new.
Overleaf, both: His colorful costumes were part of a carefully cultivated image.

His playing style was almost as remarkable as what he played, and, although many of the Fuzz Face, wah-wah, and tape delay effects he used can be readily analyzed, right down to cranking up the volume, many of his methods remain unrepeated and possibly unrepeatable. He could, for instance, produce feedback from two strings, while continuing to play the main theme on the others, giving the extraordinary impression of two guitars playing simultaneously.

Monterey 1967 brought the Experience similar status in the US, and two years of success with both concerts and recordings. *Axis Bold as Love*, which contained classics such as *Little Wing* and *If Six Was Nine*, was followed by the double *Electric Ladyland*, the only one of his records with which Hendrix was totally satisfied. It was from this LP that the Dylan track, *All Along The Watchtower*, was released to become Hendrix' most successful single.

Hendrix was arrested at Toronto airport and charged with possessing heroin. He claimed, successfully, that the package had been pressed on him by a fan and that he had no idea of its contents. He said that although he had used drugs, he had stopped taking them in any form.

At the height of his success, Hendrix began to feel increasingly introspective and musically frustrated. In 1969, he disbanded the Experience and sought a new direction.

At the Woodstock festival of 1969 Hendrix' was one of many great performances, culminating in a shattering, searing rendition of the American national anthem. Complete with bomb and machine-gun effects, this particular *Star Spangled Banner* was distinctly unpatriotic. Whether it was Hendrix' protest against the barbarism of the Vietnam war, or a product of the pressure he was under from black militant groups, has been disputed ever since. Certainly his music acquired more of a black emphasis, culminating in the formation of *Band of Gypsys*, with Jimi's ex-army friend, Billy Cox, on bass and Buddy Miles on drums. Their first major concert, at Fillmore East, San Francisco, New Year's Eve 1969, was recorded and the subsequent LP reveals a somewhat variable performance. It was followed by a despairing low point in early 1970, when he simply stopped playing during a concert in Madison Square Garden and walked off stage, a lost and lonely figure.

However, he opened his own Electric Ladyland recording studio in New York, and planned to gather together like-minded musicians for jamming sessions, which he never ceased to revel in. At least some of these ideas came to fruition in his work with Miles Davis and John McLaughlin, at the beginning of the jazz-rock fusion movement. But for Hendrix time ran out.

After a European tour in 1970 and a disappointing performance at the Isle of Wight Festival, Jimi Hendrix died in a London Hotel room from inhalation of vomit following barbiturate intoxication. He was 27.

An open verdict left endless speculation as to whether his death was suicide or just plain carelessness. Acquaintances differed on whether he was in good spirits and bubbling with fresh ideas at the time, or withdrawn and despondent. Such contradictions typify the Hendrix enigma. We know that in 1968 he tried to shake off the 'black magician/superstud' image and let his music speak without the showmanship. Inevitably, perhaps, it disappointed many of his fans, but the growing regard for Hendrix' recordings and their constant re-evaluation prove that he nevertheless could have survived.

Jimi Hendrix was an original, and, unlike most great rock musicians, suffered no imitators. By any standards, he was a difficult act to follow. ''Scuse me while I touch the sky,' he sang. And touch it he most definitely did.

RECOMMENDED RECORDINGS
Are You Experienced
Axis Bold as Love
Electric Ladyland *(double album)*
Rainbow Bridge — soundtrack album
Hendrix in the West
Band of Gypsys
The Jimi Hendrix Concerts *(live double album)*

ELTON JOHN

S uggest to the moguls of rock music that a short, podgy, balding and bespectacled lad called Reg could become one of the greatest crowd-pullers of all time, and they would most likely show you the door in no uncertain fashion. Well, most would have done in the sixties when Reginald Dwight was pounding out cockney favorites in a north London pub. Given the decade or more of worldwide acclaim and commercial success subsequently enjoyed by that £1-a-night-plus-tips pianist, they might think twice these days.

The future super-showman of rock showed early ambitions to be an entertainer, and they were encouraged by his mother and stepfather. He began to learn the piano in 1951 at the age of four and secured a scholarship to the Royal Academy of Music at eleven. However, at sixteen he began working as a messenger and teaboy for a music publishers. In the evenings he either entertained the customers at a local hotel or played with the semiprofessional band Bluesology.

Eventually they had sufficient commitments backing visiting American soul artists to warrant Reg Dwight going full-time. Appearing at the popular Cromwellian Club, they were noted by leading R&B singer, Long John Baldry, and Bluesology were adopted as his backing band. Keyboardman Dwight (he rarely got the opportunity to sing) decided a more 'jazzy' name might be useful, and taking the 'John' from Baldry, and the forename from the band's saxophonist, Elton Dean, the pseudonym was acquired. He later changed his name by deed poll to Elton Hercules (an early nickname) John.

Baldry meantime was looking for pop success and gained it (briefly) with a UK No 1 in October 1967. Thereafter he forsook R&B for cabaret work and Bluesology disbanded. Scanning *New Musical Express* magazine, Elton saw that a subsidiary of Liberty Records was looking for new talent. At the audition they asked him to sing, and he realized the only number he could put over with any vocal polish was Jim Reeves' *I Love You Because*, which did not go down well.

However, they gave him a pile of lyrics written by another applicant, Bernie Taupin. The two didn't meet for six months, by which time Elton had set twenty of the lyrics to music. It was sufficient to get them a three-year song-writing contract with Dick James Music, where they were required to churn out potential top-forty material. Anything more adventurous was not encouraged until publicist, Steve Brown, joined the company and urged them to capitalize on their own original ideas.

One result was Elton's first single, *Lady Samantha* (1969), which at least helped promote a debut album in June of that year: *Empty Sky*. It was promising, but had little impact.

Things began to happen when the pair joined up with producer, Gus Dudgeon, and arranger, Paul Buckmaster. The second album, *Elton John*, was released in April 1970, followed by a third in October, *Tumbleweed Connection*. It was a compelling, atmospheric album which gained both critical and public approval, making the UK top-twenty LP chart. Elton's first single hit (also in 1970) came with a track from the second album; *Your Song* made No 7 in the UK and, significantly, No 8 in America.

Forming The Elton John Band with bassist, Dee Murray and drummer, Nigel Olsson, and with the help of a massive publicity campaign, he scored a sensational success in the USA in summer 1970, playing in New York, Philadelphia and Los Angeles.

His next release of importance was *Madman Across The Water* (for which Davey Johnstone was recruited on guitar). Although this hinted that the duo's songwriting talents were being stretched to the full, it initiated a period of astonishing success for Elton. He had consistent singles hits, both sides of the ocean, with *Rocket Man, Honky Cat, Crocodile Rock, Daniel, Saturday Night's Alright For Fighting, Goodbye Yellow Brick Road, Bennie And The Jets, Candle In The Wind, Don't Let The Sun Go Down On Me, The Bitch Is Back*, and, surprisingly Lennon/McCartney's *Lucy In The Sky With Diamonds*.

It was while asking Lennon's permission to record the latter, that the ex-Beatle said that if it reached No 1, he would perform live with Elton. It did, and their three songs on stage at Madison Square Garden, New York, on 28 November 1976 were to constitute John Lennon's last public performance.

February 1972 saw the release of one of Elton's most lasting albums, *Honky Chateau* and the beginning of the artistic peak of his career, as he changed from fashionable cult attraction to one of the highest-paid performers in music. *Don't Shoot Me I'm Only The Piano Player*, issued January 1973, was followed in October with the superlative double album *Goodbye Yellow Brick Road*.

But the pressure of producing sufficient material for two albums per year was telling and *Caribou*, although it sold well, was poorly received. It was recorded in haste, and Elton was particularly dissatisfied with the vocals, and wanted to withdraw one track completely. Luckily he didn't because *Don't Let The Sun Go Down On Me* was nominated for the Grammy award as best vocal performance of the year! The same year he signed a contract with MCA Records reportedly worth $8 million.

1975 was an eventful year as he attained American No 1s with *Philadelphia Freedom*

Top right: The pub pianist from Pinner singing his way to stardom.
Far right: His flashy style gained Elton the title of 'the Liberace of rock and roll.'
Right: One of his more reserved stage costumes; Elton remains a great entertainer.

and *Island Girl* and reached No 4 with the re-collection of a suicide attempt, *Someone Saved My Life Tonight*. The latter was drawn from another two-record set, *Captain Fantastic and The Brown Dirt Cowboy*, a somewhat self-indulgent and self-important autobiography of Elton and Bernie's past hard times. It made No 1 in the US album charts within one week of release and stayed there all summer.

An appearance as the *Pinball Wizard* in Ken Russell's film of *Tommy* was followed by the release of the underrated *Rock of the Westies* album for Dick James (DJM) before expiry of his contract in 1976. Elton had set up his own record company, Rocket Records, some while back but it was only now he could start releasing material, including that of American rock veteran, Neil Sedaka, and British singer, Kiki Dee. It was with her that he secured a UK No 1 with *Don't Go Breaking My Heart*.

A 1976 double album, *Blue Moves*, was un-inspired (despite yielding the hit single *Sorry Seems To Be the Hardest Word*). Bernie Taupin and Elton split in 1978. *Part Time Love* did better, a top-twenty hit in Britain and America, while *Song For Guy* made No 4 in the UK. In 1979, he played to full houses in Moscow and Leningrad, using only percussionist Ray Cooper. By now he had tamed his stage act, having supposedly retired from live performance in 1977.

Although not the hit maker of the seventies, Elton remains an enduring performer with successful albums (*21 at 33, The Fox, Jump Up* and *Too Low For Zero*) and the occasional top-ten single such as *Blue Eyes*. In 1980 he toured again with Murray and Olsson, but more and more of his time was being taken up with the chairmanship of his beloved Watford football club (not to mention his much-publicized hair transplants). In 1984 he surprised everybody by marrying Renate Blauel in Australia.

Elton returned to live action in 1983 with his original line-up and played a staggering 17 nights at the Hammersmith Odeon. A 1983 album, *Too Low For Zero* was his best for years, and produced dazzling videos and singles, notably *I'm Still Standing* and *The Passenger*. He was back in the UK chart in late 1985 and early 1986 with *Nikita*.

The late eighties were traumatic for Elton. His marriage broke up, his private life was dragged through the tabloid press (though a libel case proved allegations false) and he auctioned much of his stage wardrobe for charity. Little of this affected the music, however: he scored his first ever solo British No 1 with *Sacrifice* from 1989's *Sleeping With The Past* album, the TV-advertised *Very Best Of* was a UK chart-topper and in 1991 superstars of the caliber of Bon Jovi, Phil Collins, Kate Bush and more celebrated his work on the *Two Rooms* tribute album.

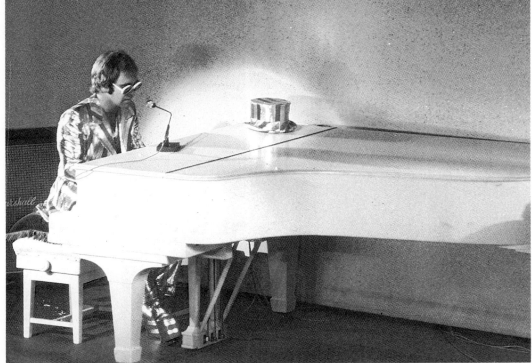

RECOMMENDED RECORDINGS

Elton John

Madman Across The Water

Honky Chateau

Don't Shoot Me I'm Only The Piano Player

Goodbye Yellow Brick Road *(double)*

Captain Fantastic And The Brown Dirt Cowboy

Jump Up

Too Low For Zero

Ice On Fire

Sleeping With The Past

The Very Best Of *(compilation)*

DAVID BOWIE

Glitter rock, disco, punk, new romanticism, all owe a debt to David Bowie music, his themes, his stage act, and his image – or rather, images: the question remains – who, which, is Bowie?

Born January 1947, a fight at school necessitated surgery on David Jones' left eye (the pupil has been paralyzed ever since). Taking up the saxophone, he played in various groups in the early sixties and, after leaving Bromley High School, took a job as a commercial artist in a London advertising agency. As David Jones and The Lower Third he cut an undistinguished album (it was resurrected and reissued in 1981), and some singles, one of which, *Liza Jane* (1964) has become an expensive collectors' item.

To avoid a clash with the similarly named member of American group, The Monkees, he adopted the surname Bowie (after the knife) and worked for a while with mime artist Lindsay Kemp, whose influence became apparent in his later stage act. An ice-cream commercial and bit parts in a TV play and two films were followed by a brief recording career with Pye Records. He moved to Decca in 1967, where the first album *The World of David Bowie* produced minor hits including the embarrassing, *Laughing Gnome* (rereleased by Decca in 1973).

In the late sixties, he briefly quit music altogether to study Zen Buddhism before returning to make the flawed but innovative *Space Oddity* album for Mercury. The title track made the top five in Britain when opportunely released near the time of the first Moon landing in 1969 (the much-admired keyboard playing on this track is the work of Rick Wakeman). However, Bowie failed to follow this success and after touring as a support act using a band called Hype, and putting together two unremarkable albums, he retired disillusioned to run an arts laboratory in Beckenham, Kent.

Pressure from Decca eventually took him back to the recording studio and *The Man who Sold The World*, issued in 1970, marked the turning point in his career. It was an astonishing album, a bleak, chilling, vision of the future: not quite what the record company had expected but it attained a considerable cult following.

His musical appetite restored, Bowie established a touring and recording band, the eventual Spiders from Mars: Mick Ronson, plus Trevor Bolder (bass) and 'Woody' Woodmansey (drums). In 1971, *Hunky Dory* was released to wide acclaim (Bowie was now with RCA). Although less trenchant than the previous album, it was equally compelling with tracks

such as *Changes*, *Life on Mars* and the anthem of beautiful youth, *Oh You Pretty Things*.

With his next recording, Bowie fashioned his most durable alter ego, and almost singlehandedly produced the blueprint for seventies glitter rock. Ziggy Stardust was the doomed rock messiah: adored, worshipped, but finally destroyed by the very fanaticism that created him. The album, *The Rise and Fall of Ziggy Stardust and the Spiders From Mars*, is one of rock's masterpieces, brilliantly conceived and executed.

As he took the Ziggy Stardust show to the USA in 1973, *Space Oddity* made a belated breakthrough in the singles charts there while *Starman* (taken from the album) reached No 10 in the UK (1972). Diversifying into record production, Bowie then revived the career of Lou Reed with the LP, *Transformer*. Expectations ran abnormally high for Bowie's own forthcoming album but, despite Ronson's inspired guitar work, *Aladdin Sane* was a little disappointing. However, it did produce a UK No 2 with *Jean Genie* and a No 3 with *Drive in Saturday*.

Above: In 1972, the alter ego of Ziggy Stardust 'became' Bowie, and gave birth to 'glitter rock.'
Left: 'Space control to Major Tom' – Bowie in the late sixties.
Right: In a guise of the thin white duke, 1974.

Above: One of rock's greatest performers, and a major influence and innovator for many years.
Left: Bowie has a tremendous, magnetic presence on stage.
Right: On stage in London during one of the stunning 'black and white' concerts of 1976, which preceded the Berlin trilogy, his most experimental music.

Pin Ups, also released in 1973, surprised his followers yet again with cover versions of favorite sixties hits, and in July of that year, at the end of a 60-concert UK tour, Bowie stunned them by announcing his retirement on stage at the Hammersmith Odeon in London.

RCA kept the hits coming with various album tracks, and in late 1973 Bowie filmed a TV special for NBC of America at London's Marquee Club, entitled *The 1980 Floor Show.* After its completion, he left to find fresh inspiration in Los Angeles.

The *Floor Show* became the framework for the 1974 recording *Diamond Dogs,* another grimly prophetic work that produced a UK No 5 with *Rebel, Rebel.* Putting together a wholly new and extravagant stage show, around *Diamond Dogs,* Bowie made a 'comeback' tour of America; the concert in Philadelphia was recorded (rather poorly) for the two-disc *David Live* set.

Philadelphia was also the venue of his next studio recording, another dramatic change of direction, this time toward black soul music. At Sigma Studio he teamed up with three of America's finest soul players, Willie Weekly (bass), Andy Newark (drums) and Carlos Alomar (guitar) to produce *Young Americans,* a blend of soul and disco that predated the disco boom itself by nearly three years.

Hit singles in 1975 came with the title track of the album, *Golden Years* and *Fame,* a surprising but memorable duet with John Lennon (it was Bowie's first US No 1, if not Lennon's).

The second Philadelphia Soul Brother recording, *Station to Station,* remains one of his best and hints at the electronic experimentation that was to follow. However, before that Bowie played the lead in Nicolas Roeg's film *The Man Who Fell to Earth* and also undertook a British tour, culminating in unforgettable performances at Wembley's Empire Pool in the

spring of 1976 – the 'black and white' shows that used only white lighting and where everything on stage was similarly either black or white.

The first of the so-called 'Berlin trilogy' with Brian Eno (ex-Roxy Music synthesizer wizard) was *Low,* an accurate reflection of Bowie's mood at the time. Relying heavily on strange, atmospheric instrumentals conceived by Eno (the story goes that Bowie simply ran out of new songs by side two) the result baffled many, not least RCA and Bowie's manager. The most commercial track, *Sound and Vision,* was a single hit, but *Low* can now be seen as an overture to the electrifying *Heroes* album. Recorded in the Hansa studio, a mere five hundred yards from the Berlin Wall, this is Bowie at his most ambitious, confident and inspired.

Heroes was an artistic triumph, as was the third 'Berlin' recording, *Lodger,* which retold the age-old myth of the figure condemned to wander the world for eternity, summed up in the track *Fantastic Voyage.*

In 1978, Bowie re-emerged in public, first in a background role playing keyboards on Iggy Pop's US and UK tours, and then to undertake a tour of his own, documented in the live two-record set, *Stage.* Since then, stage and film activities have increasingly occupied Bowie.

Despite his film commitments, he was able to conceive the excellent *Scary Monsters (And Super Creeps)* album, bringing a No 1 hit with the awesome *Ashes to Ashes,* and the destruction of another Bowie image – Major Tom of *Space Oddity.* In the same year, 1980, *Fashion* reached No 5 in the UK.

His only UK No 1 in 1981 was an unexpected collaboration with the band Queen *(Under Pressure)* while, even more surprisingly, a duet with Bing Crosby produced a top-three hit in 1982 with *Peace on Earth.* The same year, music from *Low* and *Heroes* was adapted for the powerful German film, *Christianne F.*

There was nothing nostalgic about the Nile Rodgers-produced album *Let's Dance* (1983). It was pure, unequivocal dance music and, with the title track, a UK No 1 and US No 2 hit. Controversy, however, still wasn't far away with eyebrow-raising nude scenes in the video to accompany the second hit single from the album, *China Girl* (a UK No 2). The next album release was a live double of the soundtrack for the film of Ziggy Stardust. Touring Europe and the UK for the first time in seven years also revealed that Bowie's drawing power as a live performer hadn't diminished, and the film *Merry Christmas Mr Lawrence,* demonstrated his increasing power as an actor. Of late, Bowie has become a warmer and more accessible artist, reflected in his contribution to Live Aid. *Absolute Beginners* has proved another cinema success.

After 1987's disappointing *Never Let Me Down,* Bowie's next project was the heavy metal band Tin Machine whose two albums, *Tin Machine* (1989) and *Tin Machine II* (1991), were split by a 'farewell' solo tour. With CD sales of his reissued back catalog booming, a newspaper survey suggested he was among the world's top 200 richest people.

RECOMMENDED RECORDINGS
The Man Who Sold The World
Hunky Dory
The Rise and Fall of Ziggy Stardust and the Spiders from Mars
Aladdin Sane
Diamond Dogs
Young Americans
Station to Station
Heroes
Lodger
Scary Monsters (And Super Creeps)
Let's Dance

DIANA ROSS

A colleague at Motown Records where Diane Earle worked as a typist remembers her as 'a secretary who could sing'. Thought, nothing – she could! With her friends, she became part of Motown's most popular vocal group, and alone she became the most successful female singer in the history of recorded music.

Above: The Supremes perform for a television pop show of the sixties, Diana on the extreme right taking lead vocal.
Below: 'In uniform' during the early days of success with Motown; from the left, Florence Ballard, Mary Wilson, and Diana Ross.

Right: Acknowledging the applause at an open-air concert in Central Park, NY.
Far right: Singing the blues, the most successful female entertainer in the world.
Below: Recently Diana has embraced many styles of music, from disco to jazz.

She was born into a poor family in Detroit on 26 March 1944. In her early teens she formed the Primettes with schoolfriends, and with Florence Ballard and Mary Wilson formed The Supremes. After a couple of moderate successes *Where Did Our Love Go* became an immediate US No 1, and reached No 3 in the UK. It set the pattern for an unprecedented sequence of hit singles, beginning with the worldwide No 1, *Baby Love*.

The astute song-writing and production skills of Brian and Eddie Holland and Lamont Dozier helped shoot the Supremes to fame, but Diana Ross's personal magnetism made itself felt early on.

Stop! In The Name Of Love and *Back In My Arms Again* completed a run of five US No 1s. *Nothing But Heartaches* stuck at No 11, but *I Hear A Symphony* again hit the top spot. *My World Is Empty Without You* made No 5, and the chart-toppers recommenced with *You Can't Hurry Love, You Keep Me Hangin' On* and *The Happening*. Shortly after Florence Ballard had left to be replaced by Cindy Birdsong the group became Diana Ross and The Supremes.

Holland-Dozier-Holland left Motown, and fresh songwriters brought fresh ideas. The next two singles showed a radical shift to more serious subjects, and *Love Child* ranks as one of the finest things they ever recorded. Sung with emotional intensity far removed from the carefree insouciance of their previous recordings, it was followed by the equally powerful *I'm Livin' In Shame*. Their last hit before Diana Ross went solo was Johnny Bristol's *Someday We'll Be Together*. It was their twelfth US No 1 in five years.

Her first solo single, however, was only moderately successful; *Reach Out And Touch (Somebody's Hand)* was a passionate message addressed to the parents of teenage drug addicts. *Ain't No Mountain High Enough,* a remake of the Marvin Gaye/Tammi Terrell hit, returned to more acceptable themes and was a US No 1 and UK No 6.

She also made lavish television shows, had major concerts on Broadway and in Las Vegas, and in 1973 made a stunning acting debut in

Lady Sings The Blues, which earned her an Oscar nomination.

Touch Me In The Morning, title track of a successful album, became No 1 in 1973. In 1974, she made an LP with Marvin Gaye: it produced a UK top-ten hit with *You are Everything,* and an American top-ten entry with *My Mistake (Was To Love You).*

Her second film appearance, in *Mahogany,* might also be counted a mistake. The theme song, however, *Do You Know Where You're Going To,* was Diana at her best and made No 1 in America and No 5 in Britain. It brought her total of US No 1s to sixteen. Motown decided on a hugely expensive ($23 million) 'black remake' of the Wizard of Oz, *The Wiz,* with Diana Ross as Dorothy. The musical had a lukewarm reception and is still well short of recouping its costs.

After making *The Boss* album in 1979, Diana Ross left Motown to join RCA/Capitol. It must have been a difficult and saddening decision for her; for twenty years, Berry Gordy had guided her – she once described him as 'father, mother, brother, sister, lover.'

Her success on disc was variable in the eighties, although she did have her biggest solo success of all with the memorable *Upside Down* from *Diana,* her last Motown recording. It made the top in America and No 2 in the UK. Another top-ten hit both sides of the ocean came from her first RCA/Capitol album, *Why Do Fools Fall In Love* (1981).

The 1981 US chart-topper *Endless Love* (a duet with Lionel Richie) was her last major eighties hit until the Bee Gees rejuvenated her career with *Chain Reaction,* a Supremes soundalike UK No 1 in 1986. Her spell away from Motown was otherwise disappointing in sales terms (though a 1983 concert in Central Park, New York, attracted nearly 250,000 fans), but her fame remains untarnished despite the lull.

RECOMMENDED RECORDINGS
(with The Supremes)
Greatest Hits Vols I & II
Love Child
Anthology
At Their Best
(Solo)
Lady Sings The Blues
Touch Me In The Morning
Diana Ross
The Boss
Diana

PAUL McCARTNEY & WINGS

The most energetic and productive of the ex-Beatles, and now acknowledged as the most commercially successful songwriter of all time, McCartney has not however enjoyed equivalent critical acclaim since 1970. Singles and albums have sold in consistently large numbers for Mr and Mrs McCartney – produced by a varied bunch of ex-Wings colleagues. Mull Of Kintyre sold over two million copies in Britain. Recently, Paul has enjoyed considerable success in duet with both Stevie Wonder and Michael Jackson, and certainly shows no sign yet of retiring.

McCartney, Paul's first album after the Beatles split up, was an interesting debut insofar as he played every instrument himself, and was assisted only by Linda on vocals. It has an appealing freshness, if a lack of polish, and includes the classic Maybe I'm Amazed.

Linda sang on the second album, Ram, issued 1971, and backed by New York session men. It was not well received but that didn't stop Uncle Albert/Admiral Halsey becoming a US No 1 hit.

In late 1971, McCartney formed the first Wings line-up with guitarist Denny Laine and drummer Denny Seiwell. Their opening collaboration was the indifferent, Wild Life, and Red Rose Speedway was little better, although it yielded an American No 1 with My Love.

Joining the band on this recording was Henry McCullough, one-time member of the Grease Band. Several changes in personnel took place during the seventies: Geoff Britten, Joe English and Steve Holley, for example, all had stints on drums, and Jimmy McCulloch on guitar.

The single *Give Ireland Back To The Irish* was released in the wake of the 'Bloody Sunday' massacre in Londonderry in 1972 and was banned by the BBC for its sentiments. It was a modest hit both sides of the Atlantic. The political line was unusual for McCartney and the next single could hardly have been more different – the cosy naivety of *Mary Had A Little Lamb*.

Hi Hi Hi was also banned in some places for its drug connotations. It was one of Wings' best

'A' sides and the 'B' side showed the growing influence reggae had on McCartney's music.

1973 was an eventful year with a drugs charge for McCartney, a TV special shown throughout Britain and America and a UK tour. After the tour, McCullough and Seiwell left, leaving Paul to compose the theme song for the James Bond film, *Live and Let Die*. At first the film's producers were skeptical about releasing McCartney's own version, but they were proved wrong as it made No 2 in America and No 9 in Britain.

The venue for the next recording was Ginger Baker's studio in Lagos, Nigeria. Accompanied only by Linda and the ever-faithful Denny Laine, he made his best post-Beatle album, *Band On The Run*. It spent two years in the LP charts, has

sold over five million copies, and contains many superb songs. The title track reached No 2 in the US, *Jet* also hit the charts and *Let Me Roll It* is McCartney at his smiling best.

Unfortunately, *Venus and Mars*, released in 1975, largely failed, although the track *Listen To What The Man Said* made the No 1 in the US and No 6 in Britain. The subsequent album *Wings At the Speed Of Sound* saw Paul sharing the songwriting load with the rest of the band with lackluster results. His own *Silly Love Songs* was a nicely tongue-in-cheek retort to his critics and made No 1 in the USA, No 2 in the UK.

The band began a world tour in 1975, finishing in the USA. The concerts were taped to produce the triple live album, *Wings Over America. Mull of Kintyre* (1977) became the best-selling single in history, and in 1979 he signed reputedly the most lucrative contract the music industry has ever seen. In Japan in 1980 he was arrested for possession of marijuana and was detained for ten days.

His material for Michael Jackson's *Off The Wall* album was of a very high standard. A single recorded with Michael Jackson, *The Girl is Mine*, reached No 2 in America and No 8 in Britain during 1982. *Ebony And Ivory*, a collaboration with Stevie Wonder in 1982, made No 1 in both the US and UK. Less successful was the film *Give My Regards to Broad Street* – by McCartney's standards a failure.

Songwriting collaborations with 10CC's Eric Stewart and, later, Elvis Costello spiced up his eighties output: 1989's *Flowers In The Dirt* topped the UK chart. Just when it seemed he'd done it all, Paul came up with *Choba B CCCP*, a good-time set of rock 'n' roll standards cut exclusively for the USSR, though later released elsewhere. He opened the nineties with *Tripping The Live Fantastic*, a recording of his first post-Wings tour.

RECOMMENDED RECORDINGS
Band On The Run
Wings Greatest Hits
Wings Over America (*3 disc set/live*)
Pipes Of Peace

Above: Taking first prize in the Buddy Holly lookalike competition? Paul the rocker was greatly influenced by Holly, and now owns the rights to his songs.
Left: Wings were just a threesome in 1973 when the best-selling *Band on the Run* was cut. Denny Laine (right) on guitar.
Right: Paul and Linda duet on a ballad.
Below: Paul belts it out.

ROD STEWART

To compare Rod Stewart's early recordings with the most recent is to encounter two entirely separate people with two very different sets of values. When denounced by Britain's punks in the seventies for betraying his roots, Stewart simply asked, 'What do they expect me to do with all the money? Give it back?'

Although proud of his Scottish ancestry, Rod Stewart was in fact born in north London in January 1945. His first musical influences were folk legends like Woody Guthrie and blues masters such as Sonny Boy Williamson. John Baldry heard him busking, and Stewart for a while became joint vocalist, but he left Shotgun Express after wrangling. He attempted to make it solo, but was eventually co-opted into the group led by guitarist, Jeff Beck. The band made two albums that impressed critics if not record buyers, *Truth* (1968) and *Beck-Ola* (1969), but Stewart left, signing a solo contract with Mercury Records on his way.

That contract, however, didn't prevent him also working with The Faces. This was to become his finest hour. Combining favorite folk and blues standards with equally notable compositions of his own, Rod and The Faces produced two inspired albums: *An Old Raincoat Won't Ever Let You Down* (retitled *The Rod Stewart Album* in the States) and *Gasoline Alley*. What his hoarse, scraping, gutteral voice lacked in quality was more than made up for by its unabashed sincerity and commitment.

Established in the US as a solo singer, and with two tours there in 1970, both albums sold well as a result. He decided to pursue a career that allowed one solo recording per year, and one as part of The Faces.

As lyricist, producer, and vocalist, he recorded the album which was finally to put him among the immortals: *Every Picture Tells A Story* brims with great songs, from the title track

to Tim Hardin's *Reason To Believe*, Stewart's own haunting, *Mandolin Wind*, and the classic, *Maggie Mae*, which topped the US and UK singles charts at the same time. Simultaneously, the album headed both UK and US LP charts and *Rolling Stone* magazine made Rod 'Rock Star of 1971.' Listening to his recordings, it sounded as though everyone was having a good time making them. Seeing the band on stage, you knew they were.

Never A Dull Moment (1972) was a predictable success but, for the first time, musically disappointing. *You Wear It Well* provided a single hit, but it was to be one of the last he composed himself. He relied on cover versions in 1972 and 1973. Release of the next album was long-delayed by a legal wrangle between Mercury and Warner Brothers as to who had the right to issue it. A compilation, *Sing It Again, Rod* was issued to plug the gap, but when *Smiler* finally appeared in 1974, it was an anticlimax. Only one original song maintained the previous standards, *Farewell*, otherwise the best tracks were reworkings of Sam Cooke numbers.

The cracks were beginning to show when they went to record *Atlantic Crossing* with ace producer, Tom Dowd at the Muscle Shoals studio in Alabama. It yielded a famous anthem *Sailing*, which became a hit. The same sessions also put down some tracks, which according to Tom Dowd are quite superb. They're never been released and, says Dowd, are there for when Rod needs to press the panic button.

In 1975, Stewart decided to go solo. Ronnie Lane had already left and now Ron Wood had been lured to join the Rolling Stones. Competent US session musicians filled the gap and Rod became a tax exile. America greeted him with his biggest single hit yet – eight weeks at No 1 for *Tonight's The Night*. It was taken from the successful album *A Night On The Town*, responsible for two further winners: *The Killing of Georgie* and *The First Cut Is The Deepest*. Sadly, this did not preface a major revival of Rod's composing talent.

For the next couple of years, it was his life-style, not his music that attracted the attention. Rod was having a good time. However, his concerts became grotesque, tawdry and self-parodying, but the more outrageous he became, the more people seemed to love it.

In between it all, he did get to the recording studio to make *Footloose and Fancy Free*, which also produced three good singles: *You're In My Heart, Hot Legs* and *I Was Only Joking*. In 1978, *Blondes Have More Fun* included the appalling *Do Ya Think I'm Sexy*. With another world tour, it became an international No 1.

Unremarkable albums and singles have followed but very few songs have recaptured the old glory. In December 1982 a televised show from the Los Angeles Forum is reputed to have attracted a worldwide audience of 35 million. If only they knew what they'd missed ...

Above: The return of Rod the Mod? In concert, London 1983.
Right: 'Do Ya Think I'm Sexy?' Was there ever any doubt, Rod?
Below: At his best, Rod's concerts were more like parties than performances.

RECOMMENDED RECORDINGS
An Old Raincoat Won't Ever Let You Down (US Title: The Rod Stewart Album)
Gasoline Alley
Every Picture Tells A Story
Sing It Again, Rod
Rod's Greatest Hits
A Nod's As Good As A Wink To A Blind Horse (Issued as Faces)

JANIS JOPLIN

It was a tempestuous and tragically short career, but it was enough to establish a reputation that the years have in no way diminished. No white woman has ever sung the blues quite like Janis; the joy and the hurt, nothing was withheld from her audience. She gave them everything, every time, and finally, she gave them her life.

Janis was born in Texas in 1943. She came from a reasonably well-to-do family, and began singing in the bars and clubs of Austin around 1961. She sang a mixture of country and blues which owed a lot to the two black singers she admired, and to whom she would one day be compared: Bessie Smith and Billie Holliday. Janis performed with a local folk group, the Waller Creek Boys and made her recording debut in 1962 with an advertising jingle for a bank, sung to the tune of *This Land is Your Land*. She first tasted the San Francisco scene in 1962, encouraged by producer, Chet Helms, who had been impressed by her performance at Threadgill's club in Austin, and returned there in 1966 to take the lead vocal role for a highly promising local band at the center of the burgeoning hippy cult – Big Brother and The Holding Company. Between 1962 and 1966, however, her increasing appetite for drink and drugs landed her with a spell in hospital. After being weaned off Methedrine and heroin (for a time) she returned to Texas. It was again Helms who sent a friend to Texas to recall her to California. Janis and Big Brother made a strong impression at their debut in June 1966 and, despite its rather primitive production, an album on Mainstream Records spread the message that here was a group to be reckoned with. Sam Andrew was on guitar, Peter Albin on bass, James Gurly on guitar and Dave Getz on drums.

The promise was fulfilled at the Monterey Festival of August 1967. She roared and growled her way through the set, fiery, brassy, unashamedly physical. She sang the great blues standard, *Ball and Chain* with a venom which, as the film of the festival shows, she never committed to vinyl. At Monterey she shared the spotlight with Jimi Hendrix, and Otis Redding, whom she idolized. All three turned in sensational performances and, by a chill twist of fate, three years later, all three were dead.

Now acclaimed by audiences and critics, in January 1968 the band signed with Dylan's manager, Albert Grossman, and recorded the *Cheap Thrills* album for CBS in New York. With strong interpretations of *Pieces of My Heart* (a hit single), *Turtle Blues, Ball and Chain,* and even Gershwin's *Summertime,* the album sold a million on its American release that July. Such was the phenomenal growth of their reputation. Big Brother were a driving force in the new rock music coming out of San Francisco and Janis' popularity was only comparable to that of Grace Slick of the Airplane. Yet along with the artistic reputation went one for wild, turbulent living, gross overindulgence and a stormy temperament. Her departure from the band to go it alone in 1968 left much bad feeling, but was hardly unexpected.

Her debut with the newly formed Kozmic Blues Band (retaining Sam Andrew on guitar) came at the Memphis Sound Party in December. Although it was a fairly 'untogether' performance, shortly after the album *I Got Dem Ol' Kozmic Blues Again, Mama* appeared to enthusiastic reviews. Throughout 1969 the tide of praise looked to be moving too fast even for Janis. She not only lived up to her reputation as 'the greatest white female blues singer' but also exceeded her previous excessive drinking and pleasure-seeking.

By their appearance at the Woodstock Festival in August, the personnel of the band had changed and the musicianship had considerably improved. The Janis Joplin Revue gave its final concert in December 1969 at Madison Square Garden, New York, and she then formed the Full Tilt Boogie Band in the spring of 1970. Brad Campbell and John Till (guitars) were retained from the previous line-up, and Richard Bell (piano), Ken Pearson (organ) and Clark Pearson (drums) were added to make an excellent backing band. After a summer tour, they began recording songs for a new album *Pearl,* and had finished eleven of them when Janis Joplin was found dead from a heroin overdose in a Hollywood hotel bedroom on 4 October 1970.

Pearl (it was the nickname her friends gave her) was issued posthumously, but unfinished. It contains some of her greatest work, including the unforgettable rendition of Kris Kristofferson's *Me and Bobby McGee* (US No 1). Other fine tracks include *Cry Baby, Get It While You Can* and the tongue-in-cheek *Mercedes Benz.*

Janis Joplin entered rock mythology. A film documentary *Janis* was put together in 1974 and a two-record soundtrack issued. Two biographies appeared, and the inevitable *Greatest Hits* album appeared in 1973. Material from 1963-65 was reissued in 1975 as *Janis/Early Performances,* mainly country and folk standards in unremarkable performances recorded live in Texas, and with a jazz band in San Francisco. More importantly, a double live album issued in 1972 captured the ecstasy and excitement of her concert performances as the studio albums never did.

Janis single-handedly shattered a stereotype. Before Janis, the women of rock and roll were still expected to look and act as if they'd like to make love to all the men in the audience. Janis changed that; she made love, too, but it was to everybody. Then, as she once put it so poignantly, she went home alone.

RECOMMENDED RECORDINGS
Big Brother and The Holding Company
Cheap Thrills
I Got Dem Ol' Kozmic Blues Again, Mama
Pearl
Janis Joplin In Concert
Greatest Hits
Janis *(soundtrack)*
Farewell Song

Right: They called her 'Pearl,' and on stage, she gave everything, every time.
Below: Janis on stage, with her Revue, 1969.

SUPERGROUPS

THE BEACH BOYS

Surfin', *when issued as a single in 1961, opened up a wholly original subject area of pop music. To identify with a new, fun-loving audience, the manager of their small-time record label came up with a new name: The Beach Boys. They were to outlive the brief popularity of 'surf music' to become the only American rock band, apart from The Four Seasons, seriously to challenge the 'British invasion' of the mid-sixties, led by the Beatles.*

The Beach Boys were a family affair. Brian Wilson was born in June 1942, Dennis in December 1944 and Carl in December 1946. They formed a band in 1961 to play at high-school dances, with Dennis on drums, Carl on lead guitar, Brian on bass and keyboards, their cousin, Mike Love, on saxophone and friend, Al Jardine, on rhythm guitar. They called themselves Carl and The Passions and Kenny and The Cadets (Brian was Kenny) before *Surfin'* was released, first on the one-man-and-his-dog X label, and then the slightly bigger Candix. Their father, Murray, liaised between group and record company.

They had created 'surf music' and with their distinctive falsetto vocalizing, sweet harmonies and twangy guitars, its 'sound,' too. Unusually, they had few influences, although the sound had its roots in the Everly Brothers and The Four Freshmen.

They made their stage debut as The Beach Boys at a memorial concert in Long Beach for singer Ritchie Valens in December 1961. A tour of the US followed early in 1962 with David Marks temporarily replacing Al Jardine.

Signing for Capitol Records, they notched three more 'surf' hits: *Surfin' Safari* (US No 14), *Surfin' USA* (making No 3 in America and edging into the British chart at No 34) and *Surfer Girl* (US No 1). Then Brian turned his attention to other parts of the young scene – hot rod cars and dragster racing with *Little Deuce Coupe* (No 15), and high-school rivalry with *Be True To Your School* (No 6).

By 1964 The Beach Boys had their first gold album: *Surfin' USA*, what else? They had a good measure of singles success, too, in 1964, with *Fun Fun Fun* and *Little Honda* (by the Hondells) making the top five and the inspired *I Get Around* giving them a first US No 1 and UK No 7. The 'B' side, *Don't Worry Baby*, was a minor masterpiece, as was their last hit single that year, *When I Grow Up (To Be A Man)*.

It was songs such as this that brought them serious critical interest. But the effort of composing and touring was taking its toll of Brian Wilson. He was also rapidly going deaf in one ear. In early 1965, he had a nervous breakdown and quit the band to devote himself to songwriting and production. They became probably the first rock group to be wholly self-produced.

He was replaced briefly by Glen Campbell and then by Bruce Johnston. The change didn't affect their popularity: *Help Me Rhonda* and *California Girls* making US No 1 and No 3 and UK No 27 and No 26 respectively. Brian now wrote songs of ever-greater invention and subtlety, notable on the album *Beach Boys – Today*. But two early 1966 hits were not penned by him: *Barbara Ann* (US No 2 and UK No 3) and a reworking of the folk song *Sloop John B.*

Working with lyricist Tony Asher, and utilizing innovative studio techniques, Brian produced *Pet Sounds* while the band was on tour. The songs were a far cry from the endless summer of surfing, altogether more deeply felt. *Wouldn't It Be Nice, Caroline No*, and *God Only Knows* (US No 2) were but three fine numbers. However the sheer complexity of the production made it difficult, if not impossible, to reproduce the album on stage. *Pet Sounds* was greeted enthusiastically by the critics and was a great success with Beach Boys fans in Britain, but failed badly in the US.

The American failure hit Brian badly. He began taking LSD, and tried to disown his previous music, but recovered sufficiently to compose one of the best rock songs of all time, *Good Vibrations*. It took ninety studio hours to put together but was well worth it; a US and UK No 1, it went gold with ease. Encouraged, Brian began work with lyricist Van Dyke Parks on a major concept album to be called *Smile*, but from the start it was plagued by problems. The band wanted something more commercial and resented Parks' influences. Brian's drug usage, and unpredictable behavior caused many delays and the triumphant release in 1967 of *Sgt Pepper* by their rivals, The Beatles, was the final blow. Brian despaired. Contractually required to produce something from the mess, he took three or four of the simpler songs he'd written such as *Heroes And Villains*, added some other reasonably good, new material and released the package as *Smiley Smile*, which was, somewhat unfairly, maligned.

It was a bad period for all The Beach Boys. Brian contributed less and less to subsequent albums. 1968's *Wild Honey*, a more basic set recorded in his living room, again took a critical hammering. Dennis had severe personal problems, and Mike Love took to transcendental meditation, reflected in the 1968 *Friends* album. A 1969 US tour was near-disastrous and, despite a UK No 1 with *Do It Again*, by 1970 The Beach Boys were at the nadir of their career.

Above: Augmented rhythm section in the 70s.
Far left: In the surfin' sixties: from the top, Brian, Dennis, Al, Mike, Carl.
Above left: Brian Wilson – his songs made the group successful
Right: Getting some good vibrations.
Previous pages: The Who – dynamic on stage.

They switched to Warner Brothers after an attempt to form their own label, Brother Records, and looked revitalized at the Big Sur Folk Festival. Their first Warner Brothers' album, *Sunflower*, has been consistently underrated.

In the summer of 1971 they released *Surf's Up*. The title track was an original from *Smile*, refurbished along with other tapes by their new manager, Jack Rieley. The album received many critical plaudits and put the group back among the world's top rock bands.

Bruce Johnston quit in 1972 and Ricky Fataar and Blondie Chaplin joined to fill out the rhythm section for a couple of years. Although their live performances were popular, they failed to put together an album. Then, transferring to Brother Studios (and taking Brian along), they went to Amsterdam to make *Holland*, one of the best of their later albums.

In 1974 James Guercio became their manager. During this period they had better luck in the UK singles charts than in the US, *Cottonfields* made No 5, a rerelease of *Good Vibrations* No 18 in 1976, and *Lady Lynda* No 6 in 1979.

As if to confirm the conservatism of their following, two compilation albums achieved million sales: *Endless Summer* and *Spirit of America*. 1976's *15 Big Ones* was greeted with much publicity, which in the end wasn't justified.

The Beach Boys Love You, the best album since *Holland*, appeared in 1977, with production and song writing credited to Brian Wilson. However, 1978's *M.I.U.* was a disjointed effort that sold badly.

L.A. (Light Album) was better and *Keepin' The Summer Alive* (both 1979) was much better, mainly because Bruce Johnston returned.

Johnston's *Endless Harmony* could stand as a fitting epitaph for the band. 1981's *Ten Years Of Harmony* was less inspired.

For the remainder of the eighties the group did mostly movie tie-in singles, one of which *Kokomo* from the Tom Cruise film *Cocktail* reached the US No 1 spot in 1988. The same year saw Brian's first, self-named solo album – though relations were strained when the brothers (except Dennis, who drowned in 1983) took legal action to split him from long-time guru Eugene Landy.

RECOMMENDED RECORDINGS

Pet Sounds
Smiley Smile
Sunflower
Surf's Up
Holland
Endless Summer *(compilation)*
Spirit Of America *(compilation)*
The Beach Boys Love You
Keepin' The Summer Alive

THE BEATLES

In John Lennon and Paul McCartney, The Beatles possessed the best songwriting team rock music has ever seen. Inventive and ambitious, they mastered many diverse styles: up-tempo dance numbers, ballads, comic songs, folk, country and western, rhythm and blues. The genius of their music was equalled by their imagination when making records: the novel production techniques and pioneering ideas for instrumentation which they explored had repercussions everywhere. Indeed their influence in molding the future of popular music was incalculable, and is still being felt. Every rock group that takes the stage today owes something to The Beatles.

Among the 300-odd groups playing in Liverpool in the sixties was one called The Quarrymen, named by its founder, John Lennon (b October 1940), after the Quarry Bank High School which they attended. In summer 1956 fifteen-year-old James Paul McCartney joined the group and shortly after Paul introduced George Harrison (b February 1943).

In 1959, Lennon went to the Liverpool College of Art and persuaded Stuart Sutcliffe to join the band on bass. They played under a variety of names before finally becoming The Beatles. Pete Best joined on drums and they backed Johnny Gentle on a tour of Scotland. On their return, they played long hours in a Hamburg night club until the German authorities discovered George was below the age limit to perform on licensed premises.

Returning to Liverpool, they did a regular

stint at the popular Cavern Club, and established a solid reputation in northwest England. They made some recordings in Germany under the direction of Bert Kampfaert, mostly backing Tony Sheridan, but The Beatles themselves made *Ain't She Sweet* and *My Bonnie*.

Liverpool record-shop owner, Brian Epstein became intrigued by the many requests for these discs, and went to hear the group for himself at the Cavern. Sutcliffe had stayed on in Germany, and the bass was taken up by McCartney. Epstein was impressed by the group. He arranged an audition with the Decca label, who turned them down. It was the same when he sent demonstration tapes to two of EMI's labels, HMV and Columbia, but the head of Columbia's small Parlophone label, George Martin, liked what he heard. When a recording session was fixed, The Beatles were once again

in Hamburg and Epstein telegramed them to return.

For some of the recordings they made in Germany, Pete Best was unavailable. They used Richard Starkey (b 1940), but every one knew him as Ringo Starr. However, for the first Parlophone sessions, Best was on the drum stool. George Martin was unimpressed by him, so in August 1962, Ringo Starr took a permanent job with The Beatles.

Love Me Do was their first single, a John and Paul composition that sold hand-over-fist in Merseyside but only moderately well elsewhere. It reached No 17. In early 1963 they took another new composition to Martin, a Roy Orbison-style ballad entitled *Please Please Me*. He suggested speeding it up, and they agreed. At the end of the session he declared, 'Gentlemen, you have just made your first number one.'

They had, or at least a number two, according to some charts. It was a new music, and suddenly people couldn't get enough of it. They rocketed to fame during 1963 in a manner never seen before or since. *From Me To You* and *She Loves You* went straight to No 1, and the album *Please Please Me* stayed at No 1 for 30 weeks. It was a mixture of original songs and favorites from their live repertoire, among them a blistering version of *Twist and Shout*.

In their own songwriting, Lennon and McCartney had learned a lot from the Americans. Their harmonies, for instance, were derived from the black girl groups, whose songs often relied on a call-and-response style. One of the most common responses was simply, 'yeah' – The Beatles adopted it and 'Yeah, yeah, yeah' became their trademark.

All their success thus far had been confined

to Britain. EMI's American Capitol label thought the band unsuitable for the US market. But when Capitol promoted the fifth single, including an appearance on the coast-to-coast TV *Ed Sullivan Show*, the dam broke.

I Want To Hold Your Hand went to No 1 both sides of the Atlantic, and by the time the band arrived in New York to begin their first US tour, the other singles had been rereleased and were filling the other four places in the American top five. Another seven tracks released as singles registered in the top 100. It was an unprecedented achievement.

Only one thing was going to shift their first album from the top of every chart – the second. Called *With The Beatles (Meet The Beatles* in the USA), it combined eight original compositions with six covers, among them Chuck Berry's *Roll Over Beethoven* and Smokey Robinson's *You Really Got A Hold on Me*. In Britain, it topped the LP chart for 22 weeks, and similar success was now being recorded all round the world.

The Beatles led 'the British invasion.' Other Liverpool groups made it big (usually under Epstein's guidance and with Lennon and McCartney songs) and they were followed by The Rolling Stones and the rest.

The Beatles spent most of 1964 touring, to hysterical audiences. The media dubbed it 'Beatlemania' and, for once, got it absolutely right. Single number six had the biggest advance orders of any record in music history – *Can't Buy Me Love*, naturally, went straight to No 1.

The Beatles went into films, but with as much originality as they did everything else. *A Hard Day's Night* was an amusing, quirky semi-documentary of the group's life. By now, Epstein's image manipulation was complete. The 'Fab Four' had long ago exchanged their leathers for matching suits and neat mop haircuts. Their popularity was universal. Anything The Beatles did made news.

Released, late in 1964, *Beatles For Sale* returned to the eight/six mixture of originals and covers, and had a distinctly country-meets-Buddy Holly flavor.

John and Paul's own material revealed a new maturity and sophistication: *No Reply, I'll Follow The Sun, Eight Days A Week* and *What You're Doing* were irresistible. So was *I Feel Fine*, another No 1 single, notable for John's clever 'fuzzed' guitar intro.

Thenceforth, they relied entirely on their own material, with George making an increasingly important contribution. *Ticket To Ride* broke new musical ground again but made the top spot with ease.

Released in 1965, Dick Lester's second film with the foursome, *Help*, was more self-indulgent and surreal in its humor. The title track became their biggest single hit yet and the soundtrack album, again, was full of good songs. They returned to the recording studio to produce the album which not only marked a new phase for The Beatles, but for popular music as a whole.

For many, *Rubber Soul* (1965) is the band at

their best. It's all there, from Paul's evergreen love ballad, *Michelle*, John's plaintive *Girl* and philosophical *The Word*. There was the ironic humor of *Norwegian Wood* (with George on the Indian sitar) and the poignant *In My Life*. *Rubber Soul* demanded to be judged as a work of contemporary art.

Revolver (1966) was no less an achievement, perhaps more an achievement in its innovative use of studio techniques. George Martin's contribution to their recordings can never be overestimated. Lennon and McCartney wrote most of the songs independently. *For No One* is Paul at his most wistful, and John's *Tomorrow Never Knows* explores a new sound world.

Between these two momentous albums, further US and UK No 1 singles came with *Day Tripper, We Can Work It Out* and the lyrically brilliant, *Paperback Writer*.

Toward the end of 1966, The Beatles gave their last live concert, in San Francisco, and in 1967 paid affectionate homage to their home town with what is arguably the finest pop single ever issued. On one side, Paul told of the colorful characters in *Penny Lane*, while on the other, John went tripping through *Strawberry Fields Forever*.

With advance sales of over one million, *Sgt Pepper's Lonely Hearts Club Band* was the summit of The Beatles recording career. Including orchestras, choirs and sound effects, it took a staggering 700 studio hours to record. The songs attained new levels of inspiration. *Lovely*

Rita, meter maid, Mr Kite and *Henry the Horse* entered folk mythology, the LSD-inspired imagery of John's *Lucy In The Sky With Diamonds* was like nothing heard before. Paul contributed the touching *She's Leaving Home* and the cheerful *When I'm Sixty Four. Day In The Life* is perhaps their most powerful single achievement. John's surreal vision is set against Paul's cameo of everyday life, and rarely have their own personalities been so vividly contrasted. The final screaming bars are devastating.

The summer of *Sgt Pepper* ended in tragedy. Brian Epstein died in August 1967 of an overdose of pills. It was a shattering blow to the four Beatles, although they had little need of Epstein's services now. All were deeply into Eastern mysticism (Ringo possibly with less enthusiasm than the others), and they decided to form Apple Corps, designed to encourage and support all manner of artistic ventures, including its own record label. Unfortunately, Apple went rotten. None of the four had much of a head for business. Another miscalculation was the hour-long TV film *Magical Mystery Tour*. It was too clever for its own good, and was poorly received. The songs didn't get the critical recognition they deserved, although the EP made No 2 in the UK chart. However *Yellow Submarine* has become a cartoon classic.

Prior to this, The Beatles had contributed in no small way to the flower power movement with *All You Need Is Love*. They played it live from Abbey Road studios and it was beamed by satellite to an estimated audience of 200 million around the world. It topped charts everywhere, of course, as did the next singles *Hello Goodbye*, and *Lady Madonna*.

Months were spent recording the next album, a double. Compared to *Sgt Pepper*, 1968's *The Beatles* (also known as 'the white album') is a disjointed but memorable collection of songs.

They had now switched to the Apple label themselves, releasing a seven-minute-long single, the chorusing *Hey Jude*, backed by *Revolution*: Paul the pop songsmith in uneasy alliance with political activist, John. It made No 1, and stayed there for nine weeks in America.

The next Beatles project was a multimedia presentation – record, book, film. They wanted

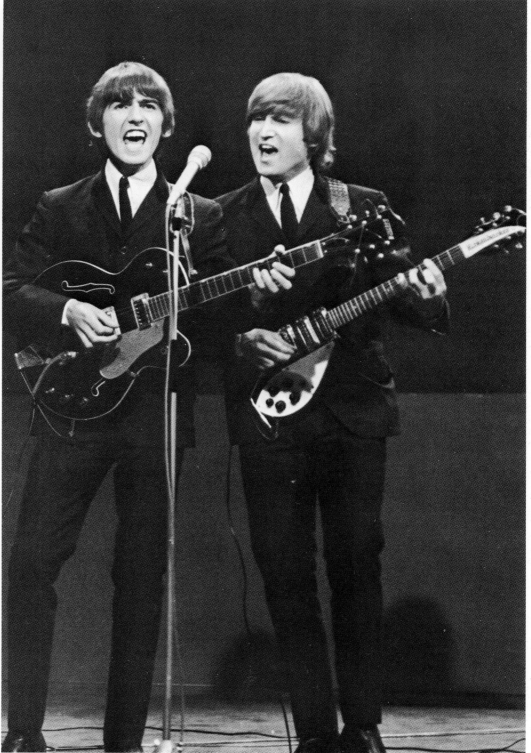

Above: Rehearsing 1963's Christmas show in London. Brian Epstein, their manager, gets an earful from George!
Above left: The Beatle suit was part of Epstein's 'image transformation.'
Right: George and John in harmony.
Below: The same pair take a break during filming of *Magical Mystery Tour*.
Previous page: The 'Fab Four' as they'll always be recalled, George, John, Ringo and Paul on bass.

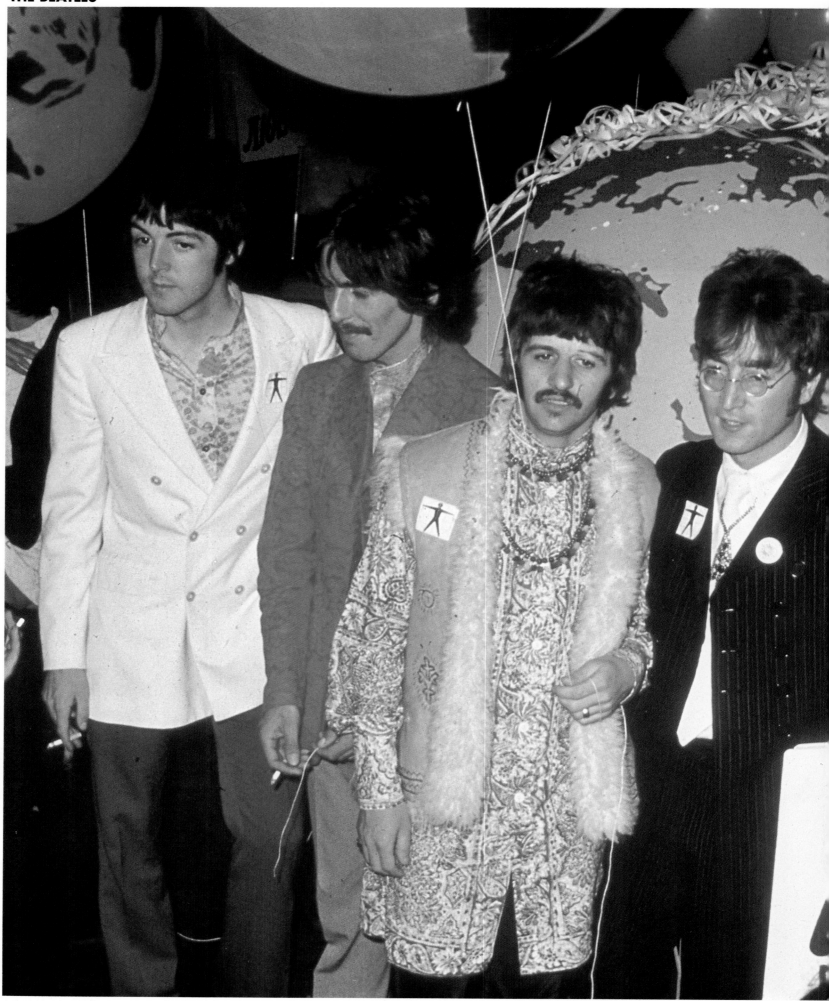

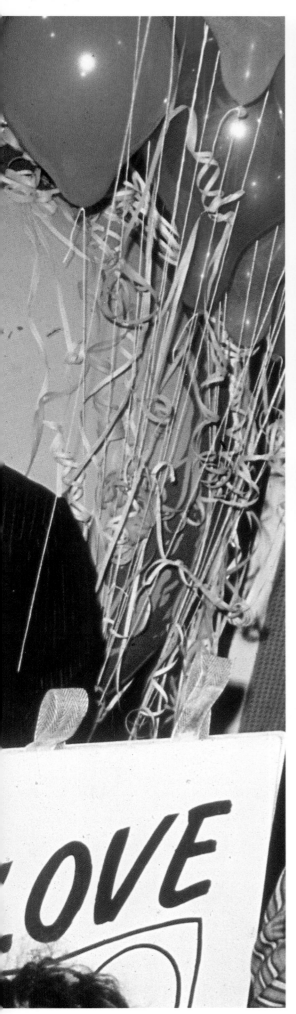

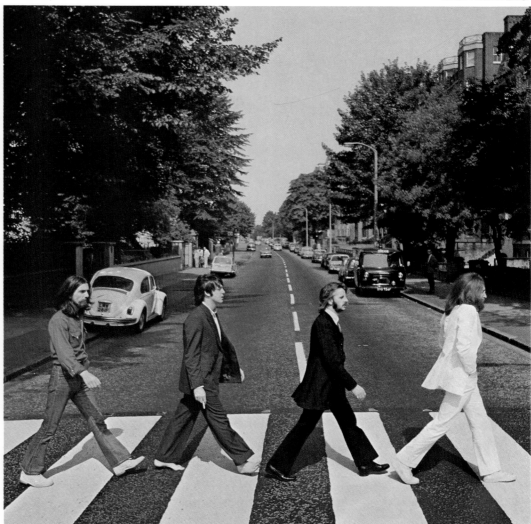

Left: On the set of 'Our World,' a worldwide satellite broadcast to 200 million and first hearing of *All You Need Is Love*.

Above: The Beatles as they appeared on the *Abbey Road* album.

the album to be as near a live performance as possible. *Get Back* contained many fine songs, but the sound tape was left 'in the can' pending completion of the whole project, although the provisional title track *(Get Back)*, and the eventual one, *Let It Be*, both became chart-topping singles in the US (No 1) and UK (No 2).

Another album was put together in the interim, the last tracks they were to lay down together. Appropriately, it was named *Abbey Road* after the scene of all their record triumphs. Ironically, *Abbey Road* has all the unity of *Sgt Pepper*, and songs of comparable quality, witness the beauty of *Here Comes The Sun* and George's *Something*.

When *Let It Be* appeared in 1970, the tapes had been remixed by the incomparable Phil Spector. The whole idea of basic simplicity was destroyed as Spector layered on the backing tracks. McCartney was annoyed that Spector, who by now was producing solo albums for Lennon, had been allowed to tamper with the tapes. It widened the already deep rift between John and Paul. Paul tried hardest of all to keep the four together, but when he saw the others no longer really cared, it was he who sued to dissolve the partnership in 1971. The Beatles era sadly ended on a discordant note, and after considerable litigation, the group wound up on 30 December 1974. John's murder on 11 December 1980 saddened the world.

The figures of the Beatles' achievements leaves one dizzy. Suffice it to say that their run of seventeen UK No 1s and twenty US No 1s has never been matched, nor is likely to be. Similarly, the list of their No 1 albums.

RECOMMENDED RECORDINGS

(The Beatles)	
Please Please Me	
With The Beatles (US: Meet The Beatles)	
A Hard Day's Night	
Beatles For Sale	
Help!	
Rubber Soul	
Revolver	
Sgt Pepper's Lonely Hearts Club Band	
The Beatles (the 'white album,' two records)	
Yellow Submarine	
Abbey Road	
Let It Be	
Magical Mystery Tour	
Live At The Hollywood Bowl	
The Beatles 1962-66 *(double compilation)*	
The Beatles 1967-70 *(double compilation)*	
A Collection of Beatles' Oldies (But Goodies) *(compilation)*	
20 Greatest Hits *(compilation)*	

THE DOORS

Jim Morrison was one of the rebels of rock music and, perhaps inevitably, one of its martyrs. In three years he declined from magnetic performer and visionary poet to paunchy alcoholic. He was twice arrested, frequently incited audiences to violence and, toward the end, often broke down in the middle of a song. But at his best, he was a unique songwriter and singer. Even though the rest of the group were accomplished musicians, Jim Morrison was The Doors.

James Morrison was born in December 1943, in Florida, into a family of military careerists. While studying theater arts at the University of Los Angeles, he met Ray Manzarek, an R&B fanatic. Manzarek had the idea of combining Morrison's poetry with music. With guitarist Robbie Krieger and drummer, John Densmore, Manzarek on keyboards (and supplying the bass line through a foot pedal) and Morrison on vocals, The Doors were formed.

They landed the job of house band in Los Angeles' fashionable Whiskey A Go Go. One night they played *The End.* Lengthy and semi-improvised, its subject matter was the psycopathic killing of his parents by their son. The club manager sacked them, but it impressed Jack Holzman of the Elektra label.

Their first album, released in early 1967, was an immediate success. Almost overnight they went from an underground cult to one of the top American rock bands. *The End* was representative of the topics that preoccupied Morrison — death, guilt, violence and sex. As well as Morrison's songs, it included *Whiskey Bar* from Brecht's *The Threepenny Opera*, and a song by Krieger that was to become one of the anthems of rock — *Light My Fire.* The original lasted nearly seven minutes and, abbreviated for single release, topped the US charts.

Morrison's stage act was a carefully cultivated mix of menace and latent animal sexuality. His off-stage image was similarly molded, even to the extent of claiming his parents were dead! He ruthlessly manipulated his audiences. Several times police were called to quell riots incited by Morrison's provocative on-stage behavior.

Album number two (also 1967) was more bizarre lyrically, but just as acclaimed. The tracks ranged from the eleven-minute *When The Music's Over* to melancholy ballads such as the title song, *Strange Days*, and *Unhappy Girl.* Throughout, Morrison's talent and poetic

flair were paramount. Whatever the uncouth image, he was widely read and deeply interested in philosophical ideas. This is most evident on the third LP, 1968's *Waiting For The Sun.* Of all the good material on this album it was the facile ditty, *Hello I Love You,* by Krieger which earned them another US No 1 (and UK No 16). Kinks' songwriter, Ray Davies, claimed it plagiarized his hit tune, *All Of The Day And All Of The Night.* Davies won, and collected the royalties on British sales of *Hello.*

On and off stage, Morrison was becoming ever more outrageous. In December 1967, performing in New Haven, Connecticut, he was arrested for using obscene language and inciting a riot; and in Miami, during March 1969, came the celebrated, but stupid incident of indecent exposure. He was acquitted, but unrepentant.

Morrison contributed little new material for the fourth album; *The Soft Parade* relies extensively on overt, and juvenile, pop songs by Krieger. It was a poor album and led to accusations that The Doors were as commercially minded as any other pop group.

They replied with a raw-edged, R&B set for *Morrison Hotel/Hard Rock Café* (1970); musically excellent, with taut, literate songs from Morrison, among them *Queen Of The Highway,* dedicated to his wife, Pamela. The same year, *Absolutely Live* finally captured Morrison's

Above: Morrison in the role of the Lizard King, potent and primeval. But in four years his lifestyle had destroyed him.
Top right: In the late sixties, the Doors lit the fires of rock and roll all over the USA. The Doors were dangerous! From the left, Krieger, Densmore, Manzarek, and Morrison.
Right: Manzarek (left) and Densmore were prime movers in putting together an album of Morrison's poetry recorded seven months before his death. The surviving Doors supplied the music.

poem *The Celebration Of The Lizard King* on tape. The band reached a creative peak in 1971 with the blues-flavored *L.A. Woman.* Among the powerful songs, with startling imagery, were *The WASP (Texas Radio And The Big Beat)* and their last single hit, *Riders On The Storm* (US No 14, and UK No 22).

However, the years of excess had taken their toll on Jim Morrison. Tired, disillusioned, in poor health, and more and more interested in poetry and theater than in rock and roll, he left the band and went to Paris. He died of a heart attack in his bath on 3 July, 1971, just twenty-seven years old. Along with Chopin, Rossini and Edith Piaf, he was buried in the cemetery of Père Lachaise and his tomb became an object of pilgrimage. Rumors spread that Morrison himself was still alive. They have remained rumors.

His poetry was published posthumously as *The Lords And The New Creatures*, while the remaining members of the band attempted to carry on. They succeeded in making two albums, the first, *Other Voices*, was better than anyone expected before drying up on *Full Circle* and subsequently disbanding.

In 1978 the survivors produced a unique tribute to Morrison, editing many hours of poetry tapes he had made and adding suitable backing tracks of their own. Issued as *An American Prayer*, it revived interest in Morrison with the result that a greatest-hits compilation achieved platinum status in the USA during 1980.

A 1991 feature film directed by Oliver Stone saw the soundtrack album lead a phalanx of Doors products back into the charts, emphasizing their continuing influence on rock.

RECOMMENDED RECORDINGS
Doors
Strange Days
Waiting For The Sun
Morrison Hotel/Hard Rock Café
Absolutely Live
L.A. Woman
An American Prayer
Greatest Hits
Alive She Cried *(live)*

LED ZEPPELIN

*L*ed Zeppelin defined what heavy metal was all about. Drawing on basic blues material and following in the wake of The Who, Hendrix and Cream, their success was almost instantaneous. Led Zeppelin's granite-hard, pile-driving sound (although frequently tempered with gentle, folksy acoustic material) provided the blueprint for all the seventies heavy-metal exponents.

Self-taught Jimmy Page was a much sought-after sessions musician, and his work can be heard on such diverse classics as The Who's *I Can't Explain* and Tom Jones' *It's Not Unusual*. Born in Heston, Middlesex in 1944, Jimmy learned note-for-note James Burton's and Scotty Moore's instrumental riffs. Other influences were American bluesman, Otis Rush, and British folk guitarist, Bert Jansch.

Resigning himself to the fact that he could never join a working rock band because of recurring sickness, he became 'house' producer and arranger for the Immediate label and an active sessions player. He was making a good living, but later joined the Yardbirds, eventually playing double-lead with Jeff Beck.

When The Yardbirds disbanded in July 1968, Jimmy Page, helped by bassist John Paul Jones, again became a sessions player. Then, together with Jones and Robert Plant (vocals) and John Bonham (drums), he formed The New Yardbirds.

Their first appearance on disc as a foursome was backing American singer, P J Proby on his 1969 album *Three Week Hero*. It was a short step from there to Led Zeppelin (the 'a' removed to avoid any confusion over pronounciation) and a management contract with manager of The Alan Price Combo and Nashville Teens, Peter Grant.

Apparently, after Dusty Springfield had confirmed the band's musicianship to Jerry Wexler of Atlantic Records, Grant was able to sign a recording contract with Wexler and Atlantic boss, Ahmet Ertegun. Jimmy Page and Robert Plant knew the band could move in either of two directions at this point: hard-rock or electric folk. They chose the former, and Page was largely the architect of the unique multi-decibel sound they produced, despite Plant's 'fronting' of the band. He became an expert producer, although the mixing on the first album might have been better left to Glyn Johns, who engineered it. Page's use of reverb and echo were put to good effect. He never underplayed the bass and drums, which gives Led Zeppelin's cuts such an emphatic attack. They decided to concentrate their commercial push on the United States.

Cream had been extremely popular there and left a gap to be filled when they disbanded. Led Zeppelin were ready to move in, after cutting their teeth in small-venue gigs

Above: Robert Plant salutes a Page solo.
Right: Blues guitarist Jimmy Page was the founder of Led Zeppelin, here playing one of his twelve-string 'axes.'

Above: Robert Plant – the voice of heavy metal.

around London, frequently billed as 'Led Zeppelin (formerly Yardbirds).'

First tour of the States was as support to Vanilla Fudge, but they were quickly back as the headliners. Atlantic mounted a massive, but ill-conceived, publicity campaign to promote their first album. As a result it was a long time before the American rock commentators took Led Zeppelin to their hearts. But it was hardly a problem. *Led Zeppelin* fully justified the hype, its mixture of blues basics and dynamic rock riffs, with strong material and high-energy delivery, was an immediate success, achieving gold status well within a year. It also gave a new form to rock and roll – heavy metal had been born, but with a good deal of finesse and expert musicianship. Page's feel for acoustic music and folk was also evident from the album, but was largely overlooked in the midst of powerhouse tracks such as *Dazed and Confused*, *The Hunter*, and a version of Willie Dixon's *You Shook Me*.

There was more than a hint of Dixon's *You Need Love* on the track which virtually became their theme song: *Whole Lotta Love*, which opens *Led Zeppelin II* (1969). For several years *Whole Lotta Love* was the signature tune of BBC's weekly TV pop show *Top Of The Pops*.

Ironically the chances of Led Zeppelin ever appearing on that programme were slim, since they never approved of Atlantic releasing singles in the UK. Grant thought singles were unnecessary in the UK, as the flourishing national music press gave all the exposure necessary. In the US, however, with its dependence on radio airplay, singles were essential and *Whole Lotta Love* was duly released, making No 4. Page's maddeningly memorable riff opens, followed by some rapidfire drumming from Bonham. The rhythm stomps on, while Plant's squealing vocals reach a height of hysteria in mock orgasm – primitive, physical, but the essence of rock music.

Led Zeppelin III (1970) was more acoustic and folk-orientated, and continued the process of world conquest. It gave a US No 16 with *Immigrant Song*, one of the tracks which always roused audiences at the group's concerts. *Stairway to Heaven*, another definitive composition from *Led Zeppelin IV* (1971), had a similar effect on their audiences. Beginning with a quiet acoustic introduction from Page, and a soft vocal from Plant, building throughout in a 'stairway-like' semitone progression, this quasi-mystical epic builds to a thunderous emotional climax. It has become another rock classic.

By March 1970, they'd toured the USA no less than five times in two years, compounding the success of *Led Zeppelin IV* (also known as the 'runes' or 'Zo-So' album, since there is no reference to the band whatsoever on the sleeve, just four occult symbols). Page had long been fascinated by mythology and mysticism, to the extent of becoming something of an expert. *Stairway* wasn't released as a single

despite its frequent airplays in the US. Grant and Atlantic shrewdly issued another superb track, *Black Dog*, instead (it made No 15).

D'Yer Make'Er, from 1973's *Houses Of The Holy* reached No 20 (it was sung to sound like 'Jamaica') and was one of the songs that provoked accusations of sexism. Plant's overtly macho stage presence also fueled them. This album was the most musically diverse to date, incorporating reggae, soul, folk and string backings.

The 1973 American tour broke all box office records, but interviews, and photocalls, were extremely rare, television and radio appearances almost always refused; the band kept deliberately enigmatic. After taking a sabbatical that lasted for most of 1974, no doubt to spend a little of the $30 million grossed from 1973's tours and concerts, they returned with a double album in 1975. *Physical Graffiti*, with its extraordinary 'tenement windows' sleeve, was musically impressive and varied, and contained one heavy-metal hymn, *Trampled Underfoot*. It was issued on Led Zeppelin's own recently established record label Swan Song.

The band was at its peak, but disaster struck in 1975 – Plant was seriously injured in a road accident. *Presence* (1976) kept them in the album charts and had the biggest advance orders ever logged in the USA, going platinum on release.

The film (and accompanying soundtrack album) *The Song Remains The Same* (1976), brilliantly captured the band's stage act and received enthusiastic reviews. Plant was back in action by April 1977, ready to start a mammoth American tour in Dallas. Midway through, they flew back to Britain to collect an Ivor Novello award.

Tragedy came when, with ten concerts to complete, Plant's son died of a virus infection. He flew home, and the rest of the tour was canceled. This prompted speculation about a break-up, which Page vigorously denied. An invitation from Swedish stars, Abba, saw Led Zeppelin recording their ninth album at Polar Studios. *In Through The Out Door* had several good tracks, including *All My Love* and *Fool In The Rain*, which made the US top thirty. Back in the UK, they topped the bill at the Knebworth Festival in August 1979.

Then, after playing to capacity crowds on a European tour early in 1980, John Bonham went on a twelve-hour booze binge at Jimmy Page's house in Windsor, Berkshire. He died after inhaling his own vomit. In December Led Zeppelin disbanded. A final album, *Coda*, appeared in 1982, but rumors of a reunion remained unfulfilled until the one-off appearance at the American Live Aid concert. Now the Zeppelin seems grounded for good.

In 1990, *Remasters* – their first ever compilation – hit the UK top ten while Page, having linked with ex-Free vocalist Paul Rodgers in The Firm, was working with Whitesnake's David Coverdale.

RECOMMENDED RECORDINGS
Led Zeppelin
Led Zeppelin II
Led Zeppelin III
Led Zeppelin IV
Houses Of The Holy
Physical Graffiti
Presence
Remasters

CHICAGO

by Donnie Dacus.

The 1980 tour also saw the release of Chicago's fourteenth album, *XIV*, followed in 1982 by three compilation sets including a second volume of *Greatest Hits*. Signing for the Full Moon label in the same year, they made their debut with an album of new material while the American Accord label released material taken from the Toronto 'Rock and Roll Revival' of 1969. A first single hit for three years came in 1982 with *Hard To Say I'm Sorry*, reaching No 1 in the US and, surprisingly perhaps, No 4 in the UK. It was their first British hit for six years, and continued a staggering sequence of world-wide success: over twenty million copies of their first fourteen albums have been sold, bringing in over $160 million.

The group carried on producing soft-rock hit singles in the eighties, but were overshadowed by departed bass player Peter Cetera who topped the US charts twice in 1986 with *Glory Of Love* and *The Next Time I Fall*. With Jason Scheff now on bass, Chicago hit back with their own chart-topper, *Look Away*, in 1988, but the innovation and inspiration of the early days was long gone.

RECOMMENDED RECORDINGS

Chicago
Chicago X
At Carnegie Hall *(live)*
Chicago IX – Greatest Hits *(compilation)*
Greatest Hits Volume 2

*W*ith hardly a change in their easy-going, inoffensive jazz/rock formula over the past years, Chicago have effortlessly amassed record sales in excess of twenty millions. Every one of their albums, including a four-disc set recorded live at Carnegie Hall in New York, has eventually achieved gold status.

The founder members formed their original band in 1968, taking the name The Big Thing. That changed to Chicago Transit Authority, which was subsequently abridged. However, having adopted the name of their home city, they then left for Los Angeles to work with a producer who was making a name as a man with something of a magic touch. And so it proved for Chicago. James William Guercio produced, packaged and promoted the band with consistent good judgment, and a rare feel for what was right for their audience.

With a strong local following in California, their debut album (a double) was an auspicious start: the rhythm line-up (Robert Lamm, keyboards; Terry Kath, guitar; Pete Cetera, bass; and Danny Seraphine, drums) integrated well with the punchy brass trio of James Punkow, Lee Loughnane and Walter Parazaider. It was a blend that produced well-contoured white blues with the brass adding spicy jazz overtones.

Instrumental solos and earthy vocals were contrasted with climactic bursts from the whole ensemble. *Chicago II*, another LP, was issued in 1970 and showed a radical change of style. The flair and energy had been dissipated into a seamless, polished but routine brand of pleasantly melodic jazz-rock, with bland, unadventurous arrangements and songs that came dangerously close to the pretentious. However, despite such criticisms, it sold well. And every subsequent album has followed the formula, becoming ever more grandiose.

In concert, stylish guitar solos were the main source of improvisation but they were hardly ambitious for the post-Hendrix era. It was big-band pop for those who were afraid of rock and liked the comfortable predictability of each successive recording. Chicago stuck unswervingly to the middle of the road.

In 1976, they scored a massive single hit with the lush, sugary ballad, *If You Leave Me Now* from the *Chicago X* album. It was a No 1 on both sides of the Atlantic, and introduced the group to a whole new audience. At this time, original guitarist Terry Kath died, to be replaced

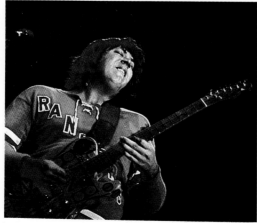

Top: Chicago's jazz-rock appeals to millions.
Above: Kath was a key element in their success.
Right: Chicago's brass section gave their music a distinctive flavor.

THE BEE GEES

In the early seventies, it seemed that the Bee Gees' time had come and gone, but, demonstrating once again a chameleon-like ability to adapt to new styles and musical vogues, they bounced back. Now, the soundtrack album from Saturday Night Fever, for which they wrote and played many of the 17 tracks, looks like becoming the biggest money-spinner the recording industry has ever known.

The brothers Gibb, mainstays of the Bee Gees, were all born in the Isle of Man: Barry in September 1946, and the twins Robin and Maurice in December 1949. The family emigrated to Australia in 1958. After winning talent shows, the brothers were offered their own weekly show on Australian television.

In August 1962 they signed for Festival Records and issued a single which made the top twenty down under: *Three Kisses of Love*. An Australian No 1 hit came with *Spicks & Specks*, and other chart success followed. With the name derived from brother Barry's initials, by 1965 the Bee Gees were the most popular group in the Antipodes.

Promoter Robert Stigwood thought they would appeal to the teeny-pop market and signed them in 1966. Before making their UK debut, the group was augmented by Colin Petersen (drums) and the talented Vince

Melouney (guitar). First chart success in Britain was with the haunting and disturbing, *New York Mining Disaster, 1941* (No 12) which, like many of their songs in this period, was better than they were given credit for. A No 1 hit came in 1967 with *Massachusetts* (US No 11). By now the Bee Gees had achieved idol status, with material very much in the melodic Lennon-McCartney vein. However, opulent orchestrations and studio effects sadly began to detract from what were well-crafted songs (mainly written, incidentally, by the brothers).

Words (US No 15, UK No 8); *I Started a Joke* (US No 6); *To Love Somebody* (US No 15, UK No 9); and *I Gotta Get A Message to You* (UK No 1, US No 8) were nevertheless major hits in America and Britain. The sentimental melan-

Above: Maurice in a melancholy mood.
Left: Maurice and Barry getting that message to you, with a little help from a friend.
Below right: The Gibbs, Maurice, Robin and Barry in harmony in 1979.
Below: Barry is now making a career as producer, Streisand but one client.

choly lyrics were enhanced by the strangled, high-pitched vocals.

In 1968 The Bee Gees toured, complete with full orchestra, but internal disagreements came to a head and Melouney departed to form his own band, followed in 1969 by Petersen. After a grandiose but largely unnoticed concept album, *Odessa*, Robin Gibb left to begin a solo career in 1969, a year which brought British chart success with *Don't Forget To Remember* (No 2) and *First Of May* (No 6). His brothers retaliated to his solo success with *Cucumber Castle*. Maurice married the vivacious Scottish songbird, Lulu (they were later divorced).

The Bee Gees reunited in late 1970 and secured a couple of million-selling singles in the USA during 1971 – *Lonely Days* (No 3) and *How Can You Mend A Broken Heart* (No 1) – but did little in the next three years. Most people had written them off when a 1975 album, *Main Course*, a creamy confection of white soul, became an American best-seller. A single from the LP, *Jive Talkin'* was the smash hit of the disco circuit that year. *Main Course* was produced by veteran Arif Mardin. The Gibbs obviously learned from him because their next LP, the self-produced *Children of the World* (1976), repeated the success. Hits came with *You Should Be Dancing* (US No 1, UK No 5) and *Love So Right* (US No 3). The Bee Gees had now assimilated the essence of the disco style and it wasn't surprising that they were selected to produce a soundtrack for the first disco movie, *Saturday Night Fever*.

Not only was the film a box-office bonanza, but the soundtrack songs dominated the air waves for months. The Bee Gees not only had a million-selling album, but three hit singles as well: *Night Fever* (US, UK No 1); *How Deep Is Your Love* (US No 1, UK No 3); and *Stayin' Alive* (US No 1, UK No 4). They also collected a host of awards including 'LP of the year.'

Their first studio album for two years, *Spirits Having Flown* (1977), rode the crest of the *Fever* success and produced two top singles, *Too Much Heaven* (US No 1, UK No 3) and *Tragedy*, an American and British chart-topper. The Bee Gees had the distinction of being the first group in the seventies to have five consecutive singles reach No 1 in America. They added a sixth in 1979 with *Love You Inside Out*.

Capitalizing on their success, a two-record live set of Bee Gees hits, *Here At Last*, was issued in 1977, and in 1978 they played a part in Robert

Stigwood's largely unloved film of *Sgt Pepper's Lonely Hearts Club Band*. Then, in 1979, the Bee Gees headlined a superstar 'Music For Unicef' charity spectacular from New York.

By now, their younger brother, Andy Gibb was well on the way with his solo career and enjoying considerable success with four hit singles. Barry, however, was busy co-producing and writing songs for Barbra Streisand's album *Guilty* and singing an award-winning performance in duet on the title track.

The LP also contained a major Gibb-penned solo hit for Streisand, the outstanding *Woman In Love*. Barry then brought Dionne Warwick back into prominence as her producer on a notable album *Heartbreaker*. The group came together again to record a new album, *Living Eyes*, and despite prolonged legal wrangles with the Stigwood organization and RSO Records, it was released in 1982. And so The Bee Gees' remarkable revival continued.

In their Miami studio the brothers Gibb worked on new material for another follow-up to *Saturday Night Fever*. Titled *Staying Alive*, the film again starred Travolta and The Bee Gees contribution totalled some six songs, although the title track wasn't one of their new compositions. Although their scores maintained the standard set by their first disco hits, the film was disappointing.

After rejuvenating Diana Ross's career with the UK No 1 *Chain Reaction*, a perfect Motown pastiche, the Bee Gees came back in their own right yet again in 1987 with the hit album *ESP* and its chart-topping single *You Win Again*. A hits collection *The Very Best Of The Bee Gees* was also well received in 1990, but the death of their younger brother Andy in 1988 after previous spells of drug use effectively took the shine off yet another glittering phase of a career that had seen them notch up more US top-ten hits than any other songwriters excepting the Beatles and Motown's Holland-Dozier-Holland team.

RECOMMENDED RECORDINGS

Main Course
Children of the World
Here at Last – The Bee Gees Live
Saturday Night Fever *(soundtrack)*
Best of the Bee Gees (Vols I and II)
Gold Vol.I
Bee Gees Greatest
Spirits Having Flown

U2

Formed as a schoolboy band in Dublin in 1976, U2 combined the pomp of stadium rock with the energy of the new wave to become Eire's biggest ever rock exports and a significant force in music through the eighties and nineties. Much of this was due to dynamic frontman Bono (real name Paul Hewson) who, with guitarist The Edge (Dave Evans), bassist Adam Clayton and drummer Larry Mullen, has been ever-present in the success story.

Their first two albums *Boy* and *October*, both produced by Steve Lilywhite, made waves in 1980-81, the latter reaching the UK top twenty, but it was the UK chart-topping *War* in 1983 that established them as Eire's biggest rock act and pushed their US-inspired brand of power-chord rock to its limit: *New Year's Day* was their first top-ten single, and encapsulated the messianic fervor Bono brought to his lyrics (all but

Clayton were committed Christians). *Under A Blood Red Sky* (1983) took *War* to the stage before the bombast (and producer Lilywhite) was dropped for a more atmospheric sound. Former Roxy Music keyboardist Brian Eno was employed with Canadian Daniel Lanois to produce 1984's *The Unforgettable Fire*. The religious aspect to the band that first surfaced on *October* was now even more obvious, though Bono claimed 'We are all alienated from most forms of organized religion.' Rather than mere preaching, they played benefits for Amnesty, the Irish unemployed and Bono cut a solo track for the *Sun City* anti-apartheid album.

Pride (In The Name Of Love) reached No 3 in the UK, the LP's title track reaching No 6 – and the album went straight in at the top. In America, the source of so many of Bono's lyrical ideas, they hit the top twenty and made the cover of *Rolling Stone* – a first for an Irish group.

After their appearance at Live Aid, the band retired with Eno to record *The Joshua Tree*, finally released in 1987. *I Still Haven't Found What I'm Looking For* was the first of three successful singles from the album, which

topped the UK charts. The band then spent 1987 touring the USA – a period documented by 1988's double LP and film *Rattle And Hum*. Cameo appearances by Bob Dylan and B B King confirmed U2's supergroup status.

Grammy Awards followed for Best Album and Best Rock Vocal Group, while Bono and The Edge guested on a Roy Orbison album, emphasizing their acceptance by all strata of rock society. Both *The Joshua Tree* and *Rattle And Hum* were US chart-toppers, while *Desire* topped the UK singles chart.

After a break from the album-tour treadmill, the band's success continued into the Nineties with *Achtung Baby* and the UK hit single *The Fly*. Their strength remained their teamwork, although Bono would clearly have little problem pursuing a successful solo career.

RECOMMENDED RECORDINGS
War
The Unforgettable Fire
The Joshua Tree
Rattle And Hum

Below left: U2, one of the biggest crowd-pullers in rock history. Right and below: Bono, the Dublin boys' frontman and vocalist, renowned for his hard-hitting, poignant lyrics.

THE WHO

O nce the most destructive and anarchic act in British music, the original line-up of The Who paradoxically outlasted that of every other major rock band. It took the tragic death of drummer, Keith Moon, to finally force a change of personnel in 1978 – some fourteen years after their historic performance in a North London pub.

All four had their roots in West London. Peter Townshend (May 1945), met John Entwistle (September 1944) at school. In the early sixties, the two were playing in a Dixieland jazz group, Peter on banjo, John on trumpet. Entwistle was the only member of The Who to receive a formal musical education; he studied the French horn.

Roger Daltrey (March 1944) was playing guitar in a band called The Detours when he encountered Townshend and Entwistle. They joined the group, and Peter's mother fixed them an audition which produced some club dates. The Detours were a five-piece and tried various vocalists before Daltrey relinquished guitar and took on the role.

They noticed another group called the Detours, so they changed their name to The Who. Playing a pub gig one evening, a cheeky-faced kid informed them that the band's drummer was a joke and he could play much better. They gave him the sticks and he *did* play better, finally demolishing the drum kit altogether. Keith Moon (August 1946) got the job.

Publicist, Peter Meaden, who managed their affairs, thought he could rework their image to appeal to the burgeoning mod movement. Renamed by Meaden, The High Numbers recorded a single in 1964. He'd re-written the 'Slim' Harpo standard *Got Love If You Want It* as *I'm The Face*, and coupled it with *Zoot Suit*. It had little success, but the band's following was growing. One night, playing in the Railway Hotel, Harrow, Pete Townshend accidentally broke the neck of his twelve-string Rickenbacker on the low ceiling. When out of frustration he smashed the guitar completely in a barrage of noise, the audience went wild.

Watching the performance were two young men who were hoping to break into film-making: Christopher 'Kit' Lambert and Christopher Stamp. They took over the band's management and encouraged them to repeat the instrument-smashing finale at every gig. It was great publicity, if expensive. No recording contracts were forthcoming. EMI turned them

down before Lambert and Stamp decided to revert to the band's earlier name.

Lambert sent a demonstration tape to producer, Shel Talmy. He was impressed with Townshend's song *I Can't Explain* and agreed to engineer it. It had little impact when released in January 1965, until The Who played it on the TV pop program, *Ready, Steady, Go*. It quickly made No 8 in the British chart.

The follow-up was startlingly different. It had a defiant lyric, crashing, discordant guitar chords, and used feedback between guitar amplifier and loudspeakers to arresting effect. The record company sent the tape back at first, convinced the noises were a fault in the mixing. *Anyway, Anyhow, Anywhere* made No 10, and attracted a much wider audience than the mods: The Who suddenly became part of pop art.

With the next single, they joined the immortals. Townshend's *My Generation* was to have an impact far beyond mere record sales (it reached No 2 in the UK, but only No 75 in America). He had written one of the most significant songs in rock music; it was aggressive, even inflammatory, and soon acquired wide notoriety. Well into the seventies, it was still the centerpiece of their stage act.

The first album was also released in 1965. It was a hybrid of traditional R&B numbers and original material, inevitably taking the title of their best-selling single (in America it appeared as *The Who Sing My Generation*). It was a good debut, exciting and spontaneous. It was followed by a string of top-ten singles throughout

1966 and 1967 from Townshend's pen. The clever and cynical *Substitute* made No 5 and *I'm A Boy* No 2. *Happy Jack* (UK No 3) took The Who into the US top thirty for the first time (No 24). In summer 1967, with the electrifying *I Can See For Miles* (UK No 10, US No 9), The Who had left the world of mods well and truly behind. Shel Talmy had also departed, and Lambert had taken on the producer's role.

It was the first of many feuds and personality clashes within the group. The disputes have continued ever since, especially the much-publicized rift between Townshend and Daltrey.

By the second album, *A Quick One* (1966), Townshend's song-writing had matured even more. It also contained his first attempt at an extended composition. The mini-opera *A Quick One While He's Away* completed Townshend's shift from anarchy to the avant-garde and the album also saw input from Entwistle, the pungent *Boris The Spider*.

The Who hit America in 1967, appearing on the *Murray The K* radio show in New York and the Smothers Brothers' TV show (an orgy of smoke bombs and destruction). Then followed a tour that finished with a superb set at the Monterey Festival.

The Who Sell Out (1967) was another ambitious album, a spoof at the expense of the advertising world. It fell short of total success despite fine songs such as *Mary Anne With The Shaky Hand*, *Armenia City In The Sky* and another Townshend mini-opera, *Rael*.

In 1969 Townshend launched *Tommy* on the

world, the first significant rock opera. It ran for an hour-and-a-half and was first performed by the group at the Metropolitan Opera House, New York. The ovation lasted fourteen minutes. For all its flaws, even the improbability of its plot, *Tommy* is a formidable achievement and a towering landmark in rock music.

Tommy virtually spelled the end of The Who as a singles band, although *Pinball Wizard* gave them a No 4 in Britain and No 19 in the USA. In 1970, an underrated Townshend song *The Seeker* just made No 19 in Britain, and was their only single hit that year.

However, 1970's *Live at Leeds* album demonstrated just how good a live act The Who were. They have strong claims to being consistently the best live rock band in the world during the seventies, rivaled only by The Rolling Stones and Led Zeppelin. *Live At Leeds* is one of the great live recordings and rock at its best, with superb extended versions of *My Generation, Magic Bus* and The Who's rendition of *Summertime Blues*.

This Eddie Cochran classic was included in the film of the Woodstock festival. It shows the visual impact of the band at its best: Townshend's acrobatic leaps and crashing, windmill-armed guitar strokes; the strutting, microphone-spinning Daltrey; Entwistle, static but punching out some of the best virtuoso bass lines in rock; and Moon's machine-gun drumming.

Moon was every bit as wild off-stage as he was on it. His crazy antics, practical jokes and penchant for wrecking hotel rooms earned him the nickname 'Moon The Loon.' It often became completely out of hand: during a pub brawl, his driver was killed.

The 1971 *Who's Next* album, produced and engineered by Glyn Johns, not only contains eight of the best songs Townshend ever wrote,

Above: They called him 'Moon the Loon' – he concluded his audition by destroying the drum kit.
Left: In 1964, The Who was carefully groomed to become the musical inspiration for the Mod movement. Soon their distinctive symbol decorated parkas and motor scooters everywhere.
Below: A 1965 appearance on UK TV resulted in The Who's first single hit.

Above: By 1971, The Who were established as one of the world's top rock bands, not least because of their Woodstock 1969 gig.
Below: Daltrey and Townshend on stage.

Right: Their stage act is never less than athletic! Townshend's leaps and windmill guitar strokes, and Daltrey's assaults on the microphone became their trademarks.

but also demonstrates his mastery of synthesizers. The track *Won't Get Fooled Again* became a UK No 9 and US No 15. *Who's Next* is arguably their most complete studio album, excellent in every respect. The same year saw the issue of a well-chosen compilation, *Meaty, Beaty, Big And Bouncy*, and the beginning of solo careers for all four members of the band.

The album *Quadrophenia* was about a mod called Jimmy who suffered from double schizophrenia. In performance, each member of The Who represented one of the four distinct facets of Jimmy's character. The material was good, but it reposed awkwardly on the band. A good single cut from the double album, *5.15*, made No 20 in the UK during 1973.

After a UK and US tour to promote *Quadrophenia*, the band returned to individual work, although Entwistle took the time to sort through various tapes left unissued over the years and came up with an intriguing collection entitled *Odds And Sods*. It was their only album release of 1974.

Above: Peter Townshend, great guitarist and composer of most of The Who's material.
Below: Roger Daltrey has had solo success as an actor and singer.

The Who regrouped in 1975 for a British tour, playing at sports stadiums as well as concert halls. *The Who By Numbers* saw Townshend voicing his disillusionment with the trappings of success, as well as the problems of getting old which he once hoped he wouldn't have. A single from this album, *Squeeze Box*, gave them a British No 10 and American No 16.

Apart from a concert with The Grateful Dead in Oakland, California, The Who did little during 1976. Record buyers had to be content with the retrospective compilation *The Story of The Who* and a single reissue of *Substitute* (UK No 7).

After more solo work The Who came together for the excellent 1978 *Who Are You* album (their best seller since *Tommy*); the long-serving management/production team was replaced by Bill Curbishley. The title track made the top twenty both sides of the Atlantic.

Moon had returned from a sojourn in California and was playing as well as ever. Then on 7 September 1978 he was found dead, killed by

an overdose of anti-alcoholism pills.

His replacement was Kenney Jones from The Faces, who had a very different temperament. Jones arrived early in 1979, and made his debut in a concert at the Rainbow, London, before the group set off for a tour of Europe and America. 1979 also saw two film ventures: an adaptation of *Quadrophenia* starring Sting, as Jimmy; and a biopic of The Who, *The Kids Are Alright* (soundtrack albums were released from both).

But, once again, the year ended in tragedy as eleven fans were crushed to death outside a stadium in Cincinatti where The Who were performing. It deeply affected them and for a while disbandment was seriously considered. Concern about the band's future was one of the factors in Townshend's decline into drugs and alcohol, although by March 1982 he was declaring himself utterly straight. Townshend's material for the album *Face Dance* (1981) was good, but somehow didn't seem to suit the band although the single *You Better, You Bet* reached No 18 in America and No 9 in Britain.

With Glyn Johns returning to produce, The Who were back to their best with the 1982 album *It's Hard*, but that year they announced a farewell tour of the United States (where they had remained one of the top three crowd-pullers in rock). The tour grossed $40 millions. They gave powerful live performances although was sadly missed.

In 1983 Pete was given a well-earned Life-time Achievement Award by the British record industry. He continued producing excellent solo work, and it was surprising that, four years after a stormy 1985 reunion for Live Aid, he, Daltrey and Entwistle returned to the road in Britain and the States with an expanded, 'big band' Who, playing acoustic guitar to avoid hearing problems, to raise money for a musical based on the Ted Hughes novel *The Iron Man*.

A triple LP, *Join Together*, was issued as a souvenir, but unlike the Stones the Who were unable to carry off the 'ageing rockers' act convincingly. Besides, Jagger had been too clever to write 'Hope I die before I get old . . .'

RECOMMENDED RECORDINGS
A Quick One/Sell Out *(double/reissued)*
Tommy *(original version)*
Live At Leeds/Who Are You *(double/reissued)*
Who's Next
Meaty, Beaty, Big And Bouncy *(compilation)*
Quadrophenia *(original version)*
Odds And Sods
The Who By Numbers
The Story Of The Who *(compilation)*
Face Dances
It's Hard

Far left: Townshend, perhaps the best spokesman rock music has ever had.
Left: Daltrey giving 100 percent.
Below: John Entwistle at Wembley in 1979, a master of the French horn and bass.
Bottom: A concert in London, 1975.

THE ROLLING STONES

Mick Jagger's bluesy whine and provocative swagger were a key factor in the success of The Stones. Utilizing those famous rubber lips to the full, he developed an unmistakeable vocal style, and a presence to match. It fronted some of the best rock and roll ever played and recorded. In the sixties, The Stones' achievements were bettered only by the Beatles.

Everything about The Stones seemed to pose a threat – from the raw, abrasive music they played, to the contemptuous, unsmiling stares which graced their early record sleeves. They spoke of rebellion, social and political breakdown, personal and sexual freedom; and were pilloried by an outraged establishment. They made their music amid celebrated drug busts, paternity suits, constant press hounding and personal tragedy. Still they weathered it all and, after The Beatles disbanded, could indeed claim to be the 'greatest rock and roll band in the world.'

While studying at the London School of Economics, Mick was also learning about American rhythm and blues from Dick Taylor and eventually the pair formed a band, with friends Bob Backwith and Allen Etherington, called, improbably, Little Boy Blue and The Blue Boys.

Keith Richard (born Richards) was an admirer of Chuck Berry and added his guitar skills to the band as well. They hung out at the fashionable Ealing Blues Club where the late Alexis Korner's Blues Incorporated was stimulating a lot of fresh interest in the music. Also attracted there was Lewis Brian Hopkin-Jones, an ex-public schoolboy from Cheltenham in Gloucestershire. Wanting to form an R&B band of his own, Jones advertised for others to join him and received replies from a singer called Andy Wren, guitarist, Geoff Bradford, and pianist, Ian Stewart. He also formed a partnership with Paul Jones (later lead singer of Manfred Mann). The Blue Boys heard Brian and his band play, and a few weeks later took the stage themselves for a jam session. They played with the great mouth-harpist Cyril Davies, and Blues Incorporated's jazz-oriented drummer, Charlie Watts.

Mick and Brian were soon rehearsing material with Geoff Bradford and Ian Stewart, and shortly joined by Dick Taylor and Keith Richard. Their music moved more and more toward the Chicago R&B of Chuck Berry and Bo

Diddley, so Taylor, something of a blues purist, felt dissatisfied and left.

Jagger, Jones and Richard moved into a small, squalid apartment in London's Hammersmith. They were almost penniless, relying on Ian Stewart's income from his job with ICI to keep going. They combined the two bands to form The Rolling Stones.

Their first break was unexpected. By now Jagger regularly sang with Blues Incorporated, and a spot on BBC radio's *Jazz Club* was fixed in June 1962. Learning that the broadcast would take place at a time when Korner's band was usually playing a regular set, at the Marquee Club in Wardour Street, Jagger offered the services of his own band to the club's management. It was the debut of Brian Jones and Mick Jagger and The Rolling Stones.

They soon acquired a loyal following, but Brian, Keith and Mick realized changes in the line-up were needed if they were to progress any further. For months they tried to persuade Charlie Watts to join them on drums, but he was wary of having to relinquish the security of his design job.

In January 1963, Charlie made the decision to join the Stones and was teamed in the rhythm section with a bass player found through auditions, Bill Wyman (aka Bill Perks), born in October 1936. It was as a six-piece that the Stones went on the London club circuit: Jagger, vocals;. Richard, lead guitar; Jones, rhythm guitar; Wyman, bass; Watts, drums; and Stewart, keyboards.

As the old line-up, they'd cut a demonstration tape (EMI had rejected it), but now went to IBC studios to make fresh ones with producer, Glyn Johns. An eight-month residency at the

fashionable Crawdaddy Club in the Station Hotel, Richmond, Surrey, elevated them to a cult attraction. One evening, Andrew Loog Oldham, PR man and music business hustler, saw The Stones. Oldham offered to take a tape to an executive at Decca Records (in the USA, the London label). Decca's Dick Rowe, who had the unenviable distinction of being the man who turned down The Beatles, gave them a recording contract.

At this time, The Beatles were being given a new, clean-cut image by their manager, Brian Epstein. Oldham countered this by making The Rolling Stones as ill-kempt and outrageous as he could. He also decided that Ian Stewart, unfortunately, didn't look the part and squeezed him out. Stewart remained in the background, playing piano on a number of album tracks and at some concerts, and later taking on the job of tour organizer for the Stones.

Decca released the first single in June 1963 – a hard-driven version of Chuck Berry's *Come On* that made the lower reaches of UK top thirty, but it got them a TV appearance and helped the band secure a spot at the First National Jazz and Blues Festival held in Richmond, Surrey, in August. In September, they played support to an Everly Brothers, Bo Diddley and Little Richard tour, and three months later released a second single, surprisingly penned by Lennon and McCartney. *I Wanna Be Your Man* rose to No 12 and was followed in January 1964 by a high-selling EP which, among other fine tracks, included a brash, belligerent version of *Money*.

As they headlined a UK tour with The Ronettes, a cover of Buddy Holly's *Not Fade Away* gave the Stones their highest singles placing yet – No 3. However, their increasing

record sales were matched by a growing notoreity. 'Would you let your daughter marry a Rolling Stone?' became a favorite press headline as stories of the Stones behavior abounded.

Released in April 1964, *The Rolling Stones* went to No 1 in the album charts and stayed there for twelve weeks. The content was mainly derived from their blues heroes, but there was also an original Jagger/Richard composition of surprising quality, *Tell Me (You're Coming Back To Me)*. The track gave them an American top-forty hit as they toured the USA in June 1964.

While there, they recorded the EP *Five By Five* at the Chess Studios in Chicago. Outside, crowds rioted – it was a measure of their rapid rise to fame in the US. However the next two singles were relatively unsuccessful there. A memorable cover of the Bobby Womack/Valentinos song, *It's All Over Now* made only No 26, while *Little Red Rooster*, in which they freely adapted Sam Cooke's treatment of the Willie

Dixon original, was banned for its sexual overtones. Both, however, reached No 1 in Britain. *Little Red Rooster* was apparently Brian Jones' favorite of all the Stones cuts.

1965 opened with a second album, recorded mainly in Chicago and Hollywood, imaginatively titled *Rolling Stones No 2*! It once again relied on strong American R&B standards, and some out-and-out pop with The Drifters' *Under The Boardwalk*. But this time there were three well-crafted Jagger/Richard efforts, prefacing their first originally-composed UK No 1, *The Last Time* (US No 9). It was a classic rock song, and a follow-up USA-only single release showed they could compose good blues numbers; *Heart Of Stone* made No 19.

A less impressive third album, *Out of Our Heads*, appeared later in 1965, and then the songwriting Stones came up with one of the all-time great rock singles. *(I Can't Get No) Satisfaction* went straight to the top both sides of

Above: Sixties Stones, with the late Brian Jones (standing).
Above left: A rare shot of Mick Jagger.

the Atlantic, their first US No 1, and has subsequently become a standard.

The same aggressive theme was extended to *Get Off My Cloud*, which enjoyed similar success later in 1965, a year in which they toured the USA twice. In 1966, a song which became a British hit for Jagger's erstwhile girlfriend, Marianne Faithfull gave The Stones a US No 6: the sentimental *As Tears Go By*.

Aftermath, their first album consisting entirely of original compositions was a masterly achievement, contains some of the most pungent songs Jagger and Richard ever conceived: *19th Nervous Breakdown* (US and UK No 2); the brutally sexist *Under My Thumb*; and the socially aware, *Mother's Little Helper* (US No 8). It also saw the most musicianly of the

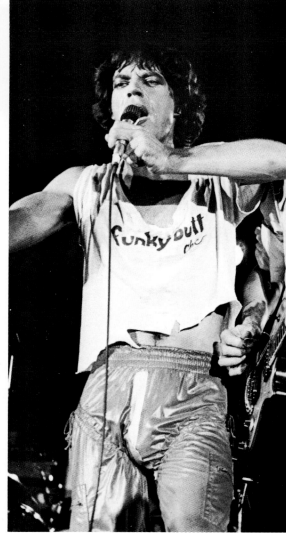

London, on 5 July.

On 11 July another sensational single was released: *Honky Tonk Woman* was the Rolling Stones at their swaggering best. The 'B' side was hardly inferior – the exquisite *You Can't Always Get What You Want* reached No 1 both sides of the Atlantic. To coincide with their first US tour for three years, in 1969 the Stones issued a second superb album, *Let It Bleed* – *Gimme Shelter*, *Midnight Rambler* and *Country Honk* were among their best-ever tracks.

In conjunction with The Grateful Dead, they held a free 'thank you' concert for their fans at the Altamont Freeway in upstate California on 6 December 1969. They paid some Hells Angels $500 to keep order. In full view of the stage, a young black (supposedly having drawn a pistol) was set upon by the Angels and stabbed repeatedly. His was the most horrifying of four deaths that occurred during the concert. Were the Stones indirectly responsible for what had happened? Whatever they concluded, they quit touring for a while.

In the seventies, The Rolling Stones became tax exiles, and moved to France. Mick played the role of the ambisexual star in *Performance*, and the band broke with Decca. They set up their own label, Rolling Stones Records, in 1971, and got off to a cracking start with another classic single, *Brown Sugar* (US No 1, UK No 2).

Their first independent album, *Sticky Fingers*, was concerned with their own hedonism and toyed with the darker side of life. *Sister Morphine* and the evocative *Moonlight Mile* were among

Stones, Brian Jones, coloring the instrumentation to great effect with the use of dulcimer, harpsichord and the like.

There was no let up in the fury of Mick and Keith's singles compositions: the resigned bitterness of *Paint It Black* (UK and US No 1) was the logical consequence of the previous songs of frustration. The next, however, didn't quite match it, but *Have You Seen Your Mother, Baby Standing In The Shadows* nevertheless was a top-ten hit.

The moral guardians were out in force once more for The Stones' following single, *Let's Spend The Night Together*. It was actually no worse than the sentiment uttered in many risqué black R&B song, but the Stones by now were seen as a serious threat to adolescent morals, and in the US the 'B' side took prominence (*Ruby Tuesday* still made No 1). On TV's *Ed Sullivan Show*, the song was censored: they sang, *Let's Spend Some Time Together*.

1967 was a bad year, with a succession of drug busts. Mick and Keith were arrested, then Brian Jones. Severe jail sentences were imposed, but eventually suspended upon appeal. It really did seem as though those in high places wanted to teach them a lesson. *The Times* newspaper published a famous leader which suggested the group was being unjustly persecuted.

Perhaps it was only to be expected that the

Between The Buttons album was below par, as was a recording from a concert at London's Royal Albert Hall, *Got Live If You Want It* (now available in a double live album *In Concert*). Jumping on the flower power bandwagon, they issued *We Love You* which, although it charted, was a vapid effort beside The Beatles' *All You Need Is Love*. Similarly, a psychedelic album, *Their Satanic Majesties Request* was utterly eclipsed by *Sgt Pepper*.

1968 started as badly as 1967 had ended: Brian was once again on a drugs charge in May, and commited for trial. But the Stones came back in style, with a single that came to be regarded as a portrait in music of Mick: the effervescent *Jumping Jack Flash* (UK No 1, US No 3).

They were once again the definitive rock and roll band, proved by the subsequent album, *Beggars Banquet* (1968). With tracks such as *Sympathy For The Devil, Street Fighting Man* and *Stray Cat Blues*, the Jagger/Richard team was in brilliant form.

Sadly, it was the last album Brian Jones would record. In June 1969 Jones left the band. On 3 July he was found drowned in his swimming pool. The verdict was death by misadventure. He was swiftly replaced in the group by 22-year-old Mick Taylor, who made his Stones debut before an audience of a quarter of a million at a free concert in Hyde Park,

Above: Keith gets a good riff going.
Left: Posing Stones – Charlie and Bill (standing), Mick, Brian and Keith (in fur).
Right: Jumping Jack Flash himself – Mick instructs his audience.
Below: Ron Wood (center) gets in on the act – he replaced Taylor in 1975.

Above: A rare smile from a young Jagger.
Right: Mick Jagger and Ronnie Wood.
Far right: Equally rare, Jagger on guitar during a 1979 concert when, despite the critics, they were as successful as ever.

the best tracks. In 1972, the Stones issued what is possibly their last great album, the two-disk *Exile On Main Street*: it offers many good tracks, including *Tumbling Dice* (UK No 5, US No 7), but was marred by a heavy production job.

Goat's Head Soup (1973) was generally uninspired, but did yield a US No 1 with *Angie* (UK No 5). In January of that year, they undertook a Los Angeles charity gig and followed with US and European tours. Afterward, Mick Taylor left and Ron Wood of The Faces replaced him. The 1975 'Tour Of The Americas' was the most elaborate (and expensive) in rock history.

Whatever critics might say about The Stones, they were grossing more at concerts and selling more albums than ever, even if 1976's *Black And Blue* was well below par. The same year, *Fool To Cry* gave them a US No 10 and UK No 6 hit, their last for two years.

Ian McLagan joined the Stones for the 1978 tour, a much less extravagant affair than in 1975. That year's album, *Some Girls,* with its controversial sleeve, brought them a single hit with the disco-style *Miss You* (US No 1, UK No 3). The title track from *Emotional Rescue* (1980) made No 3 in the US and No 9 in the UK.

Coincidentally with the release of *Tattoo You,* a better album than the previous pair. The Stones revisited the States and proceeded to break all box-office records. The payout was nothing short of phenomenal, and the album gave them hit singles with *Start Me Up* (US No 2, UK No 7) and *Waiting On A Friend* (US No 13, UK No 50). *Still Life* (1982) features recordings from that tour.

In 1983, The Rolling Stones were touring their home country again, to the usual enthusiastic audiences. Their playing may have lost some of

its bite, and at times seem distinctly sloppy, but the magnetism remains. They released an above-average album, *Undercover*, with some good rockers. The 'Greatest Rock And Roll Band In The World' rocked on regardless.

In 1985 Mick released a solo album, *She's the Boss*. Reviews were unenthusiastic, which is something that couldn't be said for Mick's solo contribution to Live Aid – with a little help from Tina Turner. He then did an unexpected, but successful, cover of the old Motown hit *Dancing In The Street* (with David Bowie). It was a great video, too.

Their 1986 offering *Dirty Work* preceded a public falling-out between Jagger and Richards, who both produced solo work in the interim. The hatchet was buried for *Steel Wheels*, a return to form in 1989, and following a triumphant tour and live LP *Flashpoint* they signed with Virgin in 1991 for a reported £20 million. . . .

RECOMMENDED RECORDINGS

The Rolling Stones
The Rolling Stones No 2
12 × 5 (USA only)
Aftermath
Big Hits (High Tide And Green Grass)
Beggars Banquet
Let It Bleed
Through The Past Darkly (Big Hits Vol 2)
Get Yer Ya Yas Out (*live*)
Sticky Fingers
Exile On Main Street
Rolled Gold (*compilation/UK only*)
Some Girls
Tattoo You
Undercover
Rewind 1971-84 (*compilation*)
Hot Rocks (*CD compilation*)
Steel Wheels

THE POLICE

A winning combination of polished musicianship, original and above-average material, a distinctive, sound, shrewd packaging and astute management has established The Police as the biggest money-spinning rock band in the eighties.

Virginia-born Stewart Copeland began playing drums at the age of thirteen, in 1965, and studied music at the University of California, Berkeley. His brother Miles was making a career in music management – among his artists was Darryl Way of Curved Air. Stewart played drums for Curved Air on a US tour and on the albums *Airborne* and *Midnight Wire*.

Stewart became disillusioned with Curved Air, and in 1976 was planning to form a band of his own. He was impressed by the simplicity, spontaneity and vitality of punk. In Newcastle he was also impressed with Last Exit's bassist, Gordon Sumner (October 1951), known to his friends as Sting.

Sting had previously played with several jazz groups, which had achieved only marginal success. Sting and Stewart were accomplished performers, but the guitarist Copeland brought along to the first rehearsals, Henry Padovani, was limited in technique. Copeland's songs were similarly limited in inspiration. However, by February 1977 they had a few gigs and had recorded the single *Fall Out* at their own expense. Two thousand copies were pressed and Copeland formed Illegal Records with brother Miles to issue it in May. It was an immediate sell-out (and registered another 100,000 sales when reissued in 1979).

Miles was very active in the burgeoning punk scene, and The Police were seen as part of it even though Sting, with his professional values, was offended by the punk bands' lack of musicianship and the banality of their material.

This first headline gig came in May 1977, at the Railway Hotel, Putney. A performance at the Marquee in June was watched with enthusiasm by guitarist Andy Summers, who had done some session work with Sting and Stewart, and he desperately wanted to play with them.

For two months, The Police played as a foursome, but Padovani was unable to play the guitar parts Sting was writing and left on 12 August. Six days later came their first gig as a three-piece, at Rebecca's club, Birmingham.

They worked with Eberhard Schoener, a German avant-garde composer; the income

virtually financed their first two years as a band. Returning to London, they asked Miles Copeland to arrange a recording deal for an album they'd put together. This he did, and *Outlandos d'Amour* was recorded at Surrey Sound between January and August 1978. They were almost ashamed of a reggae-style song with a rocking chorus, but Miles loved *Roxanne*, and by March had obtained a deal with A&M Records to release it as a single.

Roxanne's success was limited because the BBC banned it (the song was about a whore), but it made No 12 and established The Police as something of a cult band. Miles took over as manager, and he has been a vital ingredient in their success, as has been Kim Turner, their sound technician since July 1978.

Their first North American tour in October aroused a good deal of interest, with *Roxanne* and the first album becoming in-demand imports. They toured the USA coast to coast, in spring 1979, with *Roxanne* officially released by A&M. The BBC, too, were having difficulty in ignoring the single upon its reissue, and it made their top twenty. In June, The Police headlined a UK tour for the first time, playing sell-out concerts. *Outlandos d'Amour* became their first gold album, and the reissued *Can't Stand Losing*

You gave them a No 2 single (despite BBC objections to its suicide connotations.

Further UK and US tours coincided with the release of *Message In A Bottle* (their first UK No 1) in September 1979 and another successful album, *Regatta de Blanc*, ('white reggae'), which acknowledged the major influence in their music, and their obvious debt to Bob Marley.

Major shows in Germany and riotous scenes after London concerts in December firmly established The Police. The same month, *Walking On The Moon*, another arresting single, shot to No 1, with a video made at the Kennedy Space Center.

After wide-ranging tours in 1980 Sting took up residence in Ireland for tax reasons and for similar reasons recorded the next album in Holland during July. *Zenyatta Mondatta* was released in October. Although it entered the UK album charts at No 1 and achieved huge worldwide sales, the critical reception was mixed. It shows signs of strain, and the three admit parts of it had to be rushed.

Singles hits during that year came with *So Lonely* (UK No 6, a reissue from 1978), *Don't Stand So Close To Me* (UK No 1, US No 10), and *De Do Do Do, De Da Da Da* (UK No 5, US No 10).

Above: Sting sings, on a US tour.
Top left: From left, Copeland, Summers and Sting.
Left: The most successful group of the eighties.

Remarkably, a 'six pack' collection of their first singles plus a new release, *The Bed's Too Big Without You*, reached No 17.

Highspots of another lengthy tour early in 1981 were sell-out concerts in Madison Square Garden, New York. The fourth album was recorded on the Caribbean island of Montserrat. Released in autumn, *Ghost In The Machine* was infinitely better than its predecessor and produced hit singles with *Every Little Thing She Does Is Magic* (UK No 1, US No 3) and *Invisible Sun* (UK No 2) – and the BBC again banned the accompanying video which used clips of street violence in Belfast. The album, needless to add, made No 1 immediately. But after another hugely successful American tour, solo projects occupied both Sting and Andy.

In Spring 1983 Police recorded *Synchronicity*, their third consecutive LP to enter the UK chart at No 1. Comparatively modest success for their sole 1982 single, *Spirits In The Material World* (UK No 12, US No 11), was put right by 1983's *Every Breath You Take*, No 1 both sides of the Atlantic. The follow-up, *Wrapped Around Your Finger* made only No 7 in Britain. Early in 1984 The Police won Grammies for best group and best single *(Every Breath You Take)*.

Sting enjoyed the most successful solo career in the late eighties and early nineties with *The Dream Of The Blue Turtles, Bring On The Night, Nothing Like The Sun* and *The Soul Cages*: the first and third topped the UK charts. He also continued a successful acting career *(Dune,* etc), establishing himself as an all-round entertainer.

RECOMMENDED RECORDINGS
Outlandos D'Amour
Regatta De Blanc
Ghost in the Machine
Synchronicity
(Sting solo)
The Dream Of The Blue Turtles

PINK FLOYD

The most famous and successful survivors of London's hippy 'underground' of the late sixties, Pink Floyd were the archetypal 'acid rock' band. Making ever more ambitious use of lighting tricks, sound-bending techniques and other special effects, the group's spectacular stage presentation became almost as famous as its music. Although criticized in some quarters as being inflated and repetitive, their recordings have enjoyed worldwide commercial success.

As they have led the way in live performance, so Pink Floyd set new standards in record production. The band's work with engineer, Alan Parsons, on Dark Side of the Moon *was way ahead of its time and inadvertently produced the definitive disc for hi-fi freaks!*

Cambridge High School for Boys provided the starting point. It was there that George Roger Waters encountered Roger Keith ('Syd') Barrett (and Barrett's eventual replacement, Dave Gilmour). Both Barrett and Waters came to London, to study art and architecture respectively. Waters met Nicholas Mason and Richard Wright at college, and they played together as various amateur bands before forming the Abdabs (later, Screaming Abdabs) with two vocalists, Keith Noble and Juliette Gale. Gale and Wright eventually married.

Barrett, meanwhile, had worked with Geoff Mott and the Mottos, and the Hollering Blues before joining Waters in a band with Mason, Wright and jazz guitarist, Bob Close. They called themselves Pink Floyd Sound, taking the name from two American blues artists, Pink Anderson and Floyd Council. Mainly encouraged by Barrett, they moved from rhythm and blues into a more adventurous sound world, but not one that suited Bob Close, who soon quit.

By autumn 1966, the band was playing fashionable 'underground' venues in London – The Marquee Club and the Roundhouse. Then followed a top billing at UFO (Unlimited Freak Out) in Tottenham Court Road, the premier hippy club, and a weekly spot at the London Free School's sound/light workshop. It was here that an American couple, Joel and Toni Brown from Timothy Leary's Millbrook Institute, first projected color slides behind the band – the beginnings of Floyd's famous light show.

Their music was moving into startling, often discordant experimentation. Barrett was generating most of the material. He drew his inspiration from outer-space, mysticism, whimsical images of childhood, fairy tales and a surreal symbolism – partly induced by his increasing use of hallucinogens, principally LSD ('acid'), a habit which was soon to take its toll.

In October 1966, the band played at the launch party of Europe's first 'underground' newspaper, *International Times*, and did some benefit concerts in December. Managers Peter Jenner and Andrew King signed a recording contract with EMI, obtaining the (for the time) unusually high advance of £5000. Jo Gannon was recruited to devise the group's lightshows, after the Browns left.

January 1967 saw the release of Floyd's first single, the Barrett composition, *Arnold Layne* produced by UFO boss, Joe Boyd. Unfortunately, this novel tale of a transvestite who stole women's underwear from washing lines was not approved for airplay by the official radio stations, and had to rely on the 'pirates' such as Radio Caroline for exposure. It was sufficient to push it to No 20.

By May, the group had sufficient following to take over London's Queen Elizabeth Hall for an ambitious show entitled *Games For May*, complete with a primitive four-channel sound system. Retitled *See Emily Play*, the title track of the performance was issued as a single and reached No 5 in July 1967. Curiously, for a band that was to go on to superstardom, this was their sole UK top-ten entry until 1980.

Released in August 1967, the first album, *Piper at the Gates of Dawn*, contained ten Barrett (or part-Barrett) compositions out of eleven tracks, indicating the band's creative dependence on their brilliant if eccentric lead guitarist. *Astronomy Domine* and *Interstellar Overdrive* were powerful pieces of 'space rock,' while *Gnome, Scarecrow* and *Bike*

Above: Nick Mason, a founder member, on drums.
Top: Pink Floyd became famous for their spectacular psychedelic lightshows in the late sixties. In the foreground, Roger Waters on bass.
Right: Roger Waters hunched over his guitar against a background of smoke from Floyd's firework display. He has been the most creative of the four.

demonstrated Barrett's ability to invest apparently innocuous lyrics with a disturbing uneasiness and degree of menace.

On stage, Floyd had brought the April 1967 fourteen-hour 'Technicolour Dream Free Speech Festival' at Alexandra Palace in north London to a triumphant dawn close, and planned an American tour. But Barrett's behavior became unpredictable. He would barely play at all at some performances, just standing motionless on stage. By February 1968 the situation was intolerable and Waters asked Dave Gilmour to join the group. For seven weeks, Barrett and Gilmour played alongside each other, but in April, Syd departed, a 22-year-old 'acid' victim.

In 1970, assisted by Gilmour and Waters, Barrett put together two bizarre but intriguing solo albums, *The Madcap Laughs* and *Barrett*. It was his last appearance on record. Then, while Floyd were recording the track *Shine on You Crazy Diamond*, ironically dedicated to Barrett, Syd unexpectedly turned up at the studio and announced he was 'ready to do his bit.' It was virtually his last 'public' appearance. Rumor has it he lives a mole-like existence in a basement in Cambridge.

His last single with the group, *Apples and Oranges*, failed miserably in November 1967: this, and the inability to replace Barrett's inventive lyric writing, contributed to Floyd's change from a singles band to live and album performers.

The last of Syd Barrett's work can be heard on the second album, *Saucerful of Secrets*, but it also proved the band could survive without him. Roger Waters became the dominant creative force. Innovative instrumental, electronic and other effects were his specialty, as demonstrated on *Set the Controls for the Heart of the Sun*. American and European tours in 1968 allowed them to perfect their stage act in sound, light and visual effects. The culmination came at London's Royal Festival Hall, a presentation called 'More Furious Madness From The Massed Gadgets of Auximenes' and the star performer a joy-stick control known as the 'azimuth co-ordinator' which enabled sound to be directed around the full 360 degrees of the auditorium.

An interest in soundtrack music was to lead to several efforts in that field in the ensuing four years, beginning with *More*; *The Committee* (a remarkable score); *Tonite Let's All Make Love in London*; a three-track contribution to *Zabriskie Point* (1970); *The Body* (1970); and *Obscured By Clouds* (1972), a reworking of the music for the film *La Vallee* that gave them their first album success in the USA.

Ummagumma, released 1969, was a half-live, half-studio double. On the studio disc, each member of the group took half one side to experiment as he wished, but only Waters' effort emerged with true credibility.

Premiered at the Bath Festival with chorus, horn section and firework display, *Atom Heart Mother* was a promising but ultimately disappointing collaboration with electronics wizard, Ron Geesin. It did, nevertheless, reach No 1 in the UK LP charts. In early 1971 Floyd took over the concert bowl at Crystal Palace for a 'garden party.' Here they gave a first hearing of *Return To The Son Of Nothing*, a complex, extended, almost symphonic improvisation which finally surfaced on disc as *Echoes* on the 1971 album *Meddle*. The 'party,' held in driving rain, still included fireworks, and added a giant

inflatable octopus which rose from the lake in front of the concert platform. As an encore, they played a thunderous version of *Astronomy Domine*: next day, all the fish in the lake were found dead.

After touring Japan, Australia and the Far East and the US in late autumn 1971, Floyd devoted nine months to making their next album. It was time well spent. *Dark Side Of The Moon* is part of rock mythology. The material was among the group's finest ever, exploring themes of fear, loneliness, greed, even lunacy: the other side of life, the dark side. It was enhanced by some remarkable effects, airplanes droning overhead, a cacophony of clocks, and by the soaring backing vocal of Doris Troy on one track. The whole production, by Alan Parsons, was an object lesson in using studio techniques to sensational effect and immediately became a landmark in rock recording. *Dark Side* became Floyd's biggest selling album, spending two years in the UK LP charts and a No 1 in the USA, where it remained among the best sellers for many years.

After touring the US and the UK they took a six-month retirement, broken only for a benefit concert for Robert Wyatt, who had broken his back. Outside projects were also increasingly occupying them, both Gilmour and Mason venturing into production.

There were sell-out audiences for a November 1974 UK tour, but the performances were erratic. One, in Stoke-on-Trent, was illicitly recorded and issued as a 'bootleg' album. Mistaken for an official 'new' release, it supposedly sold 150,000 copies in a few weeks. The true, new Pink Floyd album was released in September. *Wish You Were Here* was a fine album but too much was expected after *Dark Side*, although the production was once again in-

comparable. 1976 tours of Europe and America were followed by the issue of *Animals* in January 1977. As well as making the top five in album charts both sides of the Atlantic, it was critically applauded, especially for Waters' impassioned, angry lyrics.

Rumors of a split followed news of other solo projects, and few were prepared for the quality and impact of the next album. Issued in 1979, *The Wall* was regarded by many as their greatest achievement to date, taking an unequivocal stance on the effects of education on children and the consequences for society at large. *Another Brick in The Wall* earned them a surprise UK No 1 single, but it was banned completely in South Africa because of its political overtones.

Wright quit amid mounting tension which solo albums from Gilmour and Mason did nothing to dissipate. The band split after 1983's *The Final Cut*, but Gilmour and Mason reformed in 1987 for the UK/US top-three album *A*

Above and left: The 1973 concerts at London's Earl Court were notable for many stunning effects including a huge 'gong' which suddenly burst into flames. From the left, Gilmour, Mason, Waters and Wright, augmented by saxophone and female backing vocalist to perform material from *Dark Side of the Moon*, their biggest-selling album.

Momentary Lapse of Reason, much to Waters' public displeasure. The former Floyd bassist reclaimed the initiative in 1990, performing *The Wall* with an all-star cast at the dismantled Berlin Wall before a TV audience of millions.

While the 'new' two-man Floyd, with Wright participating as a hired musician, was derided by some, a live LP *Delicate Sound Of Thunder* made the UK top-twenty in 1988, proving the name remained a bankable asset – even if they only played half the repertoire.

RECOMMENDED RECORDINGS

Piper at the Gates of Dawn

Saucerful of Secrets*

(*re-released together as A Nice Pair)

Relics (compilation)

Dark Side Of The Moon

Wish You Were Here

Animals

The Wall

FLEETWOOD MAC

Given their turbulent history – changes of personnel and music style, internal and external disputes – it is remarkable that Fleetwood Mac are here at all. However, they are one of the most universally popular and commercially successful bands of the past eight years.

Bassist, John McVie, drummer, Mick Fleetwood, and guitarist, Peter Green had all worked with John Mayall at one time in the sixties. When Green decided it was time to move on, he suggested to the others that they form their own band. With the addition of the elfin Jeremy Spencer on slide guitar and Bob Brunning on bass (he left in September 1967), they made their first appearance as Peter Green's Fleetwood Mac at the British National Jazz and Blues Festival in August 1967. Shortly after signing with the Blue Horizon label, the name was abbreviated to Fleetwood Mac.

Surprising success with a first album (it spent 37 weeks in the UK chart) established them as leaders of the British blues movement. The line-up was, unusually, augmented in late 1968 by a third guitarist, Danny Kirwan, giving them a formidable front-line of instrumental skill and composing talent. Then, after going to Chicago in 1969 to make a 'blues jam' session with veterans such as Willie Dixon, they amazed their

following by issuing an instrumental single, *Albatross*. Despite sounding like mid-period Shadows, it was a UK No 1. Other Peter Green compositions made the top five for them and an album on the Reprise label *Then Play On* showed a distinct shift toward a more pop style.

American success, however, eluded them, and on their first tour there, they supported Joe Cocker and Jethro Tull. Suddenly, Peter Green decided to devote his life to religion and left in May 1970. *Green Manalishi* was his last song for the band and his last UK single hit for many years.

The remaining members emerged in late 1970 with the interesting album *Kiln House*. A key factor was the inclusion of Christine Perfect (John McVie's wife and one-time vocalist and keyboard player with blues band Chicken Shack) on several of the tracks. She also joined them for an American tour which increased their popularity there above the cult status.

While in Los Angeles, Jeremy Spencer experienced a spiritual revelation and he also left. The band finished the tour with the temporary assistance of Peter Green, then returned to Britain confused and directionless.

American singer/guitarist Bob Welch replaced Spencer and soon their music was leaning toward a brand of West Coast rock, as the album *Future Games* demonstrated.

The Peter Green song *Black Magic Woman* (with Green on vocals) was rereleased in the USA with considerable success and the intriguing *Bare Trees* album of 1973 also sold well there. In Britain the band had been largely forgotten.

Following the enforced departure of Dave Kirwan, two other long-standing bluesmen, Bob Weston (ex-Long John Baldry's band) and Dave Walker (ex-Savoy Brown) were recruited and played on the bizarre *Penguin* album. To coincide with the album, *Albatross* was rereleased in the UK and, incredibly, went as far as No 2!

Personality clashes led to Walker and Weston quitting, followed by manager, Clifford Davis, who brought together a completely different bunch of musicians and promoted them as Fleetwood Mac. McVie and Fleetwood obtained a court injunction to thwart the imposters, and Fleetwood took over the band's management.

After recording *Heroes Are Hard To Find*, their first album as a Los Angeles-based outfit, Welch quit at the end of 1974 to go solo. At the suggestion of producer Keith Olsen, the three remaining members linked up with a Californian vocal/guitar duo, Stephanie 'Stevie' Nicks and Lindsey Buckingham, in January 1975.

The chemistry was exactly right this time. They had melodic invention, catchy riffs, above-average lyrics, appealing harmonies and expert production from Olsen. The first album, *Fleetwood Mac*, was a long-term best-seller throughout 1975 and 1976, yielding three US single hits with *Rhiannon* (US No 11), *Say You Love Me* (also No 11) and *Over My Head* (US No 10). In 1977, *Don't Stop* gave them their highest US placing to date, No 3.

That was followed in the same year with the outstanding *Rumours*, an album of exceptional songs and an object lesson in rock recording. *Rumours* has notched over fourteen-million sales and to support it the band undertook tours encompassing some thirteen countries and 300 concerts. One US tour kept them on the road for a year and resulted in a live double-album, released while they were camped in the studio making the next *magnum opus*. It took two years and cost a million dollars to make, but failed to live up to expectation. The well-conceived adult pop of *Rumours* had been replaced by something altogether less inspired. Tedious, self-indulgent

and loose as it was, *Tusk* nevertheless sold extremely well, giving a US No 8 and UK No 2 with the title track. *Sara* made No 7 in America.

The five-week US chart-topping *Mirage* was a shot in the arm in 1982 with a top-five single in *Hold Me*, but Nicks had already achieved a similar position with her 1981 solo debut *Bella Donna*. Individual activities continued until 1987's transatlantic chart-topping LP *Tango In The Night*. A 1988 *Greatest Hits* covered Buckingham's departure (replaced by Billy Burnette and Rick Vito), who debuted on 1990's *Behind The Mask*. Nicks and Christine then left, the others vowing to continue rock's longest soap opera.

Above: Part of the American half of the later band, Lindsey Buckingham on lead guitar.
Left: Drummer Mick Fleetwood has been in the band from the beginning. Here six-foot string-bean Fleetwood gives a conga solo.
Far left: Stevie Nicks who, with Christine McVie, has given the band a distinctive vocal sound – and a lot of glamour – on stage during a 1979 concert.
Previous page: Stevie Nicks and Lindsey Buckingham.

RECOMMENDED RECORDINGS

Peter Green's Fleetwood Mac (1967)
Kiln House
Bare Trees
Heroes Are Hard To Find
Fleetwood Mac
Rumours
Tango In The Night

ABBA

Sweden's best-known export, along with Volvo cars and Bjorn Borg, and probably the biggest money-spinner of the three, Abba's record sales outstrip those of every other group in pop history except The Beatles. Between 1977 and 1981, they were unquestionably the most popular performers in the world, and along with Australia's Bee Gees, the first to break the American-British grip on rock.

All the members of the group had established themselves individually in Swedish music well before coming together as a foursome in the early seventies. Guitarist Bjorn Vlvaeus had led a successful band called the Hootenanny Singers in the late sixties, while Stockholm-born Benny Anderson had played with The Hep Cats during the same period. Anni-Frid Lyngstad Fredriksson was born in Norway but raised in Sweden. She arrived in Stockholm in 1967, aged 22, to further her solo singing career (with some success). Also starting to make hit records at the time was seventeen-year-old Agnetha Faltskog. By 1970, Benny was living with Anni-Frid and in July 1971 Bjorn married Agnetha, something of a national event in Sweden as both were well-known figures by then.

Frustrated with the lack of progress being made by their respective groups, Bjorn and Benny quit within a short time of each other to

work for Stikkan Anderson's record company, Polar Music. Here they composed material for themselves and others and learned the art of production, which was to stand them in good stead later.

While cutting the album *Lycka*, the two girls were brought in to do some backing vocals. They did some live gigs, but it was very much a 'fun' thing at the time. Gradually, however, as Anni-Frid and Agnetha contributed more and more to the recordings, they came together as a group and between 1971 and 1973 they polished their act, and their material, with the aim of representing Sweden in the Eurovision song contest. It seemed the best way to obtain some international recognition.

In the 1973 contest they sang *Ring Ring* and got nowhere, but in 1974 in Brighton, watched by an estimated TV audience of 500 million, they were outright winners against some strong competition with *Waterloo*. This jaunty, catchy number immediately made the top of every national chart in Europe, and even reached No 6 in the United States.

Afterward Abba (they'd taken the name in 1973, from the initial letters of their Christian names) found that success in the Eurovision Song Contest was a positive disadvantage to anyone looking to break into the teenage market. Kids despised it and ridiculed those who appeared in it. To win them over, and lose the song-contest stigma, was to take Abba fully eighteen months.

They did it with a song called *SOS*, although it went up the charts slowly. But there was no denying the wide appeal of the group now. All four were attractive and wholesome, their act was superbly professional, and their material hit a winning formula. It was very tuneful, easy on the ear with its pleasant harmonies and appealing 'hooks' in the melody, and, with strong productions from Bjorn and Benny, very danceable. Their decision to write their songs entirely in English was another factor in their success, even if some of the results were fairly banal.

Left: The four famous Swedes: Benny and Bjorn, Anni-Frid and Agnetha.
Below: Abba meeting their Waterloo (it was better than most people's!).

Above: A rather coy exchange between Anni-Frid and Bjorn.
Right: Four in harmony. In 1977 they undertook a first world tour, and have since appeared in concerts for television.
Far right, top and below: Agnetha Faltskog (top) and Anni-Frid Lyngstad Fredrikkson. Both have recently embarked on solo careers, leading to rumors that Abba no longer truly exists as a group.

In Britain, *SOS* went to No 6 in 1975, but the follow-up, *Mamma Mia* made the top spot, as did *Fernando* in early 1976. Abba were back at No 1 in both Britain and America later that year with *Dancing Queen*.

With *Money Money Money* they had to settle for a UK No 2 but then came a hat-trick of chart-toppers with *Knowing Me Knowing You*, *The Name Of The Game* and *Take A Chance On Me*.

Since their sound (and, therefore, success) had been so much a product of expert studio techniques, the band were reluctant to play live, relying on equally expertly produced videos to promote their jingles. However, in 1977 they undertook a world tour, complete with fourteen extra musicians and an army of technicians.

And the hits just kept coming – *Chiquitita*, *Does Your Mother Know*, *Voulez-Vous*, *Gimme Gimme Gimme (A Man After Midnight)*, *I Have A Dream* and, in 1980, the memorable *The Winner Takes It All* and the wonderfully catchy *Super Trouper*.

In the LP charts a *Greatest Hits* compilation, using early-seventies material as well as recent successes, was in the UK top ten for most of 1976 and 1977, and *Arrival* had the distinction of more advance orders than any previous LP. *Abba, The Album, Greatest Hits Vol II, Voulez-Vous* and *Super Trouper* all kept the tills ringing, but the price of commercial success was to be the break-up of both relationships within the group. They attempted to keep their professional partnership intact and indeed scored in 1981 with two more singles including *One Of Us* and two of their best albums, *The Visitors* and

the magical *The Spanish Album – Gracias Por La Musica.*

But by the time a singles compilation appeared in 1982, Anni-Frid (calling herself simply Frida) had cut a solo album *Something's Going On)* and Agnetha followed her in 1983 with *Wrap Your Arms Around Me.*

The men, meanwhile, co-wrote the hit musical *Chess* with lyricist Tim Rice. Abba, it seemed, were no more, though Australian look/soundalikes Bjorn Again pulled capacity crowds for Abba revival shows. It seems that part of the pop world is forever Swedish.

RECOMMENDED RECORDINGS
Arrival
Abba, The Album
Greatest Hits Vol II
Voulez-Vous
Super Trouper
The Visitors
Gracias Por La Musica
The Singles

DIRE STRAITS

Just six years after their formation, but with some 70 gold records to their credit from around the world, Dire Straits are proof that excellent material coupled to fine musicianship and careful production can still triumph in the face of mere fashion.

In 1977, the band took its name from the members' financial plight, playing music whose appealing melodies and articulate lyrics were in sharp contrast to the punk sound that was rapidly gaining popularity. Eventually, Dire Straits found an audience for their brand of adult-orientated rock and it has proved to be a vast one.

English Lecturer, Mark Knopfler, was anxious to get the songs he had written performed. His flat-mate, sociology student John Illsey, suggested forming a band of their own, and recruiting Mark's brother, David, on guitar, and ex-Prairie Oyster drummer, Pick Withers, Dire Straits was formed. Illsey played bass, while Mark took vocals and lead guitar.

The band gained its first national exposure on a tour with Talking Heads in January 1978, and released a first album simply called *Dire Straits*. It consisted entirely of Mark Knopfler material, including an unlikely song about a jazz band, but one that possessed a very catchy guitar riff: *Sultans of Swing*. Released as their first single, it did nothing until it caught the ear of Radio London Disc Jockey, Charlie Gillett and through him grabbed the attention of record-buyers. A local radio station in Holland was also promoting the track vigorously, and the result was a surprising chart success at the height of the punk boom in 1979. It reached No 8 in Britain (albeit for only one week) and later attained No 4 in the USA. Sales of the album also increased rapidly, although less so in the UK than anywhere else. It became a hit in places as diverse as Canada, the USA, Holland, France, Belgium and West Germany before registering significantly in the UK.

Once again relying entirely on Mark Knopfler's material and on his rough-edged, semispoken vocals, the band recorded *Communique* under the direction of Jerry Wexler and Barry Beckett. A series of tours in 1979 increased their reputation and their following. At a time when guitar heroes were distinctly unfashionable, Knopfler's unmistakeable and highly melodic Stratocaster solos were a memorable feature of the band's performances on stage and on disc.

Far left: Lead guitar and songwriter for Dire Straits, Mark Knopfler, in concert during 1979 when the catchy *Sultans of Swing* was capturing disc jockeys' attention in the midst of the punk boom.
Left: Knopfler is one of that dying breed, the guitar hero. His solos and riffs, and the distinctive sound he obtains out of his Stratocaster characterize all Dire Straits' songs.
Below: In concert in 1982 and seemingly enjoying the success of *Love over Gold*; it topped the album charts both sides of the Atlantic that year.

Dave Knopfler left the band, to be replaced by Hal Lindes, and Roy Brittan (keyboards) was also added to record *Making Movies*. The album demonstrated Knopfler's new confidence as a songwriter.

In October 1980, Dire Straits undertook a world tour that lasted until July 1981. With Alan Clark as keyboardist they worked on their fourth album. Meantime, the almost sinister *Romeo and Juliet* made No 11 in the UK. The album *Love Over Gold* did not disappoint. It included some of Mark's most dazzling guitar work in the lengthy *Telegraph Road*. Released in late 1982, it shot to the top of the UK and US LP charts and remained in the top 100 for months. *Private Investigations* was released as a single and made No 2 in Britain.

A live album *Alchemy* preceded *Brothers In Arms*, Straits' 1985 release and the first classic album of the CD era. Twelve times platinum by 1992, it topped the album charts in the US and UK, singles including the US No 1 single *Money For Nothing* (co-written by Sting) which gave its title to a 1988 hits collection. Knopfler retreated into production and film music work, testing the waters with part-time group the Notting Hillbillies before re-launching Straits (by now Knopfler, Illsley and assorted supporting musicians) in 1991 with *On Every Street*.

RECOMMENDED RECORDINGS

Dire Straits
Communique
Making Movies
Love Over Gold
Alchemy *(double live)*
Brothers In Arms

THE ELECTRIC LIGHT ORCHESTRA

*R*oy Wood was one of the more imaginative and musically ambitious figures to emerge from the British rock scene in the sixties. His band, The Move, enjoyed a considerable following in the UK for their lively stage act and colorful psychedelia. In the US, too, they eventually achieved a kind of cult status, if not commercial success. However, as the decade closed, Wood was eagerly looking for new directions for his music. One idea that had been with him for some time, inspired by John Lennon's efforts on Strawberry Fields Forever *and* I Am The Walrus, *was to combine the best that a four-piece rock band had to offer with the potential of the classical orchestra, most especially the strings – violins, violas and cellos.*

As The Move gradually wound down, Wood worked on this format, taking the title Electric Light Orchestra. *The project also interested guitar player and vocalist, Jeff Lynne, another Birmingham-born musician who had worked with the much-vaunted Nightriders and was now with a group called The Idle Race.*

The lengthy agonies involved in producing a first album were such that Wood grew tired of the ELO and departed for pastures new. He formed Wizzard, and later a rock and roll revival and heavy metal bands, and then vanished into undeserved obscurity.

Jeff Lynne, on the other hand, conducted various permutations of ELO through a decade of unbroken and lucrative success (if not critical acclaim) on both sides of the Atlantic.

Twenty-three-year old Lynne teamed with the Move in 1971, replacing Carl Wayne. Roy Wood and Bev Bevan (drums) were the only surviving members and the group looked to be on its last legs. Wood, however, envisaged it operating in parallel to the Electric Light Orchestra, and it was the latter which mainly interested Jeff Lynne.

The band issued a single which sold reasonably well in the USA, *California Man* and Lynne penned the 'B' side, *Do Ya*. He also featured strongly on their last album of new material, *Message from The Country*. Wood's progress with ELO had been severely restricted by the Move's contractual obligations. The LP *Electric Light Orchestra* was recorded over an inordi-

Top: ELO introduced the violin and cellos to their line-up.
Top right: ELO's concerts still attract large audiences.

Above: Jeff Lynne (left) has led the Electric Light Orchestra throughout its highly successful history, keeping to its brand of pop-rock.

nately long period with an assortment of musicians and by the time it was issued in 1971, Wood had grown tired of the whole project. Although the album yielded a moderately successful single, *10538 Overture,* he quit in 1972, leaving Lynne to take up the reins along with Bev Bevan.

Together, they added seven more musicians, including three ex-London Symphony Orchestra string players, to form the second ELO line-up. Also included was Richard Tandy on keyboards, along with Lynne and Bevan (the only other member to remain with the group throughout its career).

Offering a brand of grandiose (some would say, inflated) art-rock, they released an album in February 1973. In the main, it was unenthusiastically received, but a single, an extraordinary arrangement of Chuck Berry's *Roll Over Beethoven,* made No 6 in the UK charts and began a virtually unbroken string of top-twenty hits over the next few years.

In summer 1973 ELO toured America for the first time, and issued another album later that year, *On The Third Day.* Personnel changes at the time saw cellist Hugh McDowell join from Roy Wood's Wizzard, and Mik Kaminski take over on violin.

Their music relied increasingly on a dense, multilayered production, complete with lush string sound, and could easily have passed for something coming out of the 'soul factories' of Philadelphia. Not surprising, therefore, they set out to conquer America, undertaking six tours

there in three years. They achieved a gold album in 1974 with, appropriately, *Eldorado,* and a US top-ten hit in 1975 with *Can't Get It Out of My Head. Face the Music* acquired similar album status, and produced single hits with *Evil Woman* (UK No 10) and *Strange Magic.* The release of *A New World Record* in 1976 established ELO's following in Britain as well as the USA. It remained in the American album chart for six months. *Telephone Line* was a top-ten hit in both countries, and *Turn To Stone* reached the top twenties. The latter came from another successful album, *Out Of The Blue* (notable for containing Jeff Lynne's ambitious neoclassical work, *Concerto For A Rainy Day*).

In 1978, three singles all made the UK top ten, *Sweet Talkin' Woman, Mister Blue Sky* and *Wild West Hero.* That year their spectacular stage show reached new heights of extravagance. For their US tour they had built a five-ton, 60-foot wide, white fiberglass spaceship. The top half rose some 40 feet into the air, revealing the band, and a battery of lasers, inside. It was breathtaking, if ostentatious!

Equally grand, their 1979 album *Discovery* utilized the services of a 42-strong orchestra and 30-voice male choir in ELO's most ambitious attempt yet at a classical-rock fusion. Singles from the LP, *Shine A Little Love* and *Don't Bring Me Down* made the US and UK top ten.

ELO's soundtrack was the only redeeming feature of the appalling film *Xanadu,* which they made with Olivia Newton-John in 1980. The title track went to No 1 in Britain and No 8 in

the US, although the musical itself was a miserable failure. *I'm Alive* and *All Over The World* were other hit singles from the soundtrack. 1980 also saw the issue of a four-disc compilation, *A Box Of Their Best.* In the eighties ELO remain one of rock's top concert attractions. Their latest album, *Secret Messages* achieved the status of its predecessors (UK No 4), and a 1981 hit single, *Hold On Tight* was an interesting experiment in 'rockabilly' style.

Lynne concentrated on production after 1983's *Secret Messages,* reuniting with Bevan and Tandy for 1986's *Balance Of Power* and its US hit single *Calling America.* The title spoke volumes: the now US-based Lynne produced hit LPs for George Harrison and worked with Roy Orbison, Randy Newman and others. He then joined Harrison, Orbison, Tom Petty and Dylan in *ad hoc* supergroup the Traveling Wilburys, also cutting the solo *Armchair Theatre* in 1990. In Britain, Bevan and several ex-members reformed as ELO Part 2, with Climax Blues Band's Peter Haycock taking the vocal role: an eponymous album appeared in 1991.

RECOMMENDED RECORDINGS

Eldorado

A New World Record

Out Of The Blue

Discovery

Greatest Hits *(compilation)*

A Box Of Their Best *(four-disc compilation)*

Time

THE KINKS

*T*he central figure in the up-and-down story of The Kinks has been singer/guitarist, Ray Davies, perhaps the most underrated songwriter to emerge from British pop music of the sixties. His gentle, whimsical cameos of English life and its characters were masterly if unconventional, more in the music-hall tradition than rock and roll. Curiously, for a group whose material is so peculiarly English, their following in America is now much greater than at home, where much of their best work has gone largely unappreciated.

Raymond Douglas Davies (born 1944) and his brother David (born 1947) started playing seriously in the early sixties. Ray went to art college and in December 1963 formed The Kinks with Dave on lead guitar, Mick Avory on drums and Peter Quaife on bass. One of their first jobs was backing blues singer Robert Wace (later their manager), but then producer Shel Talmy spotted them and signed the band up for Pye. They became firm favorites with the mods.

The first two singles flopped miserably. The third single, a raw slice of antique heavy metal, established them in 1964. *You Really Got Me* reached No 1 in Britain and No 7 in the US. Its basic chords and lurching rhythm owed much to The Kingsmens' *Louie Louie. All Day And All Of The Night* continued in the same vein, reaching No 2 in the UK and No 7 in the US.

A change of style in 1965 did not affect their success: the melancholy ballad *Tired Of Waiting For You* was another British No 1 and made No 6 in America. *Everybody's Gonna Be Happy* just made the UK top twenty, but *Set Me Free* and *See My Friend* were top-ten entries. *Till the End Of The Day* was their fifth British single release that year, reaching No 8. *Kwyet Kinks*, an EP released late 1965, showed Ray Davies taking a new direction. The songs had a new depth and insight, especially the social satire on middle-class conservative values, *A Well Respected Man.* In 1966, Ray made the peacocks of London the object of his humor in *Dedicated Follower of Fashion* (UK No 4).

Left: The Kinks having a whip-round! On the left drummer, Mick Avory. Then Pete Quaife on bass and Dave and Ray Davies.
Above: Ray Davies, one of rock's most original songwriters.
Overleaf: An early appearance on the leading UK TV show *Top Of The Pops.*

Sadly, The Kinks progress in America was severely limited by a dispute with the American Federation of Musicians which prevented them touring there, after a series of concerts in 1965, for four years.

In Britain, Ray Davies' wry commentaries and tragi-comic anecdotes kept the group in the UK charts through 1966 and 1967: *Sunny Afternoon* (No 1); *Dead End Street* (No 5); the classic, *Waterloo Sunset* (No 2); and the amusing tale of a suburban gardener, *Autumn Almanac* (No 3).

They began to tour less as Ray became involved in outside projects. In 1967 Pye issued the vibrantly atmospheric, *Live At Kelvin Hall* and their last Shel Talmy-produced album, the excellent *Something Else By The Kinks.* After this, they undertook their own production.

The band's ambitions continued to grow. Their first concept album appeared in 1968. *The Kinks Are The Village Green Preservation Society* was a fond appreciation of English life. The English theme was continued, albeit more sardonically, in *Arthur (Or The Decline And Fall Of The British Empire)* — a highly acclaimed narrative album that began life as a TV soundtrack.

After months of rumor, Quaife left the band to be replaced on bass by John Dalton. The group toured the US in 1969, Ray Davies stage performances becoming ever more flamboyant and theatrical.

Recent albums had produced no hit singles but the situation was corrected in 1970 with *Lola*, said to be the first rock song whose principal figure was a transvestite. It made No 2 in Britain, No 9 in America. The follow-up, *Apeman*, made No 5 at home, but did little in the US. *Lola* was included in the 1970 album, *Kinks Part 1: Lola versus Powerman and The Moneygoround*, a bitter commentary on the pop industry's manipulators.

After lengthy disputes with their management and record company, the band negotiated a contract with RCA. The first RCA release, *Muswell Hillbillies* (1971), saw a departure in style, with the addition of John Gosling on keyboards and the Mike Cotton Sound on brass. It became one of their most celebrated albums, with quintessential Kinks tracks such as *Skin and Bone*, *Alcohol* and *Acute Schizoid Paranoid Blues*, as well as the title track. It enjoyed little commercial success, however, but sales in the US were considerably enhanced by their entertaining live performances. Their American following was consolidated by 1972's *Everybody's In Showbiz – Everybody's A Star* featuring the delightfully nostalgic *Celluloid Heroes*. By now Laurie Brown (trumpet), Alan Holmes (saxophone) and John Beecham (trombone) were Kinks' regulars.

Supersonic Rocket Ship gave them a UK No 16 single hit the same year. It was followed in 1973 by their most ambitious project to date,

Above: From antique heavy metal, their songs became whimsical cameos of life and its characters, an almost music-hall quality which Dave's hat personifies!
Left: Ray Davies inevitably became the leading figure in the band, responsible for changes in the line-up as well as the material.
Top right: In the seventies, brass and reeds, and a female backing chorus, became part of the regular stage line-up as Ray's compositions became ever more conceptual and demanding.
Right: Dave Davies in a thoughtful mood.

Preservation. Intended as much as a drama as music, it exploited further the character of Mr Flash from *Village Green Preservation Society.* Originally intended as a three-album epic, part one (a double album) saw Ray Davies' inventiveness stretched to the full, although it made good theater. Part two appeared in 1974, reduced to just a single.

Mr Flash reappeared again in 1975, when his dubious adolescence was explored on *Schoolboys In Disgrace.* It was released in the USA three months ahead of Britain, but puzzled American audiences as much as it failed to stir the British. *Soap Opera,* also 1975, was better received.

The Kinks signed to Arista in 1976, and in 1977 issued *Sleepwalker,* a US top-thirty album entry, and the well-produced *Misfits,* recorded at their own London studio which they'd established in 1974 along with a record label, Konk Records.

Changes in The Kinks personnel occurred in 1977 and 1978, including Davies' dismissal of the brass section. Eventually, the three remaining founder members were solely augmented by Jim Rodford on bass, and Ian Gibbons on keyboards and this line-up has remained intact to date.

In 1979, The Kinks recorded in the US for the first time: memorable tracks on *Low Budget* (made for just that in New York!) included *Gallon Of Gas* and *Superman,* the whole a return to basic rock and roll. *One For The Road,* a live double album released in 1980, offered lively performances of old favorites.

Give The People What They Want (1982) sadly failed to live up to its name. The songs showed little of Ray Davies' usual inspiration, but recent releases have seen a return to form. *Come Dancing* made No 6 in the UK in 1983 and reached the US top ten. A good, new album was also issued, *State Of Confusion.*

The future of The Kinks obviously depends largely on the continued inspiration of Ray Davies, the most enigmatic of songwriters. Satirical or sentimental, often acutely class-conscious, his better songs appear less frequently nowadays although his imagination seems as fertile as ever.

RECOMMENDED RECORDINGS
Live At Kelvin Hall
Something Else By The Kinks
Village Green Preservation Society
Arthur (Or The Decline And Fall Of The British Empire)
Everybody's In Showbiz
Sleepwalker
Misfits
One For The Road *(live/double)*
The Kinks File *(compilation)*
20 Golden Greats *(compilation)*
Collection *(compilation)*

OFF BEAT

THE JAM

Founder-members, Paul Weller (guitar) and Rick Buckler (drums) formed the nucleus of the band while at school in Woking, Surrey. Bruce Foxton (bass) and Steve Brookes completed the initial line-up although Brookes soon departed.

After groundwork in rhythm and blues, the threesome put together a remarkable set of songs penned by Paul Weller. Their above-average quality and originality, plus the pre-requisite demonic energy, appealed to the audience of London's 100 Club when the threesome made their debut in summer 1976.

From their look (neat haircuts contrasting vividly with the styles favored by other bands!), and their material (which acknowledged a debt to Pete Townshend), the band were dubbed 'the new Who.' Later, Weller commented that if Townshend really meant the line in *My Generation*, 'Hope I die before I get old', he would have topped himself by now!

Polydor, perhaps determined to grab a slice of the punk/new wave action, signed them up and a much-acclaimed debut album, *In the City*, was issued in May 1977 making No 20 in the charts. The title track made the lower end of the UK single charts, but deserved better.

Odd men out in the British new-wave explosion of the mid-seventies, The Jam, both in their songs and their styles, displayed an obvious affinity with the early 'mod'-ish music of The Who, Small Faces and The Kinks. Their view of things was distinctly individual, and often quite different from their contemporaries. They never truly fitted any label; possibly mod-revival, but certainly not punk, and this, coupled to the outstanding song-writing abilities of Paul Weller, probably explains why they successfully survived the demise of both movements. It's interesting to speculate how much further they might have progressed had not Weller set off on a solo career in 1982, to form the successful band Style Council. He also produced for Tracie and Paul Young, equally successfully.

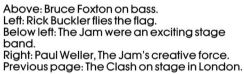

Above: Bruce Foxton on bass.
Left: Rick Buckler flies the flag.
Below left: The Jam were an exciting stage band.
Right: Paul Weller, The Jam's creative force.
Previous page: The Clash on stage in London.

In 1978, with a fast-growing following, they enjoyed three hit singles, including *News of the World* (No 13) and *Down in the Tube Station at Midnight* (No 15). A second album appeared, too, the obliquely titled, *All Mod Cons*.

In 1979, *Strange Town* made the lower half of the top twenty while the excellent and memorable *Eton Rifles* deservedly reached No 3. They hit No 4 in the album charts, too, with *Setting Sons*. The award of 'Best Group' was bequeathed to them by the readers of *New Musical Express* in the magazine's annual poll.

Going Underground (1980), *Start, A Town Called Malice* and *Beat Surrender* (1982) all made No 1 in the UK. Despite numerous accolades during 1982, December's tour was their farewell. The Jam's two final albums, *The Gift* (which entered the chart at No 1) and the live *Dig the New Breed*, made their break-up all the more regretable.

Weller remained in the spotlight first with the Style Council (15 UK top-forty hits between 1983 and 1989, operating with keyboardist Mick Talbot in white soul mold) and later with the Paul Weller Movement. The latter group commenced operations in 1991, the same year the Jam's *Greatest Hits* reached the UK top three.

RECOMMENDED RECORDINGS

In the City
Setting Sons
Sound Affects
The Gift
Dig the New Breed (*live*)
Snap

BLONDIE

*T*he inviting pout of the sultry Deborah Harry was a familiar sight in the late seventies as Blondie rose to the peak of their success in 1979. Debbie Harry's voice was as memorable as her looks; it could be effortlessly childlike and sweet-toned, or raunchy and snarling. Their most successful songs were traditional boy-and-girl themes, with a simplicity reminiscent of the unsophisticated early sixties. However, the instrumental lines were cleverly worked out, especially by Chris Stein on lead guitar and the results were irresistibly catchy. At their best, Blondie managed the difficult feat of appealing to the teenage pop/disco market and 'adult rock' connoisseurs at one and the same time.

The band came together in Manhattan in the mid-seventies, an offshoot from a group known as the Stilettoes. With Deborah Harry on vocals, Stein on lead, Gary Valentine on guitar, Jimmy Destri on keyboards and Clem Burke on drums, they cut a single in September 1976 (*In The Flesh*) and the next month were contracted to Private Stock records. An album simply entitled *Blondie* was released, but shortly after the group switched to the Chrysalis label who immediately bought out the rights to this first LP and rereleased it. Valentine left, to be replaced by Frank Infante, and drummer Nigel Harrison was taken on; this line-up toured Britain as a support group in the summer of 1977.

The same year, a second album *Plastic Letters* was released in the wake of the hit single, *Denis, Denis* (a cover of Randy and the Rainbow's mid-sixties US hit), which really set the formula for their other single hits: a steady, bouncy rhythm and well-crafted instrumental lines. The focus, as ever, was on Debbie Harry's voice which gave each song its distinctive mood and character. *Heart of Glass, Hanging on the Telephone, Picture This* and *Sunday Girl* are classics of the genre. On LP they were more adventurous, sometimes moving into the realm of art rock, and *Parallel Lines* (1978), which reached No 1 in the UK album charts, showed considerable progress in the variety and form of their songs. It remains their best album to date – and their best-selling. The album *Eat to the Beat* was the groups's second and last No 1 in the UK, and they reached a highspot in Britain by becoming 1979's best-selling performers, both on LP and single.

After releasing *Auto American* to a mixed reception in 1981, Deborah Harry and Chris

Stein quit to go their separate ways, leaving their album to chart at No 3 in the UK. Debbie made her acting debut in *Union City Blues*, but the film received a critical slating.

Unfortunately, Deborah's first solo album, *Koo Koo* (complete with change of hair color for the sleeve photograph) was also a disappointment. The material just wasn't up to it, although loyal fans helped it to No 6 in the charts. Her next film, *Videodrome*, was hardly better received.

Meanwhile, Destri and Burke were working on the other side of the mixing desk as producers, and Harrison had teamed up with new musicians. It was therefore a surprise when the band re-formed in 1982 to make *The Hunter*.

Chris Stein started his own label, Animal (signing Iggy Pop), but a wasting disease found Debbie retiring temporarily to nurse him through it successfully. In the late eighties she released two further solo LPs – *Rockbird* with the hit *French Kissin' In The USA* (1987) and *Def Dumb And Blonde* with *I Want That Man* (1989). While these broke little new ground, the 1991 UK chart success of *The Complete Picture* – a compilation of Blondie and Harry hits – proved that she retained a fond following.

RECOMMENDED RECORDINGS
Eat to the Beat
Parallel Lines

Above: Debbie Harry punches the air and Chris Stein solemnly plays on – he wrote many of their best songs.
Below: Debbie at her seductive best.

Top, and above: Her distinctive voice, and her compelling stage presence were the secret of Blondie's success, plus some classic, well-crafted hit singles.
Left: A look-in for Nigel Harrison on bass as Debbie gives a plug to Andy Warhol.
Overleaf (both): A touching moment at the edge of the stage and (opposite) the skin-tight look.

MADONNA

*W*ill she become, as many on the inside of American show-business believe, the biggest female star of rock music – or has Madonna's time come and gone, at least in the fickle and capricious world of pop? Certainly, it is going to take something pretty remarkable to match the achievements of the eighties. But it's not just Madonna's string of chart-topping hits that has ensured her such fame. She has forged a film career for herself, with varying success. And then, there was the secret wedding that wasn't so secret, not to mention the matter of the nude photographs. . .

Madonna Louise Ciccone was born on 16 August 1959 in Bay City, Michigan, just down the road from Detroit where her father worked for the Chrysler Corporation. She had a strict Catholic upbringing, along with her five brothers and two sisters, and its effect seems to have stayed with her: at the end of each stage performance an off-stage voice, supposedly that of her father, tells her what a naughty girl she's been and calls her home! But it's also part of a well-honed image, one that's been copied by her legions of teenage fans all over the globe, right down to their 'virgins' t-shirts.

Although her father paid for piano lessons, it was dancing that first attracted her (it's not for nothing that she has perhaps the best-choreographed stage show in rock music) and, apart from a few ballet lessons, she taught herself.

In 1976, she gained a place at the University of Michigan. At one of the campus discos, she met drummer Steve Bray, one of several males that were to be co-opted along the line into making a contribution towards Madonna's progress. She danced energetically to the music of his R&B band, but it was hardly the showcase for her talents.

New York beckoned, and Alvin Ailey's Dance Theater, where she trained with the beginners' troupe, and became part of the avant-garde arts scene in the city. Her now-famous navel played an early starring role as an improvised frying pan for a sizzling egg, and there was an appearance – by all of her torso – in another 'cult movie', *A Certain Sacrifice*.

Dance and drama, however, failed to provide the necessary rewards and Madonna turned to music, and a band that was being formed by Dan Gilroy and his brother, Ed. But before they'd even made their debut, the leading lady had been whisked off to Paris by

disco star Patrick Hernandez. He wanted to tutor her in the performing arts, European style, but she returned home to work with Gilroy.

Now Steve Bray returned to her life, assisting in writing and recording her own songs. She hiked a tape of one, called 'Everybody', around the New York discos, persuading those DJs she could to give it a play. One, Mark Kamins was more impressed than most and offered to produce a finished studio version of the demo tape, a tape which eventually gained her a contract with the independent New York label, Sire.

When released in the Autumn of 1982, *Everybody* wasn't over-successful – it positively flopped in Britain. 1983's *Lucky Star* did better – it reached No 171. It was with *Holiday* that things really took off. Produced by her one-time boy-friend, John 'Jellybean' Benitez, it made No 7 and did both of their careers a lot of good.

For her first album, however, now re-released with that title, she disappointed both Bray and Kamins by opting for the services of Reggie Lucas. But he was to be cast aside for the hugely-successful follow-up, *Like A Virgin*. The vote went to Nile Rodgers of Chic fame, on account of his impressive track record.

Yet no one would deny the importance of video, not just in the success of *Virgin* (atmospherically shot in Venice) but in that of all recent Madonna hits.

Visually, she has always been an original, and one with some style. On stage she's a bizarre mixture of leather and lace, a true teaser, whether it's in the strangely symbolic striptease as she erotically removes wedding dress and veil, her parody of Marilyn Monroe's *Diamonds are a Girl's Best Friend* or 'boy toy' belt buckle and 'hello sailor' message that surrounds her much-flaunted navel.

1985 proved the best year yet, with the film *Desperately Seeking Susan* released to considerable acclaim (including much directed towards Madonna herself); single hits with *Material Girl* (No 3), *Into the Groove* (No 1), *Holiday*, re-released to make No 2, *Angel/Burning Up* (No 5), and *Gambler/Dress You Up* (No 5); and marriage to film actor Sean Penn, on a wind-swept cliff, with only selected guests present

and her fans limited to viewing the ceremony on a tv film made from a helicopter.

Film work (*Shanghai Surprise*, with Penn, and *Who's That Girl?*) continued, while 1986's *True Blue* album was another US/UK No 1. The following year she became the first woman to have four UK No 1 singles: two albums, the *Who's That Girl?* soundtrack and the remix LP *You Can Dance* both made the top ten. 1989's release *Like A Prayer* was six weeks at the top in the US, while *I'm Breathless*, inspired by the film *Dick Tracy* in which she starred with paramour Warren Beatty (having divorced Penn) spawned another transatlantic chart-topper in *Vogue*. It also featured on 1990's *Immaculate Collection* hits package.

Left: Madonna hits LA in 1985.
Below: Madonna, seen here on a US Tour, gives her all on stage.
Right: A studio shot of Madonna.

RECOMMENDED RECORDINGS
Like A Virgin
The Immaculate Collection

THE
CLASH

From the beginning, it seemed The Clash had more to offer than most of the other British punk bands emerging in the seventies. So it proved: as punk burned out, the Clash were broadening the base of their musical style and widening their concerns, without losing any of the incisive fury and honesty that distinguished their rise to prominence. However, the original line up broke up in 1983 and the first appearances of the 'new' Clash were disappointing.

Legend has it that the nucleus of the band was forged just 24 hours after a meeting in London's Portobello Road street market, Mick Jones and Paul Simonon persuading Joe Strummer to join them from the 101'ers. As soon as they found a suitable drummer, Terry Chimes, they soon established a healthy reputation on the fast-growing, exuberant punk circuit. With Jones and Strummer on guitars and vocals, and Simonon on bass, the band took part in the Sex Pistols' chaotic winter 1975 tour which was headlined 'Anarchy.' Punk attacked those in power and those corrupted by power (including rock stars); and The Clash were the most uncompromising and avowedly political of the new bands. Jones and Strummer's songs were charged with frightening imagery, giving powerful voice to the anger and frustrations of living and growing up in Britain's decaying cities. *White Riot, London's Burning* and other ominous anthems had a conviction that couldn't be ignored. It was a sincere attempt to unite the fragmented punk community with a single awareness and sense of purpose, but ultimately failed as punk lost its coherent identity. Commercialism watered down punk to make it acceptable for exploitation.

However, when The Clash's first album appeared in 1977, the flame still burned brightly; some even denounced them for having signed for a major label – CBS.

It was an outstanding and successful debut. *White Riot* made the singles charts, and the band confirmed its political stance by appearing in multiracial concerts organized throughout Britain by 'Rock Against Racism.' They shared a love of Jamaican reggae, and its influence, especially in rhythm, can clearly be heard in the music of the Clash and other bands. Indeed, they recorded a reggae number, Junior Murvin's *Police and Thieves* for the first album and later used a Jamaican producer, the excellent Lee Perry.

Percussion problems continued – Chimes

left, but was replaced by Nicky 'Topper' Headon in time for the Clash to take on America (a promising confrontation as one of their most deadpan songs was *I'm So Bored With the USA!*). But they liked it there sufficiently to produce the second album in New York, *Give 'Em Enough Rope*, in late 1978 and undertake a US tour in 1979.

Rope was their first album to appear officially in the US: the first LP had only been available as a pricey import, but still accounted for sales exceeding 100,000. They had successfully expanded their audience and followed that by widening their musical style with their third studio album, *Sandinista*. Reggae, rhythm and blues and soul-funk were added to the mix now, and as the punk counterculture fizzled out, The Clash became a great rock band.

Along with regular performances in both Britain and the US, they put together a formidable double album (their third to be issued) entitled, *London Calling* which again faced up to the issues that mattered. Their musical talents, creative standards and careful production served them well.

Despite rumors of a split in 1982 (Strummer vanished for a while and upon his return, Headon and Terry Chimes returned), the band released another fine album, *Combat Rock*.

Above: The punk band with the greatest potential: left to right, Jones, Strummer, Simonon (bass), and Topper Headon (drums).
Right: Mick Jones co-wrote their powerful, uncompromising songs in collaboration with the group's other guitarist, Joe Strummer (far right).
Far right: 'London's Burning' was their cry, but eventually the fire burned out.

Jones bailed out in 1984 to form rap/rock fusion pioneers Big Audio Dynamite; Strummer dissolved the band after one more album *Cut The Crap* (1985), retiring to a fitful solo career which included film music for punk pic *Sid And Nancy*. A TV jeans ad shot the Mick Jones-composed *Should I Stay Or Should I Go?* to the top of the UK singles charts in 1991, but rather than cash in with a re-formed Clash, Strummer chose instead to front Irish rebel folk-rockers the Pogues.

RECOMMENDED RECORDINGS

The Clash
Give 'Em Enough Rope
Sandinista
London Calling
Combat Rock
History of the Clash Vol 1

THE SEX PISTOLS

*F*ive years after the demise of the band, opinions remain sharply divided about the Sex Pistols. A huge con-trick played at the expense of the record companies and the media? Just one outrageous farce, as their one-time lead singer, John Lydon, now claims? Or the heroes of a revolution in rock music, a revolution that gave it an undreamt-of political and social relevance?

The truth, no doubt, lies somewhere between all three viewpoints. The story of the Sex Pistols poses questions that extend way beyond the limits of the punk subculture of which they were leaders.

Among the providers of music for the punk-chic cult in the clubs of New York around 1974 were the New York Dolls, a strange outfit managed by a British exile, Malcolm McLaren. When the Dolls broke up, McLaren returned to London. He opened a clothes shop in the fashionable Kings Road called 'Sex' (later, 'Seditionaries') which became a kind of meeting place. It was to 'Sex' that three raw, amateur musicians calling themselves The Swankers – Steve Jones, Paul Cook and Glen Matlock – came in search of a manager. McLaren was their man. His first decision was to persuade Jones to move to guitar to make way for a more dynamic lead singer – John Lydon. Because of the condition of his teeth, he soon acquired the alias of 'Johnny Rotten.' Lydon had no singing experience but he did have a distinctive insolent look which suited the image McLaren had in mind for his band, now retitled the Sex Pistols.

At first, they crashed other people's gigs, playing brutalized versions of old Who and Small Faces numbers. Their official debut at a London art school in November 1975 lasted but ten minutes before an outraged audience had them thrown off stage. That was to be a regular pattern early on, but they were gaining a following and with it a punk philosophy was developing. It grew out of the disenchantment, frustration and boredom of seventies youth. It put those feelings into music of thunderous fury. Bondage garb, torn clothing, spiked, luridly dyed hair became the look; and abusive, irreverent, hostile cynicism the fashionable attitude. The elite of rock music were particularly hated, despite punk's obvious debt to early R&B, The Stones, The Who, Alice Cooper, Frank Zappa and others.

Despite their technical limitations, the Sex Pistols still made for compelling listening but one town council after another throughout Britain banned them. Audiences were often violent at their concerts; yet again, a trend going back to the fifties teddy boys, and the mods, rockers and skinheads of the sixties.

In just twelve months they became the most discussed rock act in Britain – so much so that, in November 1976 they signed for the UK's longest-established record company, EMI. The fee was £40,000, but it was a short-lived relationship. When the Pistols appeared on national TV a few days later they were baited mercilessly by

Left: Johnny bares the teeth that earned him his nickname.
Below: From the left, Vicious, Jones and Rotten, Cook on drums.
Right: A right pelting – shame about the suit.

the interviewer and retaliated with a few four-letter expletives which made headlines next day in the press.

EMI were ill-equipped for this sort of notoriety. When EMI workers refused to handle the Pistols' records, and 90 percent of the venues on a projected tour banned them, EMI pulled out of the deal. An EMI single, *Anarchy In The UK*, which begins with 'Rotten' declaiming, 'I am the anti-Christ!', appeared briefly and was then withdrawn. A&M Records, however, was left with even more egg on its face. Its contract with the Pistols was allegedly worth £150,000 but was terminated after seven days with a £75,000 pay-off.

In March 1977 Glen Matlock, probably its most musically talented member, was kicked out after a row with 'Johnny Rotten,' who re-placed him on bass with his friend, 'Sid Vicious' (John Ritchie) late of Siouxsie and The Ban-shees. In the May, Virgin Records stepped in with a contract for £50,000. The Pistols' second single release, *God Save The Queen* was a nicely timed 'tribute' for the 1977 Silver Jubilee and, despite a total media ban, reached No 2 (some charts left the entry blank and the record was banned outright by the BBC). A third re-lease, *Pretty Vacant* completed a staggering sequence of debut recordings and was fol-lowed in late 1977 with an album *Never Mind The Bollocks, Here's The Sex Pistols* containing all three singles and new material, including a sarcastic attack on EMI.

It was their crowning moment. In January 1978 they undertook a much-publicized but ill-fated tour of America after which the band split up in dramatic fashion. 'Rotten' was sacked and Jones and Cook went to Rio de Janeiro, to make a record with train robber, Ronald Biggs. 'Sid Vicious' met a suitably horrific end in New York. In October 1978, he was charged with murdering his girlfriend. While out on bail the following February he died of a drug overdose. His last recordings were a grotesque version of *My Way*, and the tasteless *Belsen Was A Gas*.

'Johnny Rotten,' meanwhile assuming his real name, formed Public Image Ltd, in which he continues to enjoy some success with a post-punk parody using the kind of slick session men the punks decried. *Anarchy In The UK* is still sung, however, with nostalgic venom. McLaren had been busy making a film, released in 1980, *Rock and Roll Swindle*, which caused 'Rotten' to denounce him as having sold out.

Punk released rock music back on to the streets, where it could once again become threatening, dangerous, offensive, unpredict-able, where it could break the rules. At the height of the Pistols' notoriety, Johnny Rotten declared with sly innocence, 'I don't under-stand it. All we're trying to do is destroy every-thing.' At the end, the only thing he could truth-fully consider destroyed was rock music.

Perhaps his most telling comment, however, comes during one of the band's most terrifying compositions, *Holidays In The Sun*, which lashes out vehemently at modern values and uses images of Nazism, the Berlin Wall, and concen-tration camps to gruesome effect. As the song explodes in chaos around him, Rotten ex-claims, 'I don't understand this bit at all!' And that, perhaps, was the Sex Pistols' dilemma.

RECOMMENDED RECORDINGS
Never Mind The Bollocks, Here's The Sex Pistols

FRANK ZAPPA

Z appa is the odd-man-out of rock. For nearly twenty years he has pursued a singularly individual vision, eschewing all the traditional clichés of rock music (except to parody them). As an innovator and experimenter, he has few equals, and his output of recordings is prodigious. His musical adventures have taken him into all manner of sound worlds with liberal use of choirs, orchestras and electronics, in addition to the full range of conventional rock instrumentation. His live concerts developed into theatrical events, and he is increasingly exploring the common ground between classical music, jazz and rock.

Zappa's material presents a paradox. He can pen brilliant, debunking satires, yet is also capable of putting out the most puerile, crude and apparently pointless ditties. There seems no let-up in his ideas and creative energy and his best may well be to come.

When he was ten, in 1950, Francis Vincent Zappa Jr moved with his Sicilian-Greek family from the East-coast port of Baltimore to California. Within a couple of years, he was playing the drums and he studied harmony in high school. He then formed an eight-piece band with some friends. He worked in clubs and bars where he picked up a couple of production commissions and with the money bought an electric guitar – and a studio!

Studio Z in Cucamonga was a fairly basic outfit where Zappa put together a number of demo recordings for many labels, and some for friends too. Eventually Zappa joined a group called the Soul Giants, but Zappa persuaded them to change the name to the Mothers ('of Invention' was later added to satisfy a slightly edgy MGM Records). They went nowhere until the band was heard by producer Tom Wilson, who liked their song concerning the Los Angeles race riots, *Trouble Every Day*. In the studio, Wilson was so impressed with their material that the original plan to record just a single was switched to a *double* album! It was an unprecedented debut for an unknown band, and rock's first true concept album. *Freak Out* with its sardonic, pungent observations, outrageous humor and curious interludes, was released in August 1966 and soon achieved cult status. The next recording, *Absolutely Free* was put together later that year for release in the Spring of 1967 and contained

band had a bigger following in Europe than the United States.

Weasels Ripped My Flesh, released in 1970 after the break up, is a compilation of some fine live tracks and studio material recorded between 1967 and 1969. Zappa was producing for others at this time, most notably Beefheart's *Trout Mask Replica,* and he also launched two record labels with friend Herb Cohen: Straight and Bizarre.

His second solo album *Hot Rats* (1969) featured among others the great electric violinist, Jean Luc Ponty, and is arguably his finest. But Zappa was already anticipating his biggest project to date – a film about life on the rock road. Titled *200 Motels,* the soundtrack became one of his best-selling albums, although the movie met a mixed reception.

In 1971, Zappa appeared in one of the closing concerts at the Fillmore East auditorium; on stage with John Lennon and Yoko Ono, he gave a performance which was eventually included on Lennon's LP *Sometime in New York City.* The 1971 concerts in Europe, however, were less successful: in Switzerland fire destroyed their equipment, and in London Zappa was seriously injured when the irate husband of a fan pushed him from the stage.

He recovered sufficiently to make two more albums in 1972 – and return to Europe – but by the 1973 million-seller *Overnite Sensation* his music was taking on a new simplicity, while the lyrics became weirder and more obscure. It came to a head with *Apostrophe* which confounded his fans, but they were appeased by a more typical album of good, mainly live material entitled *Roxy & Elsewhere* (the Roxy being a theater in Hollywood).

At the end of the decade Zappa was still making albums that demanded attention and sparked controversy. *Sheikh Yerbouti* was one of the most quirky and accessible, while *Joe's Garage – Act One* (1979) was the most auspicious opener of a trilogy. Unfortunately, *Act Two* and *Act Three* lost the momentum and became ridiculously self-indulgent. *Zoot Allures, Ship Arriving Too Late To Save a Drowning Witch* (1982), and *Tinsel Town Rebellion* (1980) all had their moments and Zappa's notoriety was extended further with songs like *Jewish Princess* and *I Don't Wanna Get Drafted* which his label, Mercury, refused to release. Zappa simply quit the label.

Zappa spent much of the eighties remixing his earlier work for CD and battling the Parents Music Resource Center in their bid to censor rock: his testimony to Congress was released as *Frank Zappa Meets The Mothers Of Prevention.* More conventional music included the US hit single *Valley Girl* (with daughter Moon) and a 1983 project with the London Symphony Orchestra. In 1991 it was announced that he was seriously ill, and that cancer could well rob rock of a major talent.

Above right: London 1979; Zappa still delighting, and shocking his audiences.
Above and left: Striking a ferocious chord (above), and the accomplished guitarist.
Below: Frank dressed for the ball.

some notably vitriolic satires: *Plastic People, America Drinks and Goes Home* and others. By now, the Mothers were doing a six-month stint at the Garrick Theater, Greenwich Village, NY. It was the kind of absurd and disorderly show that was to become their trademark: Zappa and the Mothers were unsavory, unlikeable and insulted their audience, members of whom were dragged into the stage act.

If you were into debunking rock idols around 1967, then the Beatles were obvious targets. *We're Only In It For The Money* was an undisguised romp at the expense of their *Sgt Pepper* album, hippiedom and the Mothers' own fans. In Britain for the first time, the Mothers played a famous first London concert at the Royal Albert Hall, London.

Zappa expanded the framework of his music in his first solo album, *Lumpy Gravy,* recorded with the Abnuceals Emullkha Electric Symphony and Chorus and a 50-strong session band. It was a serious, considered work that contrasted sharply with his next LP, *Ruben and the Jets,* an amazingly authentic re-creation of the fifties rock sound and a hugely enjoyable pastiche. Simultaneously, he worked on another recording, *Uncle Meat,* the score for a film.

Returning to Los Angeles, Zappa married Gail Sloatman, his second wife, and went to work on a kind of 'grassroots' album *Burnt Weenie Sandwich* recorded in 1969. That year he issued a press statement saying that the Mothers were disbanding, but might re-form when, and if, audiences had understood the music they'd produced thus far! Ironically, the

RECOMMENDED RECORDINGS

Freak Out *(double)*
We're Only In It For The Money
Cruising With Ruben And The Jets
Weasels Ripped My Flesh
200 Motels
Just Another Band From LA *(live)*
Overnite Sensation
Sheikh Yerbouti
Joe's Garage – Act One
Mothermania *(compilation)*

MADNESS

Infusing their music with an engaging brand of eccentric, outlandish humor, Madness offered a satisfying antidote to the all-too-serious intent of many of Britain's new-wave bands of the late seventies.

The seven-man line-up first came to attention in London at the end of 1978, combining clever and highly comic lyrics with a frantic ska beat into what they called 'The Nutty Sound.' Originally billed as The Invaders, the new name came from a much-loved song by West Indian, Prince Buster. 'Suggs' (Graham McPherson) took the vocals, aided by keyboard player Mike Barson, saxophonist Lee 'Kix' Thompson, and trumpeter Chas Smash, Chris Foreman on guitar, Mark 'Bedders' Bedford on bass, and Dan 'Woods' Woodgate on drums completed the line-up.

They found acceptance hard to get at first, but scored a top-twenty hit with their first single, *The Prince*, recorded for the Specials' Two-Tone label. At this time, Stiff Records was proving conclusively that it knew better than anyone else how to promote the British new wave, and Madness signed with them in 1979, releasing an album and single of the same name in the October. *One Step Beyond* reached No 7 in the singles list, while the LP remained in the charts for 49 weeks, peaking at No 2.

With a light-hearted, quirky stage act to suit the songs, the group toured with The Specials in the UK and then introduced the unsuspecting Americans to their crazy ways.

A second single, *My Girl*, had the distinction of making No 1 in France in January 1980. At the same time it attained the No 3 spot in the UK.

Thus began a run of fourteen consecutive hit singles — sharp-witted, nicely observed and catchy songs, expertly promoted through videos produced by the head of Stiff, Dave Robinson. Success in France continued with a No 1 EP in the spring of 1980 *(Work, Rest and Play)*; it also climbed to No 6 in Britain. A sixteen-concert summer tour coincided with the release of the superb *Baggy Trousers* single from the album *Absolutely*, and they were subsequently voted 'Singles Artists of the Year' by Britain's *New Musical Express* magazine, after no less than 46 weeks in the UK singles charts, and 56 in the album equivalent.

1981 saw singles hits with *The Return of the Las Palmas Seven* and *Grey Day*, and a massive tour of the States, Australia, New Zealand and Japan. Stiff Records produced a film about the band's formative years entitled *Take It Or Leave It*. A hits compilation, *Complete Madness*, went to the top of the UK album charts in 1982 and stayed there for three weeks, and the end of 1981 and 1982 saw five more UK chart entries: *Shut Up* (No 7); *It Must Be Love* (No 4); *Cardiac Arrest* (the only one not to enter the top ten, reaching only No 14); *House of Fun* (the band's first No 1); *Driving My Car* (No 4) and *Our House* (No 5). Rumors of internal discord were unsubstantiated and Madness went on to find some success in the US charts in 1983. 1984 saw another ingenious single hit, *Michael Caine*.

Main songwriter Mike Barson left and the band split in 1986; a partial, one album reformation in 1988 as The Madness was unsuccessful, though *Divine Madness* topped the UK chart in 1992.

RECOMMENDED RECORDINGS
One Step Beyond
Absolutely
The Rise and Fall
Mad Not Mad
Divine Madness (*compilation*)

Far left: In concert 1983, bringing some welcome humor to the pop scene.
Below left: The cover of their first LP, *One Step Beyond* (UK No 2).
Below: Lead vocalist McPherson, aka 'Suggs.'

MADNESS

ONE STEP BEYOND...

ALICE COOPER

Developing an image and a reputation for the bizarre, they released *Pretties for You* in 1969 and *Easy Action* in 1970, both with little success.

In 1971 they moved East. The break came when they teamed up with producer Bob Ezrin, and came up with the album *Love It To Death* on the Warner Brothers' label. Suddenly, they had a sensational hit recording, and a single *I'm Eighteen* made it to No 21 in the US singles charts. A second LP *Killer* continued the success, and produced minor hits, by which time their stage 'show' had attained new heights of sickening bad taste.

Alice himself cultivated a grotesque transvestism and indulged in such simulated sadomasochistic spectacles as infanticide (putting an axe through a child's doll), necrophilia, maltreatment of animals, and topped it with demonstrations of the gallows, guillotine and electric chair. Nothing, it seemed, was too repulsive to reproduce.

No doubt out of curiosity, people made the band a top American box-office attraction. The 1972 *School's Out* album spawned a million-selling single in the US and made the top of the British charts.

S ome win through on talent; some succeed on charisma; some get there by being creatively original; and some bluff their way to the top because, for a while at least, no one quite knows whether to take them seriously or not. Alice Cooper is a case in point.

Top right: A dismembered doll is but one of Alice's props.
Right: On occasions, real women took part in his simulated stage horrors.
Below: Vincent wonders what the future holds.

Clergyman's son Vincent Furnier was born in Detroit (February, 1948) but raised in Phoenix, Arizona. A band formed with school friends, crashing out mainly Rolling Stones' material, played under various names between 1964 and 1966 (The Earwigs, The Spiders and Nazz) before trying their luck in Los Angeles in 1967. As Todd Rundgren had also chosen the name Nazz for his band, the group were forced to retitle and so emerged Alice Cooper – collectively, and singly as an alias for Furnier.

Work in bars and clubs, where they acquired the unenviable accolade of the worst band in LA, culminated in an appearance at a memorial party for the late American avant-garde comedian, Lenny Bruce. Though most of the party audience rapidly deserted them, promoter Shep Gordon noted some potential, as did Frank Zappa. Gordon became their manager and the band signed for Zappa's Straight record label in 1969.

In 1973, the band went on tour with a lavish stage show called *Billion Dollar Babies* (and released an album of the same name). The tour was a huge money-spinner, but Alice took the whole spoof less than seriously. In 1974, he sacked all the members of the original band and replaced them, under Ezrin's prompting, with a five-piece outfit that had worked with Lou Reed. They put together a review entitled *Welcome To My Nightmare* and toured the US and UK, following it up with an album of the same name. The most notable track was a rendering of *Only Women (Bleed)* and two more moderate hits ensued from succeeding albums. But their popularity was on the wane and a live album flopped miserably. However, further singles and albums appeared during 1978 and 1979, increasingly concerned with Alice's well-publicized alcoholism (and subsequent cure). His stage props now included bottles, hospital gear and a huge syringe.

Cooper's eighties were less than successful, but a link with Bon Jovi's writing and production team kickstarted his ebbing career in 1989 with the transatlantic top-twenty album *Trash*. Another epic, *Hey Stoopid*, followed two years later, bringing his brand of blood-spattered rock theater to a new, equally fascinated, generation of fans attracted by guest stars ranging from Kiss and Mötley Crüe to Ozzy Osbourne.

Considered aside from his stage persona, Alice Cooper did cut many good tracks, of which *School's Out* is probably the most memorable. His 'showmanship' is best consigned to rock history.

RECOMMENDED RECORDINGS
Love It To Death
Killer
School's Out
Greatest Hits (*compilation*)

BOB MARLEY

Mention reggae, and the first name everyone thinks of is Bob Marley, to date the only reggae musician to achieve international acclaim among white as well as black audiences.

At his death at age 36 in 1981, Marley was far more to the Jamaicans than just a musician; he was a national hero, a political symbol and the embodiment not just of many Jamaicans' aspirations, but also those of people throughout the Third World. His body lay in state in Kingston – the town where fifteen years earlier they'd put nim in gaol. But in that time, Bob Marley, aided by a variety of musicians who collectively made up generations of The Wailers, popularized a music that on the face of it seemed unintelligible beyond the shores of his native island. He made such a good job of it that for a while it looked as though reggae might become *the* driving musical force of the seventies, influencing rock musicians as diverse as The Grateful Dead, Eric Clapton, Police and The Clash.

Although the exact origin of the word 'reggae' remains unrecorded, its roots can be traced to the ska and rock-steady music that had everybody jumping in Jamaica in the early sixties. That music almost certainly developed out of the records played by local radio stations in the southern states of America, easily picked up in the Caribbean on a transistor radio. The sounds coming out of New Orleans were especially popular, and Fats Domino's style of up-tempo boogie-woogie was a favorite in Jamaica.

Born February 1945, Bob Marley was the half-caste son of a British army captain and a Jamaican. He cut his first single record *Judge Not* as long ago as 1962, and formed the original Wailers in 1964: Peter Tosh, Bunny Livingston, Junior Braithwaite, and Beverly Kelso. A ska single, *Simmer Down*, produced at Coxone Dodd's Studio One, the island's first recording studio of any note, was the first of several Jamaican hits. The series culminated in 1966 with *Rude Boy*, a number that told the story of the young delinquents of Kingston's ghettoes. After this, Kelso and Braithwaite departed, and Marley also elected to quit the Coxone label. An attempt at forming his own label, Wailing Souls, failed after just six releases but his musical career was salvaged for a while by singer Johnny Nash.

Returning in 1969 from being an unwilling guest of the government, Marley made two albums, *Soul Rebel* and *Soul Revolution* and these, together with some hit singles, re-established him in his homeland. A second try at the business side of record-making proved more successful: the Tuff Gong label had many local hits – including *Trench Town Rock*, a none-too-flattering portrait of Kingston's worst ghetto. The religion of Rastafarianism also gripped Marley around this time. The plaited hairstyle (dreadlocks) was one emblem of this new faith, and two albums – *African Herbsman* (1973) and *Rasta Revolution* (1974) – show its profound influence on his music.

The brothers Barrett (Carlton, drums, and Aston on bass) were now added to the line-up and the first recording, financed by Chris Blackwell of Island, was *Catch A Fire* (1972). It was more sophisticated and multilayered than previous recordings, but Blackwell realized that white audiences were only going to come around to liking Marley slowly and promoted him accordingly. Tours of the USA and Britain were followed in late 1973 by the release of a new LP, *Burning*, and one of its finest tracks, *I Shot the Sheriff*, became an international hit for Eric Clapton. Much as it helped publicize Marley's music, Clapton's cover version has none of the sharp bitterness of the original.

Natty Dread, released in early 1975, contains some of Marley's best songs, including the classic, *No Woman, No Cry*, a live version of which became a UK hit single. By now he was touring regularly, not just Europe and the United States, but Africa as well. An exciting live album, plus the studio-produced *Rastaman Vibration* and *Exodus* had, by 1977, established Marley's international status as a musician and songwriter: he was no longer purely a reggae artist. His first UK top-ten hit came with *Jamming*, followed by a week of sell-out concerts at the Rainbow in London.

By this time he was in voluntary exile from Jamaica; not only had his views on events there made it too hot for him, but a gunman had come close to killing him. However, he did return in 1978 to play at the *One Love Peace Concert* at the request of the then Prime Minister, Michael Manley. It was also the year that *Kaya*, a surprisingly romantic album, went to No 4 in the British charts in its first week of release, and the British punk movement discovered that reggae voiced their feelings as effectively as it did those of oppressed Jamaicans. To further this unexpected alliance, Marley recorded *Punky Reggae Party*, and followed this in 1979 with perhaps his most intense statements to date on the LP *Survival*.

The band appeared at one of the cathedrals of American black music, the Apollo Theater in Harlem, New York. Further recognition came with an invitation to play at the Zimbabwe independence celebrations in 1980; a lengthy and successful European tour; and the release of the controversial *Uprising*.

Above: Bob Marley fronts the Wailers at a London gig, complete with Rastafarian banner draped across the stage.
Right: The King of Reggae. Dreadlocks are a symbol of a Rastaman.
Previous pages: Bob Marley brought reggae to white audiences.

As he came home to receive his homeland's highest award, the Jamaican Order of Merit, Bob Marley was battling for his life; clinics in the United States and West Germany had been desperately trying to rid him of a brain tumor. It was to no avail. On 11 May 1981, Bob Marley, the great rastaman, the living essence of reggae, and its most successful exponent, died in Florida. The loss to music was enormous but, to his country, he was to prove irreplaceable.

RECOMMENDED RECORDINGS
Catch a Fire
Burnin'
Natty Dread
Live!
Exodus
Kaya
Babylon by Bus *(live double)*
Survival
Uprising
Confrontation

EARTH, WIND & FIRE

*B*y the late sixties, the spark had deserted soul music. The impetus had shifted to a new brand of black music, funk, a form invented and pioneered by James Brown. Prime mover of the new music was George Clinton, who saw his task as rescuing dance music from the 'blahs' as he called them.

Not far behind him was a talented, Memphis-born, session drummer, Maurice White. Working on recordings for the Motown and Chess labels, in 1971 White, while based in Chicago, assembled a kind of black musicians' co-operative, collectively known as Earth, Wind and Fire. It was an impressive array of talent, nine musicians offering a dazzling range of instrumental colors. As well as being a fine percussionist, Maurice White soon revealed himself as one of the best producers in the business. He established a highly successful formula and has rarely veered away from it: a sleek, polished, but high-energy, jazz-funk fusion of rhythm and blues, mainstream jazz, soft soul, and Latin and African folk rhythms. Almost without exception, the songs were uncomplicated messages of happiness, and if on occasions they became simply banal, White's production expertise was adept at distracting the critical ear. It's a formula which has brought Earth, Wind and Fire over a decade of unbroken success.

White and co-producer, Charles Stepney, first signed the band with Warner Brothers and they made two moderately successful albums for that label before moving to CBS, a move that coincided with the arrival of vocalist and percussionist, Philip Bailey.

Although the second CBS album *Head To The Sky* set the standard for what was to follow, and has proved one of their most durable albums, it wasn't until the fourth that E, W & F were really established as the slickest outfit on the jazz-funk scene: *That's the Way of the World* not only produced two hit singles (the title track and *Shining Star*) but was the soundtrack to a film in which the band played a small part. The production – which put the jingle of cowbells side-by-side with vibrant Latin riffs, for example – was masterly.

Gratitude was a double-album, three sides of which were devoted to typically exuberant live performances, while the fourth, studio-originated side, turned up a couple more hit

Above: Colorful, vibrant soul-funk from the band founded by Maurice White, here on lead vocal.
Above left: Andrew Woolfolk joined in the mid-1970s.
Far left: Maurice White enjoys the contribution of his fellow vocalist.
Left: Verdine White plays bass.

singles, *Sing a Song* and *Can't Hide Love*.

After the death of Charles Stepney the 1976 best-selling album *Spirit* was dedicated to him. White now produced for other artists; one of his most successful efforts was *This is Niecy* for Deniece Williams, giving her a British No 1 Hit in 1977 with *Free*.

For the band, success continued with automatic gold-award albums in 1977 and 1978, including a *Best of* LP and more hit singles such as *Serpentine Fire, Fantasy, September*, and Lennon-McCartney's *Got To Get You Into My Life*.

After a 1979 tour, taking in Europe and Japan, White followed the lead of many black artists before him and sought total creative independence. He formed the American Recording Company (although retaining distribution through CBS) to handle the production and recording not only for his own band, but also for Deniece Williams, The Emotions and others. A single, recorded with The Emotions, was a hit for Earth, Wind and Fire (*Boogie Wonderland*) and *After the Love Is Gone* won a

Grammy award for best vocal performance by a group. Single hits *Let Me Talk* and *Love Goes On* emerged from the 1980 *Faces* double album, and 1981's *Raise* continued the trend.

That year's transatlantic top-three hit single *Let's Groove* was their last major success, and E, W & F split in 1984. The following year, vocalist Philip Bailey topped the UK chart (and reached US No 2) with *Easy Lover*, a duet with Phil Collins (who used the E, W & F horns on his own solo albums). A re-formation in 1987 as a quintet with ex-Commodore Sheldon Reynolds failed to restore their cross-the-board success of the late seventies, though *Touch The World* and *Heritage* both proved big sellers in the black music charts. Nevertheless, Earth, Wind and Fire could look back on a career that saw them straddle the music world like a colossus, taking Sly Stone and James Brown's funky fusions to a commercial peak.

RECOMMENDED RECORDINGS
Head to the Sky
That's the Way of the World
Gratitude
Spirit
All 'n' All
Best of Earth, Wind and Fire Vol 1
Faces
Raise

RAY CHARLES

If Ray Charles had followed the path of his first great influence, Nat King Cole, it's doubtful if he would have merited a mention here. When he finally discovered the music that he really wanted to play – a magical blend of emotionally charged gospel, rhythm and blues, and jazz – the results were sufficient for no less than Frank Sinatra to describe him as 'the only genius in the business.' But it wasn't the genius of originality, more a gift for taking the best of the earthy music around him and fusing it into something quite different from the cool detachment of his early work. In this way, Ray Charles can justly claim to be one of the founding fathers of soul.

Ray Charles Robinson was born in Albany, Georgia, in September 1930, but soon moved to Greenville, Florida where a neighbor started him off playing the piano. Before he was six years old he suffered the shock of seeing his brother drown in, of all things, a washtub, and it's possible that the experience worsened the glaucoma which led to him becoming permanently blind soon after.

He was enrolled at the St Augustine School for the Deaf and Blind and there learned to read and write music in braille, as well as play a variety of instruments. The death of his mother left him an orphan at fifteen and two years later he took his $600 savings and moved to Seattle, Washington state. Forming his own band, he did the rounds of the West Coast clubs and made a few recordings for some independent labels such as Swing Time.

Above: Ray Charles, 'The Father of Soul.'
Left: *What'd I Say* – his evergreen showstopper.
Below: The Raelettes joined in the early 1960s.
Right: At Carnegie Hall with writer James Baldwin.

After signing with Atlantic in 1952, his music developed more of an outright blues feel, but it was a cultured and refined kind of blues. However, sessions in New York produced the boogie-woogie classic, *Mess Around*, among other great numbers and a new emotional and physical involvement in the music was detectable. It increased when Charles went to work with 'Guitar Slim' (Eddie Jones) in New Orleans. Jones' music was artless and uninhibited, but had what Ray Charles' music was missing – a fiery, rousing spontaneity. New Orleans also awakened him to the secular possibilities of the exuberant music played in its black churches.

In a December 1953 recording session, Ray Charles demonstrated how much he'd learned, and how much he'd changed. The songs and arrangements were his own, so was the backing band, and the result was a stunning single, *Don't You Know*. In a second session, he made an electrifying version of Jones' *Feeling Sad*, and with *I've Got A Woman*, recorded in Atlanta, the fusion of the elements was complete. The gently rocking voice of the crooner was unrecognizable: now he roared and shrieked with unrestrained exhilaration. It was ecstatic and it was exciting; if his subject was profane, it had an almost religious fervor.

A string of hit singles and albums followed, culminating in the feverish abandon of *What'd I Say?*, a number which summed up everything that made Ray Charles the unique performer he was. It had it all, and for years afterward was the traditional closing item at his concerts, guaranteed to have the audience dancing and clapping wildly. At the end of 1960 he left Atlantic for ABC/Paramount and continued to make classics like *Hit The Road, Jack* and *Georgia On My Mind*.

By now his concerts had become events, a complete show with his own band and his own, very fine, female backing group, The Raelettes. He was also enlarging his musical horizons: making recordings with the Modern Jazz Quartet, and master of the vibes, Milt Jackson; performing at the Newport Jazz Festival; and, much to the initial astonishment and dismay of his fans, issuing an album in 1962 titled *Modern Sounds in Country & Western*. Despite those who thought he had 'sold out' and gone commercial, the album was successful and produced a hit version of Hank Williams' *I Can't Stop Loving You*, which went on to sell over three million copies. Indeed, it is a measure of Ray Charles' following at the time that he sold some $8 millions worth of records in 1962 alone. Throughout the sixties he had a succession of hits with great songs such as *Take These Chains From My Heart, Your Cheatin' Heart, Crying Time* and *Busted*.

Busted had special significance because in 1965, Ray Charles was convicted of possessing heroin (he had been an addict for over twenty years) and spent an enforced lay-off in a sanatorium. He was able to kick the habit, but it was a very different figure that re-emerged – the old

spark, the verve had gone. The content drifted more and more toward inconsequential and tedious middle-of-the-road material, liberally sugared and complete with heavenly choir.

Once in a while, the spirit returned, often in thoughtful interpretations of great songs by other writers, Paul McCartney's *Yesterday* being a prime example. His own song, *I Don't Need No Doctor* was poignant and pointed. Then, in 1976, he collaborated with British jazz songstress, Cleo Laine, in a compelling version of Gershwin's *Porgy and Bess*, music obviously close to his heart. However, it is for his earlier achievements that Ray Charles will be remembered with most affection, not least by a generation of black (and white) vocalists whose style owes so much to his influence: the like of Joe Cocker, Eric Burdon, Steve Winwood and, of course, Stevie Wonder who put his appreciation into song with *Tribute to Uncle Ray*. At his best, Ray Charles was the very heart of soul.

RECOMMENDED RECORDINGS
What'd I Say?
Ray Charles Live – The Great Concerts
Genius Sings the Blues
Modern Sounds in Country & Western
Soul Meeting *(with Milt Jackson)*
A Man and His Soul
Focus on Ray Charles *(compilation)*
Tell The Truth

PRINCE

Prince Rogers Nelson has been called many things in his brief, bright career. With a guitar style owing something to Hendrix, the most overtly sexual gyrations since Michael Jackson and more than a touch of Bowie's androgyny, he's amalgamated soul and rock in a way few have been able to categorize, let alone emulate. His originality, technical prowess and showmanship have won for him a global following, whilst earning a reputation as one of the hardest working musicians in the business.

From the beginning, the career of the young Minneapolis-born guitarist (born 7 June 1960) was full of contradictions: his first album – *For You*, released in 1978 – bore a dedication to God, while song titles like *Soft And Wet* suggested a healthy sexual appetite. Conflict between the sacred and secular, a constant thread in black music, was a problem Prince never quite resolved.

Prince (1979) contained the US No 11 single *I Wanna Be Your Lover*, a track which brought the flamboyant artist to the attention of a wider audience. But the aptly titled *Dirty Mind*, released in 1980, shocked many would-be fans with songs of incest and oral sex. Such outrageousness was better accepted by a rock audience.

1981's *Controversy* predictably created just that, Prince chanting the Lord's Prayer during the title track which stood alongside such sexually explicit cuts as *Do Me Baby*. The following year's double *1999* brought the commercial breakthrough he'd waited for. MTV took to him immediately: the video for his US No 6 single *Little Red Corvette* was one of the first by a black performer to be played regularly on the network.

Purple Rain (1984) was not only an album but a full-length film, naturally starring Prince himself. Low-budget and patchily produced, the film merged live footage with a vague showbiz plot. Nevertheless within weeks, *Purple Rain* headed for the box-office charts.

Prince was also writing and producing other artists including Sheena Easton, the Bangles, Chaka Khan and Sinead O'Connor. Though *Purple Rain* and its hit singles – *When Doves Cry* and *Let's Go Crazy* were US chart-toppers, the title track a No 2 – brought Prince to a wider audience, long-time followers saw his music as a dilution of his earlier work.

This was inevitable, but the rewards were obvious. In early 1985, Prince announced his retirement from live performance – but this resolution was not to last.

1985's *Around The World In A Day* spawned two US hits in *Raspberry Beret* (2) and *Pop Life* (7). It was his own first album on his own Paisley Park label, and was followed by the more consistent *Parade* in 1986 which contained a US chart-topping single in the superb *Kiss*.

1987's *Sign O The Times*, a double set inevitably compared with *1999* – but Prince's next project, known as *The Black Album*, was not to see commercial release, allegedly due to its controversial lyrical content. Instead came *Lovesexy*, an album whose compact disc was one long track!

His soundtrack for the 1989 film *Batman* topped the charts on both sides of the Atlantic, while 1990's *Graffiti Bridge*, another movie soundtrack, repeated the feat in Britain. This continuing success, which blossomed with 1991's *Diamonds And Pearls*, suggested that he would continue to be a musical force with his powerful rock/funk fusion.

Above: *Purple Rain*, one of the great classics delivered with unrelenting passion.
Above right: Looking particularly cheeky, one of the many faces of Prince Rogers Nelson.
Right: The 1991 tour saw Prince adopt a more conventional style on stage.
Far right: At once provocative, daring, irreverent and inspired, Prince is simply unique.

RECOMMENDED RECORDINGS
1999
Around The World In a Day
Purple Rain
Lovesexy
Diamonds And Pearls

STEVIE WONDER

Genius is a much overworked word, not least in rock music, but nothing less describes the talents of Stevie Wonder: writer of so many memorable and lasting songs; master of a huge variety of instruments; skillful arranger and producer, not only of his own albums but those of several other black performers; and an exuberant and exciting stage artist.

For all the bubbling, extrovert vitality of his concerts and records, Stevie Wonder remains something of an enigma. He is a private, even mysterious, person, who shuns publicity, revealing his thoughts only in his music, which is why no one can predict where the next phase of his musical development will take him. From the simple love-ditties of his early days, Stevie Wonder's most recent songs have combined an increasing social awareness, a deep desire for universal peace and love with an irresistible celebration of life itself. He remains not only the most talented rock musician of the present era, but one of the most potent.

Right: The man with inner visions, the enigmatic but always exciting Stevie Wonder.
Far right: His many talents, as musician and songwriter, were recognized in the name Motown gave him at the age of twelve, 'Little Stevie Wonder.' He went on to become one of the five greatest artists the label has produced.

Steveland Judkins, born in Saginaw, Michigan in 1950, was blind from birth. He first began to play the harmonica at five (by which time he was living in Detroit) and followed this with piano lessons at six, the drums at eight, and a first attempt at songwriting at ten. With such gifts, it is hardly surprising that Berry Gordy Jr signed him immediately for Tamla Motown after just one brief audition. According to legend, Gordy described the young boy as 'a miracle, a real wonder' – and the name followed, except in those days it was 'Little Stevie Wonder.'

His first US hit record came in 1963, an extraordinary harmonica instrumental entitled *Fingertips*. Recorded live and lasting seven minutes, it was split over two sides of a 45rpm single. The second side, complete with mistakes and the despairing cries of fellow musicians ('What key? What key!') remains one of the most exciting displays of technique and improvisation ever.

For Motown the problem then, and for some time to come, was exactly how to harness this unique talent, a problem left unsolved by the unexciting *Tribute to Uncle Ray*. The album *Little Stevie Wonder, Twelve-Year Old Genius* is also best left in the archives.

By 1965, however, he had grown up in more ways than one. Gone was the 'Little' and every-

thing associated with that tag. The second phase of Stevie Wonder's progress was underway with powerful, punchy numbers such as *Up Tight (Everything's Alright)* (1966), *Nothing's Too Good for my Baby* and – most surprisingly – Dylan's *Blowing in the Wind*. It shouldn't have worked, but it did, and, together with a version of the cabaret standard *For Once in my Life*, established that there were many faces to the music of Stevie Wonder.

His first self-produced album, *Signed, Sealed and Delivered*, produced four chart hits including an exhilarating rendition of Lennon and McCartney's *We Can Work It Out*.

The third, and most important phase of his career began in 1971 with a new contract, and, at the age of 21 the addition of one million dollars to his bank account from the trust fund set up years previously by Berry Gordy to take care of his ensuing royalties. It was a far cry from the two-and-a-half dollars per week allowance he had received on first joining Motown. The rewritten contract more-or-less released him from all the artistic and commercial restrictions the label normally imposed on its performers, an acknowledgment that Stevie hadn't enjoyed the success his talent merited.

He immediately formed his own music publishing company, Black Bull Music, and production company, Taurus Productions, and the first fruit was *Music of my Mind*, first of a quartet of outstandingly successful albums. Stevie played every instrument and co-wrote all the songs with his wife, Syreeta Wright, but only one

single hit emerged from the LP – *Superwoman (Where Were You When I Needed You)*.

In 1972, he toured with the Rolling Stones, a repeat of a 1964 concert tour except that then the Stones had been number two on the bill! But even playing 'second string' brought Stevie Wonder to the attention of a much greater audience, and gained him a huge following among whites as well as blacks.

Talking Book must rate as one of the supreme achievements in seventies rock music, and two of its songs, *Superstition* and *You Are the Sunshine of my Life* are all-time classics. The next album, *Innervisions*, is possibly greater still. From the poetry of *Visions* to the bitterness of the black anthem *Living in the City*, each of its nine songs is full of melody, rhythm, color and that urgent vitality that underpins even the slowest ballads.

In August 1973 he was seriously injured in a car accident and spent several days in a coma, close to death. Upon recovery, the full meaning of the lines in his song *Higher Ground* came home to him: 'I'm so glad that he let me try it again, 'Cause my last time on earth I lived a whole world of sin.'

He saw his recovery as a second chance, and he was determined to make the most of it. *Fulfillingness' First Finale* was an auspicious beginning, but then after a winter 1974 tour, he virtually retired from the road to work on another masterpiece. In 1976, *Songs in the Key of Life* appeared, prefaced on the sleeve with a note to his fans, 'Thank you for being so patient.'

Above: A young Stevie in lively mood in the studio.
Left: When finally freed from the creative ties imposed by Motown, his genius flowered, in producing recordings as well as making them.
Right: On stage in 1982, colorful and exuberant.

He needn't have apologized. It was yet another stupendous recording with such songs as *I Wish*, *Sir Duke* (a tribute to Duke Ellington) and the joyous *Isn't She Lovely* – his new-born daughter being the object of affection. The song possessed a simple, disarming happiness that has made it a worldwide favorite.

His next project was his most inaccessible and misunderstood. Asked by a film producer to produce some music to accompany a documentary on plants and their inner workings, Stevie produced an entire score, added further songs and lyrics, overdubbed appropriate natural sounds, and issued *Stevie Wonder's Journey Through the Secret Life of Plants*.

Significantly, perhaps, Stevie used very little from his latest recording for his 1980 concert tour, and returned to the fold in the eyes of most of his fans with *Hotter than July*, a selection of typically diverse, richly melodic and memorable songs such as the poignant ballad *Lately* and his ebullient tribute to the late Martin Luther King, *Happy Birthday* (an effort to have King's birthday made a public holiday in the United States, an effort that has now succeeded).

The eighties saw only two new albums, *In Square Circle* (1985) and *Characters* (1988), yet he remained active with soundtracks (notably *The Woman In Red*, containing the transatlantic No 1 *I Just Called To Say I Love You*) plus duets with Paul McCartney (the equally successful *Ebony And Ivory*), Michael Jackson and Julio Iglesias. He also found time to participate in charity recordings like *We Are The World* and the US chart-topping Aids fundraiser *That's What Friends Are For*. Despite slowing down his musical output, Stevie Wonder remains a unique talent.

RECOMMENDED RECORDINGS

Signed, Sealed and Delivered
Music of my Mind
Talking Book
Innervisions
Songs in the Key of Life
Hotter than July
Musiquarium Original (*compilation*)

TINA TURNER

As her most recent concerts have demonstrated, Tina Turner continues to be just as exciting and sensual a performer as ever. Pulling no punches, physical as well as vocal, Tina's sizzling stage act is the kind that's impossible to capture fully on record. Although many of her studio recordings have achieved classic status and enduring popularity, the visual impact is as essential as the aural. Both as part of the duo with ex-husband, Ike, and solo, Tina has enjoyed equal, if not greater acclaim in Britain than in her native America – perhaps because the UK has never produced anyone quite like her itself! Her rip-roaring, outrageously entertaining brand of soul make Tina a consistent favorite on the Las Vegas casino cabaret circuit, as well as someone who can guarantee full houses in major rock venues.

The sexiest purveyor of black soul, and responsible for two of rock's all-time-great singles, the world first heard the voice of Annie Mae "Tina" Bullock in a Tennessee church choir. Born in November 1938, she moved, taking her sister with her, to St Louis in the mid-1950s looking for work as a professional singer. There she encountered sometime rhythm and bluesman, talent scout, and disc-jockey, Ike Turner. After an audition she was recruited to Turner's traveling revue in 1957. In fact, Ike was so taken with Tina he married her a year later.

In 1960, Ike had arranged a recording session and when the booked vocalist failed to arrive, Tina stepped into the breach producing a million-selling single, *A Fool In Love*. It was the first of a string of hits on the R & B-oriented Sue label for the team of Ike and Tina Turner, including *I Idolize You* and *It's Gonna Work Out Fine*.

Touring mainly the Southern States 'chitlin' circuit, the revue had become only one step removed from an orgy! With a three-girl backing trio called The Ikettes dressed in barely respectable miniskirts, Ike and Tina embellished their songs with suggestive movements and ribald interplay, with Tina flaunting her sexuality and feigning orgasms. Somehow they got away with it, and the audiences loved it.

The song Tina is best remembered for was the result of a chance meeting with producer Phil Spector, while doing the soundtrack for a film called *The T'N'T Show*. Spector wanted to produce a single with Tina, and given Spector's track record, Ike was quite happy to bow out for

Above: Tina gets her kicks on stage, the sassiest soul queen of them all.
Above left: Performing for US TV, Ike on guitar.
Left, lower: Ike and Tina – a dynamic duo!

this one. The result was *River Deep, Mountain High*, probably the greatest thing Spector ever put on vinyl.

Although it reached No 3 in the UK (and deserved to go to the top), it failed in America, a disappointment which so disillusioned Phil Spector that he went into retirement – albeit briefly.

A 1969 tour supporting the Rolling Stones brought them nationwide popularity in the United States. For all its risqué clowning, their stage show was a dramatic, exciting and professional piece of work which not even live recordings truly do justice to. After the Stones tour, they concentrated on playing major rock venues and the Las Vegas circuit, coming up with another hit album in 1971, *What You Hear Is What You Get*.

In 1973, Tina wrote, and the duo recorded, *Nutbush City Limits*, a pulsating, energetic number in the same vein as *River Deep* . . . Again, curiously, this was a bigger hit in the UK (No 2) than in the US.

The revue, backed by a group called The Family Vibes, kept going until 1976 when Ike and Tina's marriage broke up, with their professional association soon following. Tina continued with a successful career as a leading lady of soul, including a shattering performance as the Acid Queen in Ken Russell's film of Pete Townshend's rock opera, *Tommy*. Ike, in contrast made a back-to-grass-roots blues album, but the pair reunited eventually for a new LP, *Airwaves* (their thirtieth album).

Tina achieved a UK top ten hit with a raunchy reworking of Al Green's *Let's Stay Together* and was in good form on a 1982 album *Hot 'N' Sassy*. She showed she had lost little of the old magic during a 1983 UK tour, and her version of *Help* hit the charts.

Tina finally broke as a huge international star in 1984 with the album *Private Dancer*, and two hit singles, the superb *What's Love Got To Do With It* and *Let's Stay Together*. In 1985, she undertook a staggering 155-date world tour – a sell out in Britain – and starred in *Mad Max III*.

Break Every Rule (1986) and 1989's *Foreign Affair* continued her run of multi-platinum albums, celebrated in 1991 by the aptly-titled compilation *Simply The Best*. By now, Ike was in jail for drug trafficking, and threatening to sue Tina for use of her name!

RECOMMENDED RECORDINGS
River Deep, Mountain High
The Hunter
'Nuff Said
Nutbush City Limits
What You Hear Is What You Get
Acid Queen
The Very Best of Ike and Tina Turner (compilation)
Sixteen Great Performances
Hot 'N' Sassy
Private Dancer
Break Every Rule
Simply The Best (compilation)

Left and top: Still enjoying enormous popularity in Britain, and well able to keep pace with her youthful dancers, on tour in 1982.
Above: The Beatles' *Help* gave Tina a surprise 1984 hit.
Right: The 'stone-age' look for her successful UK 1983 tour.

SMOKEY ROBINSON

Favorite son of Motown, Smokey Robinson has been writer and producer of over 60 of its biggest-selling hit songs. In 1967, in recognition of his enormous contribution to the label's fortunes, founder Berry Gordy appointed Robinson 'Vice-President in charge of artist development,' a role which assumed more and more of his time and led to a virtual retirement from live performance in 1972.

However, by then he had a list of successes to his credit which could have filled a Motown 'Greatest Hits' album twice over; classic, unforgettable love songs sung in his plaintive, trembling falsetto and backed by the glowing sounds of the Miracles.

Detroit-born, William Robinson was making his first attempts at song writing in 1945 – at the age of five. Ten years later he joined with four friends in a vocal group called The Matadors and, when joined by Claudette Rogers, the name was changed to The Miracles. At a 1957 audition, Berry Gordy was at first interested in Claudette, but the potential of the lead singer didn't go unnoticed.

Their first hit, and the first for the Motown label proper, came in 1960 with *Shop Around*. The story goes that Gordy didn't like the first cut, but couldn't identify just why. It finally hit him late one night – the tempo was too slow. He immediately got the group out of their beds, and into the studio at three in the morning to rerecord the song which established them, and Motown, as forces to be reckoned with.

Other well-crafted Robinson songs kept the hits coming: *Ooh Baby, Baby; Mickey's Monkey; Going To A Go Go* (the first British hit); and *You Really Got A Hold On Me* (notable for being covered by The Beatles on their second album).

By now, he was also writing and producing for other Motown artists, his creative energy showing no bounds. The serene *My Guy* was a massive hit for Mary Wells, and a profitable two-year partnership with The Temptations culminated in their first No 1 in 1965, the exquisite *My Girl*. A temporary lull in Marvin Gaye's career was ended by two Robinson songs, *Ain't That Peculiar* and *I'll Be Doggone*. In the same year, Claudette, now married to Smokey, left the Miracles and wasn't replaced. They recorded *The Tracks Of My Tears*, arguably the highspot of Robinson's songwriting career. It was an immediate American hit, but didn't

score in Britain until 1969, despite the Miracles presence on a 1965 Motown 'all-star' tour. He certainly never rested on his laurels, and his output during these years shows that, even if the inspiration for a song came by chance (in the case of *Tracks* from hearing an improvised guitar line), they were worked out with enormous thought and care. The depth of feeling in *Tears Of A Clown* is one example. This emotive song was astonishingly overlooked when singles were being plucked from the excellent *Make It Happen* album of 1967. When finally released three years later, it made No 1 on both sides of the Atlantic.

Although he still made hit records, Smokey became increasingly involved with his executive role and by 1972, the group was to all intents and purposes defunct. Smokey and his friends went their own ways after a farewell concert tour (although he continued to produce for them). He went on to make a series of solo albums – ambitious attempts to extend his musical horizons. Many of his best songs in the seventies went to other artists, for instance Kim Carnes sang *More Love* (1980). In the singles charts, *Baby Come Close* (1974) was an American best-seller, and did it largely unpromoted. He worked on a film score and did

some recording with his own Quiet Storm band, making a selective return to touring in 1975. The 1977 *Deep In My Soul* album was a surprising tribute to his fellow songwriters, with none of his own material, and in 1979 the LP *Where's The Smoke* realized a US top-ten hit with *Cruisin'*.

When *Billboard* magazine judged that the seventies was his 'lost decade,' Smokey merely pointed out the failure of 'white' radio in America to take notice of what he was doing. It's a valid point, but it has to be admitted that he has never recaptured those heady days of the sixties when his influence as a writer, producer and performer was at its peak, his

Left: Smokey (center) surrounded by the Miracles. A great voice and a gifted songwriter, he later became a key figure in the fortunes of the Motown empire, sadly at the expense of his stage career.

creative power seemingly limitless, and when an album such as *Going To A Go Go* could yield no less than four top-twenty hits. Great names continue to make successful cover versions of his first songs, but then what singer wouldn't with lyrics to interpret such as: 'I've got sunshine on a cloudy day. When it's cold outside, I've even got the month of May.' Nothing less than sheer poetry!

Above: Back in England for concerts in 1983 and as great an entertainer as ever.
Top: Songs like *Tears Of A Clown* were pure poetry, and no one could sing them as expressively as Smokey himself.

RECOMMENDED RECORDINGS

Going To A Go Go
Make It Happen (*reissued as* Tears Of A Clown)
Live On Stage
Greatest Hits
Where's The Smoke

MARVIN GAYE

*F*or some twenty years, the rich, satin-smooth tenor voice of Marvin Gaye was one of Motown's most lucrative assets. Comfortably adapting from the neo-gospel style in demand in the early sixties, through a highly polished and successful blend of soul-pop, he then slipped easily into the disco mold. Gaye was one of the few performers to have broken away from the stringent artistic disciplines the label imposes on its recording artists.

Marvin Gaye won his independence with an album which still resounds as an explosion of black anger and a heartfelt attempt to highlight the malaise of American urban society. At first Motown, to whom social problems meant broken hearts and unrequited love, were loath to issue it and only did so with skepticism. But it became one of their biggest sellers, and for Marvin Gaye his passport to creative freedom.

His musical apprenticeship began when playing the organ in the church where his father was minister. That was in Washington, DC, where Marvin Gaye had been born in April 1939. At school, he studied piano and drums and played in the orchestra, then developed his singing style with a leading local vocal group, the Rainbows (led by the great Don Covay). The group also contained Billy Stewart who also went on to a successful solo career, cut tragically short by a car crash in 1970. Leaving in 1957, and taking two of the group with him, Gaye formed The Marquees.

Their break came when Harvey Fuqua, leader of the disbanded Moonglows, came to Washington in search of a new line-up and adopted the Marquees *en bloc*. Two records for Chess followed in 1959, but the key introduction for Gaye came at a Detroit concert, where Berry Gordy signed him straight away.

However, it wasn't his voice which was first heard on Motown, but his drumming – he backed on all the early Smokey Robinson and the Miracles recordings and toured with them for six months. His own career took a significant step forward with a single hit, *Stubborn Kind Of Fellow* (with Martha and the Vandellas on backing vocals), making the US rhythm and blues charts, as did further releases.

Throughout 1964 and 1965, he scored a series of well-produced, up-tempo pop hits such as *How Sweet It Is,* mainly written by Motown's resident Holland-Dozier-Holland

team. Then the label had the idea of teaming Marvin Gaye with their leading female singers: Mary Wells, Kim Weston, Diana Ross and, most successfully, with Tammi Terrell. *Ain't No Mountain High Enough* and *Your Precious Love,* were just two of a string of hit US singles they made together. Their highest UK chart placing was No 9 with the treacly *Onion Song.*

In 1968 he topped the American and British charts with a number which will always be associated with him – the almost sinister *I Heard It Through The Grapevine.*

Follow-up singles, if not as distinctive, were similarly successful. Then tragedy struck; Tammi Terrell collapsed into his arms on stage one night. A brain tumor was diagnosed, and she later died – Marvin Gaye gave no public performances for six years. He did make productive sorties into the studio, first to make the revolutionary *What's Going On,* a series of uncompromising songs depicting the decay and poverty – both material and spiritual – that was destroying urban America and its people. Motown were aghast at issuing such a document and despaired of its commercial prospects. But Marvin Gaye proved them wrong: it was the first significant concept album by a black artist, and three tracks (including the fiery *Inner City Blues*) made single hits.

Now writing, arranging and producing his own recordings, the next effort was the mainly instrumental soundtrack to an indifferent film, *Trouble Man,* followed in 1973 by *Let's Get It On.* The social themes had been exchanged for unabashed sexuality, and what has been described as the closest Motown ever got to outright eroticism has become Marvin Gaye's most popular album. The same year, he teamed with Diana Ross for an LP that produced the hit single, *My Mistake (Was To Love You),* and then finally returned to the road with a 1974 concert at the Oakland Coliseum in California. It was recorded and issued as *Marvin Gaye Live* and was successful enough to warrant a two-record live album being issued from his 1976 tour of Britain (the London Palladium concert). Side four of this set contained the disco stormer, *Got To Give It Up, Part 1,* which was a hit both sides of the Atlantic.

The US top-five success of *I Want You* (1976) was soured by divorce proceedings chronicled in 1979's *Here My Dear,* apparently recorded to raise the necessary alimony. Gaye's declining years, hampered by drug problems, were punctuated only by the excellent *Midnight Love,* cut for CBS in 1982 which included a UK/US top-five hit in *Sexual Healing* and a Grammy-winning Best Vocal Performance in *Midnight Love.* Tragically, the come-

Above: The death of Tammi Terrell kept him off the stage for six years. He first returned to the UK for concerts in 1976.
Top left: Motown first took on the young Marvin as a sessions drummer, but soon discovered that fabulous tenor voice.
Right: Marvin was a great performer until his tragic end in April 1984.

back was not to continue, for on 1 April 1984 he was shot dead by his father, a church minister. It was a tragic end for one of Motown's premier singer-songwriters and a man who broke the black music mold.

RECOMMENDED RECORDINGS

How Sweet It Is
That's The Way Love Is
You're All I Need To Get By (with Tammi Terrell)
Greatest Hits (with Tammi Terrell)
It Takes Two (with Kim Weston)
What's Going On
Trouble Man (soundtrack)
Let's Get It On
Anthology (compilation)
Live!
I Want You
Live At The London Palladium (double)
Here, My Dear
Midnight Love

OTIS REDDING

Otis Redding's career was tragically cut short just as the Memphis soul sound, of which he was the undisputed master, made a significant impact on the white audience as well as the black. The charts were no longer exclusively 'vanilla,' as the record industry termed it, and the best soul artists, such as Otis and Aretha Franklin, were able to make the charts without diluting their music for white ears.

Then, at the peak of his career, Otis Redding's private aircraft crashed on to a frozen lake. Otis was killed, with four of his musicians, and although he was to enjoy his biggest single success posthumously, soul music began to die that day, too.

Many of the turning points in rock music have occurred by accident, and the debut of Otis Redding is no exception. He was 21, a minister's son living in Macon, Georgia, where he'd been brought up. Like virtually every major black artist, the church was where he found his voice.

He had a good friend in Phil Walden, who found work for Otis in the local clubs, where he mainly entertained in the 'shouting' style of Little Richard. At one gig, he encountered a rhythm and blues group, Johnny Jenkins and the Pinetoppers and, with Walden as manager, joined them as general dogsbody and occasional singer.

Jenkins' group had a session booked in Memphis and Otis went along. It was a fairly uninspired affair and finished some 40 minutes early. Redding asked if he could lay down a track in the time left and proceeded to hit them with *These Arms of Mine*. Stax Records' boss, Jim Stewart was encouraged, and released the track on his new Volt label. It crept slowly up the US charts in 1963, warranting a second single eight months later, *Pain In My Heart*. The success of this led to an album of the same name, still with several Little Richard-style tracks. However, Otis was now more influenced by Sam Cooke, whom he much admired, and Ray Charles. Touring mainly on the black circuit from 1964 to 1967, Otis scored with a succession of co-authored singles, both ballads and up-tempo stompers. He handled their very different moods with equal skill; *Respect, Mr Pitiful, That's How Strong My Love Is, I Can't Turn You Loose*, Sam Cooke's *Shake* and the intensely emotional; *I've Been Loving You Too Long* were but six of the most memorable. His first British hit came with a classic version of The Temptations' *My Girl*, and

after touring Europe in 1965 his popularity there was greater than in the US.

All had the distinctive 'Memphis Sound,' a very different mix from the satin-smooth Motown formula. Otis was backed by Booker T and The MGs (superb performers in their own right) and by the Mar-Key horn section in a way which perfectly complemented his songs. The result was a bright, spontaneous sound. Otis' baritone was marvellously expressive; he could pace a lyric perfectly and convey its mood instantly. When he turned to covering major rock numbers, as a way of broadening the audience for his own soul music, his skill didn't fail him. He breathed new life into the Stones' *Satisfaction* and The Beatles' *Day Tripper*.

Below: Relaxing between concerts, the greatest exponent of the Memphis sound.
Right: Giving it all he's got, Otis' skill spanned gospel and modern rock and his loss to music was incalculable.

His biggest moment, his confirmation as 'King of Soul,' came just four months before his death. At the Monterey Festival in 1967 Otis earned superstar status (as did Jimi Hendrix and Janis Joplin). He was to have some nine posthumous chart hits, including his biggest of all: *Sittin' on The Dock Of the Bay* which made No 3 in the UK and No 1 in the US. His album *Otis Blue* is generally acknowledged as one of the finest, if not *the* finest soul record ever made. There is little argument that he was the greatest soul artist of the decade.

RECOMMENDED RECORDINGS
Otis Blue
Best of Otis Redding
History of Otis Redding
Dock of The Bay
Immortal Otis Redding
Dictionary of Soul

THE DRIFTERS

Y ou could have first seen The Drifters in 1953, and you could have listened to a vocal group of the same name 30 years on. The singers would have differed, as they'd differed so many times during the group's history, and so would the music: in the fifties, a refined but emotional gospel sound; more recently, pleasant and inoffensive middle-of-the-road pop.

The Drifters' story is one that involves many singers, most especially their four great lead vocalists, and many of the best songwriters, producers and arrangers over three decades. It also inescapably involves manager George Treadwell and his wife, Fay, because it is the fact that the Treadwells own the name, The Drifters, that has permitted it to continue through so many permutations of personnel.

In 1953, the sweet, falsetto voice of Clyde McPhatter was to be heard in a reasonably successful vocal group called The Dominoes. However, he fancied the idea of a solo career, and Ahmet Ertegun of Atlantic Records was willing to take him on. Using his friends, the Thrasher Wonders, a hot-gospelling team from Harlem, New York, McPhatter assembled a gospel-style vocal group. Their first release, *Money Honey* was a top hit for eleven weeks in the American rhythm and blues chart.

McPhatter was undoubtedly the most original, and ultimately most influential, of their lead vocalists, but his reign was short. After six hit records he left to go solo leaving, among his successes, *Such A Night* which became a No 1 hit for Johnnie Ray (the original would have been unknown to white audiences at the time), and an eyebrow-raiser, the sensual *Honey Love*, which did much for Clyde's personal female following.

He was replaced by Johnny Moore, but his tenure was brief (the US Army claimed him for military service, as it also did McPhatter). Bobby Hendricks took over between 1955 and 1958, and the number of hits declined. Manager George Treadwell disbanded the group but wisely retained rights to the name, enabling him to revive it by renaming another Harlem band titled the Five Crowns. Their lead singer was also outstanding: he was called Ben E King, and with him came a profitable change of style.

King and Treadwell had co-authored a song called *There Goes My Baby*. During the recording session, a lot of ideas were thrown around about the treatment and the final mix

ended up as a collage of lush orchestration, Latin rhythms and a smooth pop-cum-soul vocal. This Leiber and Stoller production was a huge hit, and it was to be a huge influence. Many subsequent 'sound styles' such as that of Motown can be traced back to this point. After, The Drifters were more than happy to pander to the tastes of the white teenage market, and that market responded by giving them hit after hit, of which the best was *Save The Last Dance For Me*.

Gaining a 1961 hit on his own with *Spanish Harlem*, Ben E King followed McPhatter into a solo career, and the new front man became Rudy Lewis. The Drifters entered yet another successful era with *Sweets for My Sweet, On Broadway* and the superb Jerry Coffin and Carole King number *Up On The Roof*. Then, on the day of another recording session, Lewis was found dead (rumor has it from a drug overdose). The session went ahead, with Johnny Moore once again stepping up to take the lead, and the event explains why one of their most relaxed, sunny songs, *Under The Board-walk*, comes over with such surprising melancholy.

Performing mainly in cabaret, they continued to score with the likes of *Saturday Night at the Movies*, and *At the Club* and, in 1972, suddenly found themselves in the middle of a nostalgic fifties revival in Britain and rising up the charts with reissues such as *Come On Over To My Place*. They cashed in by recording new songs in the same vein written for them by the British songwriting team of Roger Cook and Roger Greenaway, *Kissin' in the Back Row of the Movies* (1974) being one of them. It was popular easy listening, evidenced by the success of their double album *24 Original Hits*.

Above and right: The group made the most of the nostalgia for the fifties with some immaculately presented concert tours.
Top: The Drifters have survived several styles and many personnel changes.
Top right: All smiles before a concert: just a foursome then.

In 1982, veteran Johnny Moore left and formed his own group, Slightly Adrift and was replaced once again by Ben E King, although by this time there were actually several groups of singers touring around billing themselves as The Drifters.

RECOMMENDED RECORDINGS
Clyde McPhatter and The Drifters
Save The Last Dance For Me
24 Original Hits
The Drifters Story

SAM COOKE

Sam Cooke came to enjoy huge success both as singer and songwriter, with a string of hit US singles spanning seven years. Performers as diverse as Otis Redding and the Rolling Stones covered his songs. To blacks, he became a hero: his own man, controlling his own destiny, making fine music for everyone.

By 1964, his status was indisputable and the music world was at his feet. Then, on 10 December of that year, the manageress of a Los Angeles motel found herself menaced by a guest who'd become violent when his unwilling female roommate had given him the slip. As he attacked her, the manageress grabbed a revolver and shot three times, finally felling her assailant with a blow across the head. By the time medical help arrived, Sam Cooke was dead.

Cooke was one of eight sons of a baptist minister and by the age of nine was in the family's gospel quartet, The Singing Children. He sang with the Highway QCs before joining America's most popular gospellers, The Soul Stirrers. He eventually replaced the reverend R H Harris as lead vocalist, but won over his audience immediately, earning a standing ovation at his first performance. The group toured extensively and cut a number of discs for the Specialty label; on them Cooke sings with rare feeling and sensitivity. They remain among his greatest recordings.

But Sam sensed he could reach an even greater audience, as did his manager. He decided to cut a couple of non-gospel tracks using the pseudonym Dale Cooke. These first attempts were largely unsuccessful, but he persisted, encouraged by his friend-cum-manager, J W Alexander, and producer, 'Bumps' Blackwell. Blackwell decided to try a session using a white female backing group, a format which most definitely did not meet with the approval of the head of Specialty, Art Rupe. Rupe told them to take their contract elsewhere, and Blackwell found a ready buyer in Keen Records, Again, the first single releases failed, but then the track which had appalled Rupe was released; *You Send Me* spent three weeks at No 1 in the US, selling a total of 1.7 million copies in 1957.

Sam Cooke's sudden rise to fame, especially after a top-spot appearance on television, took most of those around him by surprise,

not least Keen Records who were most unaccustomed to pressing seven-figure quantities. Cooke spent two years with Keen before setting up a record company of his own, Sar/Derby Records, and signing a lucrative contract with RCA. Sam Cooke's bread-and-butter was stil R&B, and RCA's only black artist at the time was the calypso singer Harry Belafonte. Could he hold his black following while expanding the white pop audience that songs such as *Wonderful World* and *Only Sixteen* had brought him? The answer came with his second RCA single release, *Chain Gang*, a smash hit both sides of the Atlantic (his first in Britain). It was a quirky, out-and-out pop number, but he followed it with a quiet blues ballad called *Sad Mood* which showed just how successfully he could satisfy both audiences. The song also indicated how broad the appeal of the gospel/blues mixture could be. It was the music they would soon be calling 'soul.'

In the next four years, Sam Cooke enjoyed a run of memorable hits: *Twistin' The Night Away* was an international top-ten success, as were *Cupid, Another Saturday Night* and the powerful *Bring It On Home To Me* in which Lou Rawls

Above: Sam, smiling after signing a big contract with RCA, 1959, only the label's second black artist.
Below: He held audiences in the palm of his hand.
Right: His success came to a tragic end.

sang the 'call-and-response' style backing vocal. He personally notched 43 entries in the American Hot 100. He also had innumerable successful cover versions of his songs; as a provider for others, he was equaled only by Chuck Berry.

Idolized by black and white audiences alike, Cooke's 1964 hits indicated the broad range of his music. *Good News* was rooted in gospel, while *Good Times* was an out-and-out party popper. Then, just for good measure, he had a hit with the evergreen *Tennessee Waltz*.

His career, so secure, so rich in promise, came to a terrible end in a moment of madness. Whatever the circumstances, Cooke died a martyr in black eyes and the scenes at the funeral parlor in his home town of Chicago were extraordinary. Doors were smashed as grief-stricken fans tried to gain one last glimpse of him.

But Sam Cooke's legend lived on. *Shake* was a posthumous hit early in 1965, but the B-side became even more of a classic, especially in view of the tragedy that preceded it. *A Change is Gonna Come*, sang Sam Cooke. In music, he was one of the prime movers in that change, opening many doors for others, and he made a contribution to the greater cause of black America, too.

Wonderful World took him back to the UK top three in 1986 thanks to a film and jeans commercial, but Cooke's music was beyond fad or fashion.

RECOMMENDED RECORDINGS
This is Sam Cooke
The Golden Age of Sam Cooke
The Soul Stirrers Featuring Sam Cooke
The Best of Sam Cooke
The Man and His Music

JAMES BROWN

ful black rhythm and blues recording thus far, critically and commercially, and earned Brown the tag, 'Mr Dynamite'!

James Brown was now setting new box office records all over the US, playing to huge, wildly enthusiastic black audiences, mainly in ghetto areas, and hoping to add a new white following with an outright pop number, *Prisoner of Love*. However, King Records were not getting Brown the coverage on radio or the record sales that his popularity justified, and he was forced to break his contract with them. In 1964 he recorded *Out of Sight* on the Smash label (a subsidiary of Mercury) and it became, deservedly, a massive hit.

He did re-sign with King, but only after a legal battle in which he secured total inde-

*F*ew would dispute that James Brown is the greatest showman in the history of rock and roll. His high-voltage, nonstop stage acts, with some 40 musicians, singers and dancers supporting him, are colorful, noisy, unflagging, but highly polished and hugely entertaining productions. He's been delivering such performances to delighted audiences around the world for decades now and neither his stamina nor his enthusiasm show any sign of wilting. It's a staying power that's also clearly seen in his personal drive and ambition: the drive that took him out of abject poverty, made him fight for (and get) total control of his career, and still ensures he never merely goes through the motions in concert, or resorts to making mediocre records. He continues to put everything into every song he sings, a total, passionate commitment every time.

The odds against him could hardly have been worse. Born into a desperately poor black family in America's deep South during the Depression (May 1933 in Augusta, Georgia), he took up piano, followed by drums and bass. He learned music the hard way, busking on the streets. It wasn't until 1956 that he got the break he was looking for: a demonstration disc for King Records of Cincinnati. They liked his energetic blend of fiery gospel and rhythm and blues which, as with so many performers, was firmly rooted in the music of the black churches of the South. The track was re-cut, with his long-standing backing group, The Famous Flames, and *Please, Please, Please* became a modestly successful hit. But he had difficulty following it up and, despite touring widely in the South, managed only a few local hits in Georgia. Brown reached a much wider audience with the lugubrious, gospel-influenced *Try Me* in 1958.

By now, his stage shows had become the kind of all-singing, all-dancing spectacular revue that was to become his trademark everywhere, and as the leading black American performer, he gave a shattering display at the New York Apollo Theater in Harlem. The album *Live at the Apollo* is a classic – not only as one of the first live rock albums, but also as one of the best. It became the most success-

Top: 'Soul Brother Number One,' and a shattering performance every time.
Right: Brown became his own man – and a rich one – admired by blacks everywhere.

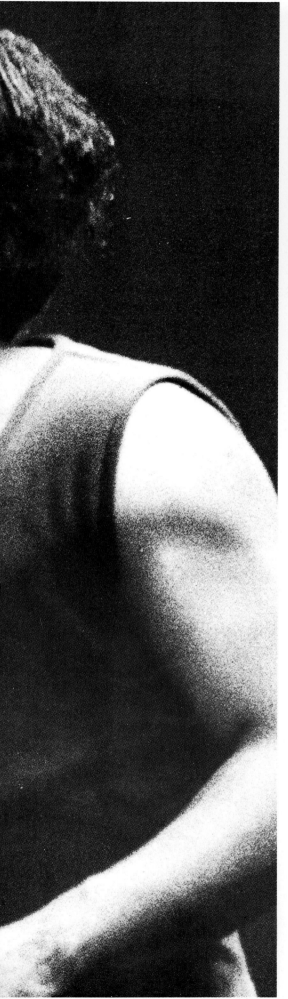

Above: The face of the hardest-working man in show-business.

Left: Capturing the frenzy, vitality and exuberance of every James Brown performance. Now the elder statesman of soul, he shows no indication of cooling his high-voltage stage act.

Far left: 'Say it loud, I'm black and proud,' and certainly his influence on black music was profound, all the soul singers that followed owing him a great debt.

pendence (the first black performer to achieve it), leaving the label simply to cut and press the records. It worked, with *Papa's Got a Brand New Bag* becoming his first US top-ten hit in 1965 and *I Got You (I Feel Good)* and *It's a Man's, Man's, Man's World* making a million sales worldwide in 1966.

The new mood of black self-awareness in the United States was well-represented in Brown's 1968 release, *Say it Loud – I'm Black and I'm Proud*. His rags-to-riches story, his hard-won commercial and creative freedom, and the fact that he'd achieved it without compromising in his attitudes or his music, put him in a powerful position among black Americans and he almost became caught up in their politics. In 1968 he used his considerable influence to help cool racial tensions after the assassination of Martin Luther King.

But it was on black *music* where the influence of James Brown was supreme. His chugging motor-rhythms, and clever use of jazz and African elements, laid the groundwork for the popular street funk of the seventies and the dominant disco sounds of today. He has been fêted as the 'Godfather of Soul' and it is true he opened the door for the likes of Otis Redding and Wilson Pickett to follow.

By the late seventies his popularity began to diminish, although the 1974 album *Payback* and 1976's *Body Heat* were among his biggest sellers. Ironically, for someone who supplied its basic ingredients, he has been unable to capitalize on the current disco boom, despite the authentic claim of his 1979 LP release *The Original Disco Man*. Surprisingly perhaps, he has had only six hit singles in the US and never secured a No 1.

Even now, he shows no sign of slowing down, especially since his film appearance in *The Blues Brothers* reawakened an appetite for his music. In recent years he left Polydor and signed briefly with PK to produce *Soul Syndrome*, his best album since *Payback*. He was even more briefly with Churchill/Augusta Records.

James Brown's importance as a black artist cannot be underestimated either. He has probably been black America's most popular musical son, durable enough and inventive enough to survive the change from R&B to soul, through funk and on to disco. To prove the point, 1986 saw him singing the theme song for *Rocky IV*, and gaining his first worldwide hit for years with *Living in America*, off the *Gravity* album.

In 1989, Brown was jailed on bank robbery and firearms charges, but on his release two years later was soon back in the studio, anxious as ever to reclaim his crown. Meanwhile Soul II Soul and others had emphasized his influence, emulating or sampling his music to create new soul history.

RECOMMENDED RECORDINGS
James Brown at the Apollo Vol 1 (1963)
Live at the Apollo Vol 2 (1968) Vol 3 (1971)
Papa's Got a Brand New Bag
Say It Loud, I'm Black and I'm Proud
Soul Brother Number One
The Payback
Body Heat
Soul Classics Vols 1-3
Sex Machine
Solid Gold (compilation)
Can Your Heart Stand It (compilation)
Live – Hot on the One
Soul Syndrome
Gravity

FATS DOMINO

*I*t must have provoked a wry smile on the genial face of Mr Domino when, in the early fifties, they began to talk of the 'new music' – rock and roll. It wasn't new at all: he had been pounding out these percussive rhythms ever since he could play the piano. And that wasn't long after he was born into a musical family in New Orleans during February 1928. His father was a well-known violinist, but it was his brother-in-law, Harrison Verrett, an accomplished guitarist, who taught the young Antoine to play piano. It must have been good tutoring because, by the age of ten, the boy had his first professional engagements. Leaving school at fourteen, he worked by day in a factory and played the clubs at night.

The key year was 1949. Domino shared regular work with bandleader/trumpeter Dave Bartholomew and they established a profitable partnership, with Bartholomew becoming his musical arranger and co-composer, that lasted over twenty years. The same year, he signed for Imperial Records and the debut single sold a million. It was entitled *The Fat Man* and, given the performer's roly-poly physique, the subsequent nickname was inevitable. The melody was a straight eight-bar blues, very much in the New Orleans' tradition that was to characterize everything Fats produced.

In 1952, his piano playing was a vital ingredient of one of the first rock and roll hits, Lloyd Price's *Lawdy Miss Clawdy*. By 1955, with a string of hit singles behind him, Fats Domino took on the mantle of rock and roller with no trouble at all. It was made for him, and he was soon established, through concerts and records, with this new audience. *Ain't That a Shame* and *Blueberry Hill* became (and remain) rock classics, much covered by other performers.

Fats' affable charm graced two early rock movies, *The Girl Can't Help It* and *Shake Rattle and Roll*. Although he was no great innovator, he sustained his popularity with songs of good-humored simplicity, a rich, unmistakeable voice and equally distinctive boogie-woogie piano style.

Walkin' to New Orleans earned the last of several gold discs in 1960, and the rest of that decade was to prove comparatively lean for him, at least in the United States. In Britain, Beatles' manager, Brian Epstein, persuaded him to play what was surprisingly his first British concert, in London. Further UK shows, plus a

general reawakening to early rock and roll, earned a revival of interest in his music and he secured a part in the film, *Let The Good Times Roll*.

In the seventies, he was still touring up to ten months of every year and in 1976 made a return visit to the UK. Simultaneously, United Artists issued a *20 Greatest Hits* album and a definitive six volume set of his work. In 1981 he had a small country hit with *Whistling Heaven* from the Clint Eastwood movie, *Any Which Way You Can*.

Now semiretired in New Orleans, mainly playing the Las Vegas casino circuit with re-workings of his past successes, Fats Domino can look back on a long and remarkably consistent career – and record sales topping 65 million. And who hasn't at some time stood round an upright piano at parties and sung *Blueberry Hill* or *Ain't That a Shame*? It's been a pleasure, Fats.

RECOMMENDED RECORDINGS

Rollin' and Rockin'
Live at Montreux
Live in Europe
Fats is Back
20 Greatest Hits
Boogie Woogie Baby

Above left: In the autumn of his years, Fats relaxes at home in New Orleans, his family roots and his musical ones were there.
Left: The hands that pounded out the rhythms that became rock and roll.
Below: His size never stopped Fats playing his energetic, frantic style of boogie-woogie. It didn't change much over the years, but who wanted it to?

LITTLE RICHARD

Little Richard's raucous rocker Tutti Frutti marks a watershed in the development of rock and roll. Recorded at the back end of an otherwise undistinguished session in New Orleans in 1955, it belonged in none of the existing categories of music. More than that – it fulfilled what the man called 'his first law of youth culture' – attract the kids by driving their parents up the wall! Trace a line back through all the showmen of rock – Jagger, Hendrix, Otis Redding, James Brown – and you inevitably end up at Richard Penniman.

One of twelve children of a family of Seventh Day Adventists, he was born in December 1935 in Macon, Georgia. The church taught the young Richard how to sing and play the piano. Unfortunately, when he was at·home, it wasn't gospel songs his family heard from his room, but rhythm and blues. Disapproval of his musical tastes and his outlandish ways led to Richard leaving home to join a traveling 'medicine show' at the age of fourteen. He won a talent contest in Atlanta in 1951 which led to a contract with RCA and some unmemorable gospel-style 'jump-up' blues recordings with them and other labels.

However, a privately made demonstration tape which he sent to Art Rupe of Specialty Records in Los Angeles, created more interest. Rupe eventually arranged a session at Cosimo Matassa's J & M Studios in New Orleans, using 'Bumps' Blackwell as producer and a good local rhythm section. Matassa's technique as a recording engineer was essentially to put down a live performance. His mixing desk, his miking, were kept simple; there were no effects, no overdubs, no edits. The results were electric. They had a vitality and atmosphere which has never been recaptured and is no better heard than on *Tutti Frutti.*

It became a 1956 million-seller and earned Little Richard a five-year contract. Others, all in the same furious, frantic style, were gold records. Little Richard, pounding the life out of his piano, screeched and shouted his way through *Long Tall Sally, Rip It Up, Keep A-Knockin', Lucille, The Girl Can't Help It* (title song of a film in which he appeared), and his last major hits, *Good Golly Miss Molly* and *Baby Face* (UK No 3).

It was his last because, in 1957, Little Richard went to study theology in Alabama, recording only gospel music for five years. When he returned to rock and roll in 1963, he signed with Vee-Jay Records and immediately recut his old hits for rerelease. Almost without exception, they lacked the spark and drive of the originals. He was more successful recording blues and soul for the Okeh and Modern labels (as well as Vee-Jay) but made little impact again until 1970 when the general revival of interest in early rock, plus a new contract with Reprise records, brought him prominence with songs like *Freedom Blues* and moderately good, new R&B albums such as *The Rill Thing* and *The King of Rock and Roll.* He also recorded with admiring newcomers such as Canned Heat, and Delaney and Bonnie Bramlett.

There had always been a certain sexual ambivalence about Little Richard's stage act, but in the seventies, he left no one in any doubt, camping it up for all he was worth with gaudy costumes and thick, lurid, makeup. Sadly, his ego seemed to rise as rapidly as the quality of his act went down. Although his vain attempts to capture the old magic were pitiful, he retained a surprisingly loyal following, especially in Britain. In the late seventies, the church claimed him again, and he was once more telling revival meetings, 'God wants you to give up rock and roll.' He usually goes on to warn how the music is irrevocably linked to drug-taking and homosexuality – citing his own experience as evidence.

Whatever he now chooses to recant, in his day he was the wildest rock and roller of them all, one of the true originals. He will be remembered belting out each song at full blast, gyrating, shaking, clambering over the piano, and reaching a kind of Dervish-like frenzy with his eyes rolling insanely in their sockets.

Above: Little Richard remains one of the great rock and rollers, even if more recent appearances have been disappointing. His on-off relationship with God led him to reject his own music and advise others to do the same; but his following is loyal.

RECOMMENDED RECORDINGS

The Original Little Richard
Rock Hard, Rock Heavy
All-Time Hits
Here's Little Richard
Little Richard, Vol. 2
The Fabulous Little Richard
Well Alright!
Get Down With It

ROOTS

BUDDY HOLLY

*T*he mid-fifties saw the arrival of the two most widely influential singer-songwriters in rock music. For Chuck Berry, it has led to two decades of success; Buddy Holly had but two years to make his mark. But what a mark! He set the precedent for the self-sufficient group, writing and playing its own material, deciding its own recordings and arrangements, and concerning itself with production. The impact of his song-writing, vocal, and guitar-playing style is enormous, influencing artists from Bob Dylan to the Beatles. However much popular music changes, Buddy Holly's stamp remains indelible.

The music of Charles Hardin Holley is a synthesis of many elements, some of which he encountered as a child in Texas (country and western, swing, baptist hymn tunes) and some of which he heard when star names visited his home town of Lubbock or came across the airwaves (Elvis Presley, Bo Diddley, Ray Charles). His first stage appearance was at the age of five, in 1941, at a local talent show. At first he took up the violin, changing later to guitar. By the age of thirteen he had teamed up with Bob Montgomery to play a brand of 'country bop' at school dances. In 1953 the duo were well enough known to merit a show on local radio KDAV: *The Buddy and Bob Show.* Adding Larry Welborn to the line-up, they cut eleven demonstration tracks in 1954/5 (subsequently issued as *Holly In The Hills*) and the band regularly supported big-name tours visiting Lubbock (Elvis and Bill Haley were but two). A talent scout spotted Holly at one of these, and Decca Records offered him a contract.

The first sessions, held in Nashville in 1956, produced sixteen solo tracks. There were mainly rockabilly material, which went unremarked at the time, although they were among the freshest, most exhilarating recordings he ever made. The first single release on Decca appeared in July 1956, *Love Me* coupled with *Blue Days, Black Nights.* At this time he was also putting in some memorable live performances just backed on drums by his friend, Jerry Allison.

Augmenting Allison with Don Guess (bass) and Sonny Curtis (guitar), he formed a backing group called the Three Tunes. Playing pure rock and roll, they returned to Nashville where one of the new tracks cut was the Holly-Allison composition *That'll Be The Day.*

Above: The Crickets arrive in London for their first UK tour in February 1958.
Left: Buddy Holly (center) with Jerry Allison (drums) and Joe Maudlin (acoustic bass).
Previous pages: Buddy Holly on stage.

Feeling that he wasn't progressing with Decca, Buddy Holly turned to producer Norman Petty whose work at his studio in Clovis, New Mexico, was attracting attention. For the first session, Holly and Allison were joined by Niki Sullivan (guitar) and Joe Maudlin (bass), the entire group calling themselves The Crickets. Petty recut *That'll Be The Day*; Bob Thiele of Brunswick liked it enormously and issued it immediately. His judgment was impeccable: it made No 3 in the US and the UK.

Norman Petty became manager, sessions leader and occasional keyboard player as well as producer. He decided to issue Crickets recordings on Brunswick and discs credited solely to Buddy Holly (although still backed by the same team) on the Coral label. Both secured a succession of million-selling singles, although some of the solo singles veered toward pure schmaltz, while group releases tended to be brighter, and more raw.

From the Crickets came *Maybe Baby, Think It Over* and *Oh Boy*, while Buddy Holly took sole credit for the classic *Peggy Sue*, which demonstrated his distinctive 'hiccuping' vocal presentation to the full. *Peggy Sue* has become one of the fictional heroines of rock and roll, although curiously the song says precious little about her.

Holly was one of the first country-oriented musicians to use percussion, coupled to the pounding back-beat that characterized black rhythm and blues. In collaboration with Petty, he experimented with overdubbing and multi-tracking, which allowed him to make more of his (for the period) highly developed guitar technique.

In 1957 and 1958, he had seven US top-forty hits, with more in Britain, where his popularity was reinforced by a 1958 tour accompanied by Jerry Allison and Joe Maudlin (Sullivan had left the band the previous year). He impressed musicians too, especially those who hadn't heard the Fender Stratocaster guitar before.

His return from the UK saw important changes. First he married and moved to Greenwich Village, New York. Second, he broke away from The Crickets and took to recording with the Dick Jacobs Orchestra and Chorus, producing very different material, as a comparison between *Peggy Sue* and *Raining In My Heart* soon evidences. It was pop, even if superior pop. He also recorded with a new backing group, featuring two of the finest musicians around, saxophonist King Curtis and guitarist Tommy Allsup, whose imaginative playing enhanced many of Holly's tracks.

Second only in popularity to Elvis Presley, in both the US and the UK, Buddy Holly joined a 1959 show titled The Biggest Show of Stars. Holly and fellow bill-toppers Big Bopper and Ritchie Valens decided to charter a light aircraft to take them on to Clear Lake, Iowa. It took off from Mason City airfield just after half-past-one on the morning of 3 February 1959, and crashed minutes later on to a frozen lake.

They called it 'the day music died.' After his death, Holly's popularity and reputation grew unabated. A posthumous single, coupling *It Doesn't Matter Anymore* with *Raining In My Heart* stayed at No 1 for six weeks and, although his name gradually slipped from the US charts, he registered constantly in the UK. An inevitable album, *The Buddy Holly Story* immediately sold in vast quantities, and back in New Mexico, Norman Petty was busy unearthing every unreleased Buddy Holly tape he could think of — demos, rehearsal cuts, the lot. He overdubbed orchestral backings and the like as he thought necessary. It generated sufficient new material for compilation albums to be issued up to ten years after his death.

Top left: Sending those 'Words of Love' down the airwaves.
Far left: When you're with me, oh boy – Buddy and Joe enjoy a duet.
Above: Second only in popularity to Elvis, 1958 saw a change of style to a more lavish and sophisticated backing. The edges were smoothed down, but he still made some of the finest music around.
Left: The Holly look that will always be remembered. His influence extended right through the sixties and seventies.

The Crickets, whose lyrical and musical ideas had contributed to Buddy Holly's success, continued recording for some years after, including a tribute album of their late vocalist with Bobby Vee.

Buddy Holly's songs have hardly dated at all. As late as 1978, Blondie were recording *I'm Gonna Love You Too*. An overtly sentimental film, *The Buddy Holly Story*, aroused yet more interest in his music, and Denny Laine of Wings completed a tribute album entitled *Holly Days*. Paul McCartney bought the rights to all of Holly's work. In *American Pie* Don McLean pinpoints the beginning of rock and roll's decline to the day of Holly's death.

RECOMMENDED RECORDINGS
Legend
Chirping Crickets
Buddy Holly's Greatest Hits
The Buddy Holly Story
Twenty Golden Greats
The Nashville Sessions

BB KING

B B King's distinctive style of blues guitar playing has been the model and the inspiration for most of the great rock guitarists to have emerged in the past twenty years. His use of 'bent' and rapidly picked notes, his beautifully shaped solos based on single-string runs, and his sheer purity of sound have left their mark in no uncertain way on the likes of Eric Clapton, Mike Bloomfield, Alvin Lee, Jimmy Page and the late Jimi Hendrix.

For almost 40 years now, King has worked at becoming the master of the blues. He is its greatest ambassador, introducing the music to audiences in America, Europe and even the Soviet Union. However, his present widespread popularity is largely due to the rock musicians whose respect and admiration he has gained. They repaid their debt to King by introducing him to their own audiences, and now he enjoys the recognition his unique contribution to music deserves.

Influential as *he* was, B B King had several important influences himself. His mellow, well-honed, jazz-like style owes much to the great Charlie Christian, and even Django Reinhardt, whose Paris recordings he heard during the forties. He is also indebted to Robert Johnson and the original master of the electric blues guitar, T-Bone Walker. King's style became much more refined than that of other early bluesmen.

Riley B King was born on a plantation in Itta Bena, Mississippi, on 16 September 1925 and raised by a foster family. He sang with gospel quartets in the early forties, an experience that was to shape his later vocal style, and formed The Elkhorn Singers to play to local black clubs. It was around the time he was drafted into the US army, in 1943, that King first began to seriously work at the blues guitar. That interest was furthered in 1947 when he went to live in Memphis with is cousin, the country blues musician, Bukka White.

At that time Memphis was a blossoming center of music and could even claim the first black-operated radio station in the South, WDIA. Through his friendship with Sonny Boy Williamson II, King earned a ten-minute stint as disc jockey for WDIA on the *King Biscuit Boy Show*. Between these turns he jammed with the jazz and blues artists coming to the studio and soon formed a band with some of them, The

Beale Streeters. King was nicknamed 'The Beale Street Blues Boy,' later shortened to just B B, the initials by which he has been known ever since.

At first, the Streeters used the popular 'shouter' style of delivery, but this soon took on a lighter, gospel complexion, acknowledging the success at the time of saxophonist-singer, Louis Jordan.

B B King's first record was made in 1949 for Bullet Records, but shortly after the release of *Miss Martha King* he moved to Modern Records (Ike Turner actually signed him), appearing on RPM.

With a band that included, for the first time, the horn section that was to feature in most of his concerts, King undertook almost ceaseless tours around the 'chitlin' circuit. In 1956, he played no less than 342 gigs in the black R&B clubs, big and small, that made up the circuit.

Most of his best-selling recordings were covers, but he succeeded in putting his individual imprint on each of them. *Three O'Clock Blues*, a cover of the Lowell Fulson original, was a major R&B hit in 1951 and was followed by classics such as *Woke Up This Morning, Sweet Little Angel, Eyesight To The Blind, You Know I Love You, You Upset Me* and the 1955 million seller that became his signature tune, *Every Day I Have The Blues*.

Below and right: B B King feeling every note; the greatest virtuoso of the blues guitar yet a man who has never stopped learning.

Firmly established as the leading black urban bluesman, and certainly one of the most imaginative, he first made the pop charts in 1957 with *Be Careful With A Fool*. After this the RPM label folded and he was forced to switch to Kent for singles and Crown, United and Custom for albums. Kent released one of his catchiest hits, *Sweet Sixteen*.

King's 'crossover' appeal was cemented in the early sixties with a huge response from both black and white audiences to his album, *Live At The Regal* – arguably his best recording. Single hits in this period came with *Rock Me Baby*, *Don't Answer The Door* (an American R&B top-ten entry in 1966) and *Paying The Cost To Be The Boss* (1968).

King got together with rock producer, Bill Szymcyck, to make *Live and Well* in 1969. One side of the album features the BB King Band during a live gig at the Village Gate in New York, while for side two King went to Los Angeles to record with a white rock session group, among them Al Kooper.

The same line-up (minus Kooper) recorded the pulsating album *Completely Well*. It included several dazzling solos from King and ended with the potent *The Thrill is Gone*, which went on to become a major hit in the US in 1970, his second million-selling single. It also featured a superb jam session based on the songs *Crying Won't Help* and *You're So Mean*.

With these last two albums King virtually became part of the rock elite! Ironically, much of King's recognition was due to the British 'invasion' of the sixties with Clapton, Alvin Lee and the rest paying homage.

Although he took account of this new following in his music, King remained loyal to the blues. This can be heard in the album he made with Joe Walsh, Leon Russell and Carole King,

Below and left: B B has been a regular guest at the New Orleans jazz and blues festivals, and similar events around the world. In 1979 he gave a series of concerts in the Soviet Union.

BB KING

Indianola Mississippi Seeds, a best-seller, and the live recording he made in Cook County jail. Another live album emerged from a London concert with Peter Green, Alexis Corner and Ringo Starr, but his most extraordinary blues journey took him to the Soviet Union in 1979 for a successful twenty-concert tour.

Other notable albums with leading rock musicians included *LA Midnight* cut with Joe Walsh and Taj Mahal, and *To Know You Is To Love You,* featuring Stevie Wonder on keyboards. His biggest success came in collaboration with Bobby 'Blue' Bland: *Live Together For The First Time* made gold-record status in 1975.

During the late seventies BB King was a regular attraction at jazz and blues festivals around the world – New Orleans, for example, and the Hammersmith Blues Festival in London,

Far right: Demands of the club circuit have broadened his range, to the disappointment of blues purists.
Below: B B King greets New Orleans.

where he once again appeared with Bobby Bland and shared the bill with another veteran blues master, John Lee Hooker. He guested at the Capital Radio Jazz Festival (with his own backing band) and then toured Britain with top US jazz-funk band, The Crusaders, during 1982. A product of the tour was a fine live album, *Live in London.*

During this period, much of what he played was disappointingly middle-of-the-road, although undeniably giving him a broad, all-ages appeal. Little pure blues was included in his repertoire, and of that some was puzzlingly obscure. The influence of his manager, Sidney Seidenberg, seems to have been paramount in widening the range of his music, to the extent of recording everything from country and western to Broadway show standards, and working with such diverse partners as famous rock artists and top orchestras. In truth the range at times has seemed *too* wide, and the programing ill-conceived, although BB's contributions have been never less than excellent.

B B King's audience these days is mainly the

Las Vegas casino crowd, although he's still cutting hit records. He achieved a Grammy in 1987 for Lifetime Achievement, and U2 featured him on their *Rattle And Hum* LP/tour/film project two years later, just two examples of the veneration in which this ever-youthful bluesman is held.

RECOMMENDED RECORDINGS

Live At The Regal
Live And Well
Completely Well
Live in Cook County Jail
Indianolo Mississippi Seeds
B B King In London
To Know You Is To Love You
Live Together For The First Time (with Bobby Bland)
The B B King Story Chapters I and II (compilations)
The Best of B B King (compilation)
The Great B B King (compilation)
Blues 'n' Jazz
Six Silver Strings

CHUCK BERRY

The influence of Chuck Berry can be heard in some part, great or small, in the music of every white rock band of the sixties, seventies and even the eighties. The subjects of his songs; the wit and sophistication of his lyrics; their structure and rhythmic excitement; his unique and much-imitated guitar style and vocal delivery – all constitute the bricks and mortar of rock and roll. He was the first major rock performer to write almost all his own material, another precedent for those that followed.

Yet his personal success was comparatively brief and he never truly recovered from the criminal charge which put him behind bars for two years at the height of his fame. He went to prison a star (and possibly a victim) and emerged, much to his surprise, as a legend.

The exact date of birth of 'The Father of Rock and Roll' is unknown, because Chuck Berry variously gives it as 15 January 1925 and 18 October 1931. Shortly after his birth, Charles Edward Berry's family moved to St Louis, Missouri, where he sang in school glee clubs and church choirs, saved up to buy a second-hand six-string guitar and a pile of guitar tutors, and listened to country music on local radio. Early influences were the blues-swing of Louis Jordan and the innovatory electric-guitar techniques of T-Bone Walker. Music was still very much a side interest, especially while serving three years in a reform school for attempted robbery. Released in 1947, he worked first for General Motors and then trained as a hairdresser, supplementing his wages by performing with the Chuck Berry Combo at weekends.

Not until 1955 did he think about taking up music professionally. With his pianist Johnnie Johnson, he made an audition tape and headed for Chicago. He contrived a meeting with the great Muddy Waters who recommended to Leonard Chess, head of Chess Records, that he give Berry an audition.

Of the two tracks on the audition tape, Chuck and Johnnie Johnson preferred the typical slow blues number, *Wee Wee Hours*. But Leonard Chess thought the proposed 'B' side was outstanding: an up-tempo blend of country and western and R&B called *Ida Red*. It was unlike anything he'd ever heard before, a true original.

A few changes were suggested (rumor has it

by disc jockey Alan Freed), and the title was changed to *Maybellene*. Freed at that time was the chief promoter of black R&B through his radio show. He gave plenty of airplay to *Maybellene* and the song not only sat on top of the American R&B chart for nine weeks but also made the top-ten proper.

Yet it was a success Berry found hard to follow, even though his next two singles were far better songs. *Too Much Monkey Business* and *Brown-Eyed Handsome Man* were astute and penetrating statements – too much so for the white teenagers of America who had loved (and bought) *Maybellene*. So it was the concerns and preoccupations of that audience that provided the themes for his next singles. Girlfriends, boyfriends, cars, clothes, music, dancing, parental frustrations and aggravation at school became the staple diet of his compositions.

Yet *Roll Over Beethoven* still only made the top thirty, and it took the autobiographical *Johnny B Goode* to give Chuck his second top-ten US hit. It is one of the standards of rock and

roll. It was followed in 1958 by *Sweet Little Sixteen*, the greatest and most affectionate portrait of a teenage rock fan, and one of just two British hits during the fifties.

He produced an incomparable sequence of inspired song writing: *Carol, School Days* and *Rock and Roll Music* were added to the list of hits. Such was the quality of his single releases that classic tracks such as *Memphis Tennessee* appeared solely on his albums.

For his live act Berry had developed the strange 'duck walk' that was to become his trademark; he strutted around the stage, bent like a jacknife and clutching his Gibson 335 to his midriff. It's nowhere better seen than in *Jazz on A Summer's Day*, a documentary of the 1959 Newport Jazz Festival.

Top: A wry smile from Charles Edward B.
Above: Any requests? Encores come payable in advance at Chuck's concerts.
Right: 'Long distance information . . .' and at the other end of the line groups like The Beatles were taking it all in.

Overleaf (both): The leaps into the air and, of course, the extraordinary and unique 'duck walk' all go to make Chuck's act vividly entertaining, even though rock fans see little of him now. But someone's always playing *Johnny B Goode* somewhere in the world.

Although immensely popular with white youth, the American musical establishment was not quite so enamored with him. There were grounds to suspect racism at work when he was accused of abducting and violating a minor in 1959. His first trial was declared null and void, but at the end of the second trial, in 1961, Chuck Berry was found guilty and sent to prison for two years. He has protested his innocence ever since.

When he emerged in 1964, his marriage was ruined, but his music lived on. Rock music had changed, but changed to his advantage. Up-and-coming British groups were hammering out his songs. The Beatles sold a million copies of *Roll Over Beethoven* in the US and The Rolling Stones had just released *Come On* as its first single, and were to go on to record over twelve more. Moreover, he could hear his guitar style in just about everything they and all the other bands were playing.

Chess Records took note of his popularity. After his release, they issued *Memphis Tennessee* as a single and quickly arranged studio

Left: That hunted look – surely not the Internal Revenue Service again!
Above: Singing of his ding-a-ling brought Chuck long-overdue No 1s in America and in Britain, but the song was hardly his best.
Below: Tuning his legendary Gibson 335 prior to a recent US concert.

sessions (the first for five years). The new songs were every bit as good as those of the fifties: *Nadine, No Particular Place To Go,* and *You Never Can Tell* scored chart success in America and Britain. But were they *new* songs? Many suspect Chuck had them written before his prison term, because after those three his songwriting abilities deserted him completely, and chart success faded away. He concentrated on his still popular tours and music festivals, including a trip to Britain with Carl Perkins.

After four undistinguished years on the Mercury label, he returned to Chess in 1970 and, quite out of the blue, made three outstanding albums: *Back Home, San Francisco Dues* and *Bio.* The first of these produced at least two tracks to rank with his fifties classics: *Tulane,* about the life and times of a pair of dope pushers, and perhaps his best-ever pure blues, *Have Mercy Judge.*

He worked rock revival shows, played a major part in the rock movie, *Let the Good Times Roll* and, in 1971, an appearance in Britain produced the live half of a double album entitled *London Sessions.*

It was perhaps the supreme irony that he should score his biggest single success in 1972 with the childishly risqué *My Ding A Ling* from that live LP. A ditty that had been in his repertoire (as *My Tambourine*) for twenty years became a US and UK Number one. Around the same time, Elvis Presley made a cover version of Berry's outstanding *Promised Land,* and the comparison was pointed.

After starring in the film *American Hot Wax* in 1978, Chuck Berry once again found himself a guest of the US government, this time with four months for tax evasion. In 1979, he signed a short-lived contract with Atlantic, producing only one album. *Rock It* was almost Chuck Berry at his best, but it failed, as had his previous LP release *Live At The Fillmore,* where he was backed by The Steve Miller Band.

At the beginning of the eighties, Chuck received a long-overdue 'achievement award' from the American recording industry, and continued to appear regularly at jazz and blues events around the world, although it has to be admitted that some of his performances were no more than embarrassing self-parody. For his repertoire he relies heavily on his evergreen standards (not that most audiences expect anything else). He still retains his reputation for ruthless, hard-headed dealing with promoters, and everyone else in the music business.

In the UK, he appeared at one of the jazz festivals staged by London's Capital Radio, and an annual 'Chuck Berry Week' at a London theater proved a highly successful venture, hugely popular with Britain's rocker community.

Since *Rock It,* his album releases have concentrated on compilations, and it's difficult not to conclude that the Chuck Berry of the 1980s is living off the past.

Looking back over Chuck Berry's achievements, it's easy to say that all his best compositions are written to the same pattern, but he managed to repeat the formula without becoming tedious. First, he wrote great lyrics, employed an imaginative vocabulary, and drew on a rich stock of subject matter – and he never took himself too seriously. Chuck's music was, above all, fun. However, he had a reputation for a stormy temper, and as an extremely tough businessman. As many promoters find to their dismay, he plays only what he is paid for. If the audience wants encores, that means a bigger fee.

Berry's style drew heavily on country and western, and on long-established guitar tricks, adapted for blues-style playing. To this he added innovative 'shuffle' rhythms and chord changes, and thus created a unique instrumental accompaniment for his equally original lyrics. And the breathless, chattering piano accompaniment to his recordings from Johnnie Johnson was almost as influential.

Chuck Berry is arguably the most important influence on rock and roll of all. Not only are his greatest songs regularly covered, but also many original compositions still echo Chuck Berry. *Johnny B Goode,* one suspects, will be alive as long as rock and roll itself.

RECOMMENDED RECORDINGS
Golden Decade Vols I, II, III
Motorvatin'
Berry Is On Top
Chuck Berry Volumes 1/2
Back Home
San Francisco Dues
One Dozen Berry's

BILL
HALEY

For most Europeans rock and roll began with Bill Haley, and particularly with Rock Around The Clock which gained success from being selected as the theme song for the film Blackboard Jungle. Somewhat ironically, the movie dealt with the problem of teenage delinquency. Haley, by this time approaching 30, was an unlikely candidate for rock idol number one: an affable, rather podgy, purveyor of exceptionally exciting dance music. After a dozen or so huge worldwide hits in the mid- to late fifties, Haley and various line-ups of Comets settled into a round of increasingly nostalgic concert tours which continued right up to his death in Texas in February 1981.

William John Clifton Haley was born on 6 July 1925 and spent his childhood in Pennsylvania. His first musical love was country and western. In the late forties he toured the mid-Western C&W club circuit singing and playing country music like hundreds of other aspiring musicians. In 1949 he formed a band called the Four Aces of Western Swing and they obtained regular broadcasts on local radio stations and a recording contract with the Cowboy label.

While doing the rounds of the radio studios Haley noted an increasing interest in black R&B among young whites, which offered energetic dance music. Renaming his band The Saddlemen, he gradually introduced an element of

Right: Bill reads about himself in a UK magazine.
Below: The original Comets.
Previous page: One of the legendary stage tricks.

Above: Although by 1960 he'd cut his last record, Bill Haley continued touring for twenty years, growing a little broader in the beam, but still able to punch out all the old favorites for loyal fans.
Left: Still sporting the famous kiss-curl.
Right: 'Shake, rattle 'n' roll' – he was still doing it up to his death in 1981.

R&B into his material and soon noticed the effect. Some danced, some clapped their hands, others tapped their feet, and it was all down to rhythm and tempo. The more it was stepped up, the more excited everyone became. Haley cut a few, largely forgotten, singles including a cover version of Jackie Brenston's R&B hit *Rocket 88*. This song has strong claims to being the root stock of rock and roll; certainly in Brenston's version, if not Haley's, all the fundamentals of rock can be heard.

Another name change – to The Comets – and Haley was playing exclusively a catchy new music which fused elements of white country and swing with black R&B. An early hit single, and first to make the pop charts, was *Dim, Dim The Lights*, which made the black R&B chart, probably the first white rock-and-roll recording to do so. Other minor hits came with *Rock The Joint* in 1951, and in 1953 with his own

composition, *Crazy Man Crazy*, which was arguably the first rock and roll record to enter the American listings. Like many of his songs, it drew on teenage hip talk for its (fairly basic) lyrics.

In 1954 Bill Haley and The Comets left the small Essex label for Decca. Their producer was Milt Gabler, who had enviable experience in rhythm and blues. Gabler drew out the best Haley's band had to offer: lots of instrumental color, driving energy and an unwavering beat. With Fran Beecher on electric lead guitar; Billy Williamson on steel guitar; Al Rex, acoustic bass; Ralph Jones, percussion; Johnny Grande, piano-accordion; the superb Rudy Pompilli on tenor saxophone; and Haley himself on rhythm guitar, they became the first performers to bring rock and roll to the attention of the masses.

Rock Around The Clock was actually recorded in 1954 and was released to an un-enthusiastic reception, but by the time *Shake Rattle and Roll* was issued in 1954, America was more than ready for rock and roll. It stayed in the US top twenty for twelve weeks and scored in Britain, too. Indeed, the band had six UK chart entries by May 1956.

It was then that The Comets' manager persuaded MGM to include *Rock Around The Clock* in the film soundtrack of *Blackboard Jungle* and with the rerelease of the single, Haley had a global hit and world stardom. It went on to sell an astonishing 22 million copies over the decades that followed. It remains the first anthem of rock, as well as one of the biggest-selling singles ever.

Soon Haley's 'kiss-curl' hairstyle was being widely imitated, as well as his music. He starred in several early rock movies, including *Rock Around The Clock*, which had the dubious distinction of causing uproar in the cinemas of America and Britain, especially among the teddy boy cult in UK. Bill Haley's music was responsible for many a torn cinema seat. He got the kids dancing and, even if he sometimes seemed bewildered by all the hysteria, he stuck to the formula and kept the hits coming: *See You Later Alligator* and *Don't Knock The Rock* were but two of the more memorable.

Haley was always more popular in the UK than in the US. But his European tour in early 1957 exposed the fact that Haley and his boys were no spring chickens and certainly didn't have the charisma of Elvis Presley, who was attracting considerable attention by then.

As the decade drew to a close, The Comets were in the descendant and wisely relinquished recording for concert tours, which for the next twenty years were unchanging evocations of the fifties. That alone always assured him a popular reception, especially in Britain.

He wasn't an especially remarkable musician, or an innovative songwriter, and was certainly miscast as a revolutionary, but Haley nevertheless rates as the man who had the wit to see the way music was moving and adapt to meet the new demands. Along with Jerry Lee Lewis, Carl Perkins, Gene Vincent, Buddy Holly, and of course Elvis, he hammered out the earliest white rock and roll. As cinema managers of the fifties no doubt bitterly recall, Haley was the first to have his audience rolling (and rocking) in the aisles.

RECOMMENDED RECORDINGS
A Tribute To Bill Haley
Golden Hits

JERRY LEE LEWIS

Jerry Lee's reputation rests largely on just two, possibly three songs, which are unique rock classics, and on a stage act that for relentless, uncontrolled frenzy has no equals among the white rock and rollers. His impact and importance have been far greater than mere arithmetic suggests: if not the king of rock and roll, he's certainly its greatest survivor.

Born in the town of Ferriday, Louisiana in September 1935, Lewis was taught piano by his father. The story goes that by the age of eight he was showing such promise that his parents mortgaged their house to buy him a $900 piano. Unfortunately, they couldn't keep up the repayments. Jerry Lee kept his paino; they lost the house.

His was a religious family and the church provided his first musical influence. In his early teens, he even studied in Texas to be come a pentecostal minister, but soon returned home. The influence of sacred music was now replaced by that of boogie exponents, such as Moon Mullican, and blues and honky-tonk musicians. After his first public performance at the age of fourteen, Jerry Lee played locally for four years before becoming a professional. Adept at drums as well as piano, he became a resident performer at numerous clubs and bars along the Mississippi river. The extrovert stage act, however, was yet to arrive.

In 1956 Lewis gained an audition at Sun Studios in Memphis; Sam Phillips liked Lewis' tape and called him back for a second session. The result, *Crazy Arms*, was a hit in the country charts; but it was the second single, released in 1957, which shot Jerry Lee Lewis to stardom. *Whole Lotta Shakin' Goin' On* was actually recorded as a fill-in at the end of the recording session, and this frenetic boogie quickly made No 3 in the American chart and No 8 in Britain.

By this time, Lewis, apparently in an effort to overcome stage shyness, had been encouraged to let go a little. This he certainly did, developing an act where he literally assaulted the piano, pounding the keys, playing sweeping glissandos, hammering the notes with his feet and elbows, clambering over and under the instrument, and all the time ecstatically yelling the lyrics. It was nothing if not spectacular and soon made him a celebrity on American TV and radio.

The follow up to *Shakin'* was even more successful and *Great Balls of Fire*, probably the number for which he will always be re-membered, reached No 2 in the US and No 1 in the UK. His fame broadened with appearances in films such as *Disc Jockey Jamboree* and *High School Confidential* and Lewis looked set to rise to the top.

In 1958, with a version of Otis Blackwell's *Breathless* (Blackwell composed many early rock classics) rising rapidly up the charts, Jerry Lee Lewis came to Britain for what should have been a highly successful tour. Unfortunately, although legal in Louisiana, his marriage to thirteen-year-old second-cousin Myra Brown caused outrage in Britain. It was also Lewis' third marriage (and one of the previous two had been bigamous). The organizers had to cancel the tour after just five days.

Unfortunately it didn't end there. Suddenly he, and his records, were being banned all over the place, not just in Britain. His progress came to an abrupt halt. For three years he was a forgotten man, and had to wait until 1961 for a hit record: a fine cover version of Ray Charles' *What'd I Say*. But rock music was changing and his chance had gone.

In the early sixties, however, he felt the furore had died down and began touring again. There were several successful visits to Europe and endless engagements across the United States. He would play just about anywhere to

Right: 'Nobody cuts The Killer,' was Jerry's warning to the audience.
Below: Assault on a piano, and a whole lotta shakin' is goin' on! Once he was stage shy . . .

get exposure. He certainly remained convinced of his own pre-eminence. When persuaded reluctantly to play second billing to Chuck Berry, he finished his act by setting fire to the piano, declaring, 'Let's see anybody follow that!' However, despite large audiences for his concerts, his recordings didn't sell too well. Lewis had always been able to mellow his act with a good weepie, and a new role of country crooner didn't prove too difficult for him to accept.

By 1968 Jerry Lee was back in the fold. A succession of country hits had brought him back into favor, good songs such as *What's Made Milwaukee Famous (Has Made A Loser Out Of Me)*; *Another Time, Another Place*; and *She Even Woke Me Up To Say Goodbye*. He then made a triumphant return to rock and roll at a revival concert in Toronto, and turned in a superlative performance in Jack Good's production of *Catch My Soul*. *Chantilly Lace* hit the UK charts and the marvelous Kris Kristofferson song, *Me and Bobby McGee*, became a hit in the US. A 1973 session in London with guitarists Rory Gallagher, Alvin Lee and Peter Frampton produced a top-selling album.

Switching to the Elektra label, his debut LP produced a country hit with the title song *Rocking My Life Away*. Although his second period of success had begun to wane by the mid-seventies, Lewis kept up an astonishing aver-

age of 200 live performances a year until, in 1981, his lifestyle finally caught up with him. A stomach rupture necessitated emergency surgery. He came close to death, but seemed unrepentent when discharged from hospital and immediately ordered cigars and whisky.

His arrogant and irrepressible personality have ensured a continuing cult following into the nineties. Fellow artists, too, hold him in high regard: as recently as 1983 he was invited to guest on a Rolling Stones album, but recuperation from his recent surgery made this particular engagement impossible to fulfil. His life was made into a 1989 biopic, *Great Balls Of Fire*, starring Dennis Quaid as the Killer himself.

Before the ill-fated 1958 tour, he had already made a lasting contribution to rock music, and on remarkably little recorded material. Despite ten years in the wilderness he has survived: 'As long as they gimme a piano, I'll be out there!'

RECOMMENDED RECORDINGS

The Original Jerry Lee Lewis
The Essential Jerry Lee Lewis
Live At The Star Club Hamburg
The Greatest Live Show On Earth — Vols 1 & 2
Country Songs for City Folks
The Killer Rocks On
Killer Country

Above: Jerry, the young Killer at the keyboard.
Right: Back in concert in 1982 after the serious stomach surgery.
Below: Jerry in his new role of crooner.

BO DIDDLEY

*A*s much for his sound as his songs, British R&B bands of the early sixties owed a considerable debt to Bo Diddley. The Yardbirds, The Animals and The Rolling Stones (to name but three of the most famous) delved into his work for material, and freely adapted his distinctive riffs and hammered rhythms. Although he never had quite the influence of his companion at Chess Records, Chuck Berry, echoes of his primitive, energetic style can still be heard today.

Although the blues originated in the Southern States of America, by the mid-1930s, the center of the music's development had shifted north, principally to Chicago and Detroit. Thrown out of work by the great depression, the McDaniel family moved north from McComb, Mississippi, in 1933 to look for work. Their five-year-old son, Elias, had already shown a musical aptitude and by the age of seven had taken up the violin, soon to be followed by the guitar (largely self-taught).

Growing up in Chicago, and exposed to the new urban blues, generally louder and more raucous than its Southern counterpart, Elias formed his first group at high school. Then, taking the name Bo Diddley, he got together a band which included Otis Spann (half-brother of the great Muddy Waters) on piano; Frank Kirkland on drums; Jerome Green on maracas; Billy Boy Arnold on harmonica and

Bo's half-sister, 'The Duchess,' on vocals.

In the early fifties, he played an incalculable number of gigs in the black clubs of Chicago, appearing either with his band or solo. Many of these clubs were owned and run by Leonard and Philip Chess, and in 1950 they started their own record label to capture the wealth of musical talent among the negroes of the city. In 1955, now with a stock of his own distinctive blues material, Bo Diddley cut his first disc for Checker, a subsidiary of Chess. *I'm A Man* coupled with the autobiographical *Bo Diddley* were major American rhythm-and-blues hits. The latter contained one of the most famous and recognizable riffs ever penned, and has been a starting point for many a subsequent rock song.

The same year, Bo scored again in the US with *Pretty Thing* and *Diddy Wah Diddy*, and, along with Muddy Waters, was one of the first

Above: Bo, famed for punchy, chopped guitar riffs.
Left: In the film *Let The Good Times Roll*.
Right: One of Bo's distinctive axes.

R&B performers to go electric. Exploring the range of sounds available from the electric guitar, with small rhythm sections, and making up for lack of numbers with sheer amplification, the duo were among the forerunners of the basic rock group. In their emphasis on raw simplicity, the punk bands of the late seventies were unwittingly paying homage to Bo Diddley and his fellow bluesmen. Indeed he toured the UK with The Clash in 1979 and returned to play further concerts in 1982. He even started the interest in experimental guitars; much of his custom-made hardware adopted unusual geometry for the bodies long before this became the vogue.

Above: Bo delivering his driving brand of rhythm and blues in a studio session.
Left: 'I'm a roadrunner, baby' – riffs from his classics are widely imitated.
Right: The guitar man.

In 1957, Bo had another hit (and penned another R&B standard) with *Mona (Now I've Got A Witness)*, now best-known for the cover version on the Rolling Stones' first album. His music, with its emphasis on thumping rhythmic vitality, stimulated the burgeoning R&B scene in Britain. In 1959 he scored his only pop hit when *Say Man*, a record in which Diddley and Jerome Green trade insults over a chopped guitar riff, made No 20. Bo Diddley enjoyed much acclaim in the sixties during his tours of Europe. Hit records came with driving R&B numbers like *Road Runner* and *You Can't Judge A Book By its Cover*.

Sadly, as the decade ended, his song-writing invention seemed to desert him, although he was a popular artist on various rock-and-roll revival tours and gave a memorable performance in the film *Let The Good Times Roll*.

Bo Diddley's style was never sophisticated; rather it was a raw-boned, rugged sound that derived much from the rudimentary folk music of his native South. His unique crisp, chopped guitar sound is now widely used.

RECOMMENDED RECORDINGS
Golden Decade
Chess Masters Vols 1 and 2

EVERLY BROTHERS

F or five years, between 1957 and 1962, Don and Phil Everly enjoyed a succession of marvellous hit records. They were one of the phenomena of early rock music, adapting elements of bluegrass and country for the pop market and succeeding handsomely. No wonder their appealing, and distinctive, style found its way into much of sixties rock music. Sadly for the Everlys, by 1963, through disputes and bad decisions, they had been eclipsed by their imitators.

The brothers were born in Brownie, Kentucky, Don in February 1937 and Phil in January 1939. Their parents, Ike and Margaret, were well-known country singers and the boys appeared on stage with them from an early age. They toured the southern states, and appeared on local radio shows (including their parents own) from 1946 onward, playing a synthesis of hillbilly and gospel.

In 1956, they came to the attention of guitarist Chet Atkins and cut an unsuccessful single, *The Sun Keeps Shining*, before signing with one of the shrewdest managers in the business, Wesley Rose. At the same time, Archie Bleyer, head of Cadence Records in Nashville, Texas, was desperately trying to revive the label's fortunes. Rose urged him to sign his young country vocal duo. They were very much in the tradition of other established duos but once contracted to Cadence, the Everlys very quickly put their country and western style to the service of rock music.

Also contracted to Wesley Rose was a skillful husband-and-wife songwriting team, Boudleaux and Felice Bryant. One of their songs had so far been rejected by no less than 30 artists – *Bye Bye Love*. With Chet Atkins producing, placing the Everlys' fine, shining harmonies over their emphatic, full-bodied acoustic guitar sound, the result was a million-selling single. The Bryants then obliged with another classic, *Wake Up Little Susie*, and these two hits gained them regular US TV appearances and national fame.

With their first British tour in 1958 came a No 1 on both sides of the ocean, *All I Have To Do Is Dream*. The tempo was slower, the mood gentler, but the formula was identical. The sessions in Nashville were never casual affairs. The whole team contributed ideas to the mix, rehearsals were exacting, and the production team knew exactly the polished, seamless result it wanted. It was underpinned by a slick rhythm section of bass, drums and piano, Don and Phil punching out glittering guitar lines and their clear-cut voices doing the rest. The magic worked time after time.

As well as songs from the Bryants, they recorded their own compositions, and those by other performers, such as Roy Orbison's *Claudette*. Hits came with *Bird Dog, Problems, Let It Be Me, (Till) I Kissed You,* and *Take A Message To Mary*, which included the odd, but effective, sound of a screwdriver tapped against a Coke bottle, and was recorded with Buddy Holly's band, The Crickets. The Everlys also toured constantly, performing one-nighters all over the United States.

In 1960, after a row with Archie Bleyer over royalty payments, the brothers switched to the new Warner Brothers label. It was a lucrative deal for them and they saw it as a chance to broaden their musical horizons. At first their popularity remained undiminished.

However, they did lose the Nashville sound team. In 1961, when they fired Wesley Rose as manager, they also lost the songwriting talents of the Bryants. It didn't seem to matter. Their own composition, *Cathy's Clown*, went to No 1 in Britain and the US. Phil's song *When Will I Be Loved* (their first to be recorded with a string accompaniment), *So Sad* and *Lucille* produced further hits. *Ebony Eyes* went to No 8 in America, and *Walk Right Back* to No 1 in the UK.

Their luck changed with the compulsory spell in the US Marines. Relations between Don and Phil went sour and their career lost its momentum. Their last major record successes came in 1962. On a British tour in 1963, Don Everly suffered a nervous breakdown and other problems; he was in and out of hospital until 1966, and even attempted suicide. Phil completed the UK tour alone, but it was the turning point for them. Despite British hits in 1965 with *The Price of Love* and *Love Is Strange*, the duo never recaptured its previous status.

The irony was that, as they declined through the sixties, many of those replacing them at the top were doing so thanks to the Everlys' groundwork. Their influence on The Beatles, Bob Dylan, The Hollies, The Byrds, Beach Boys, Lovin' Spoonful and Simon and Garfunkel, especially in the use of vocal harmonies, was plain to hear, and then there were numerous successful cover versions of their best songs.

Far left: Early on, all they had to do was dream.
Left: A unique duo, Don (left) and Phil Everly.

In 1968, Don and Phil made something of a comeback with a remarkable documentary album, *Roots*. Produced by the excellent Lenny Waronker, it saw them returning to their country and bluegrass origins, and certainly deserved to do better than it did. Sadly, other albums in this period warranted being the failures they were.

Joining RCA in the early seventies, they did produce a good recording with the assistance of friends such as John Sebastian, Delaney and Bonnie Bramlett, David Crosby and Graham Nash. *Stories We Could Tell* was intended to be the start of a new career, working together and separately, but the quarrels and friction continued. However, their tours were successful and they retained a loyal following in the UK.

Then, on stage one night in July 1973, they argued yet again. Don smashed his guitar and walked off, declaring, 'The Everly Brothers died ten years ago!' Their subsequent solo careers never approached their success as a duo, although a 1976 compilation, *Walk Right Back With The Everly Brothers* put their name back in the album charts.

Don Everly signed with Hickory Records

Above: Pressures and disagreements took their toll and, by the early seventies, a break seemed inevitable.
Left: The brothers in rehearsal.
Below: Still in fine voice, a triumphant 1983 reunion in London.

back in Nashville in 1976 and cut an LP, *Brother Juke Box*.

Phil, meanwhile, recorded with several labels, including a duet with Cliff Richard on *She Means Nothing To Me*, which took his name back into prominence, albeit briefly. Then, much to everyone's surprise, the duo came to London and gave some great concerts. In 1985, the brothers again reunited for concerts and also released a studio album produced by Dave Edmunds, *Born Yesterday*.

They have left a legacy of memorable, effervescent, uncomplicated recordings; the driving energy of rock brilliantly harnessed to the harmonic disciplines of country music. It remains one of the most unmistakable sounds ever created in popular music.

RECOMMENDED RECORDINGS
The Everly Brothers
The Fabulous Style Of The Everly Brothers
Walk Right Back With The Everly Brothers (compilation)
The Very Best Of The Everly Brothers
Born Yesterday

LOU REED

Of all the important influences in rock music, few have experienced so little commercial success and public acclaim during their so-called 'heyday' as The Velvet Underground. The Underground explored a sinister, twilight world of bizarre characters and relationships. Mainly through the imagination of founder-member John Cale, they ventured widely into avant-garde musical ideas and sounds. Lou Reed was the principal lyricist and vocalist, and as such a chief inspiration for the likes of David Bowie and Roxy Music in the seventies.

The Velvets were a direct stimulus to the punk and new-wave movements in both Britain and the United States. Even the electronic Euro-pop of, for instance, Kraftwerk, owes much to the early experiments of the Velvets.

Reed and Cale got together in New York in 1966. Reed recruited Sterling Morrison on guitar, and, unusually, a female drummer, Maureen Tucker. Cale completed the line-up and they took their name from an obscure pornographic novel. Their first gig, suitably enough, was at the Cafe Bizarre in Greenwich Village in the winter of 1966.

Their music aroused immediate and passionate controversy. They were soon fired from the Bizarre, their songs of drugs, death and decadence too much even for Greenwich Village. However, they had been noted by pop art 'guru,' Andy Warhol, who was looking for a rock band to participate in his multimedia touring extravaganza, *The Exploding Plastic Inevitable*. Warhol added German-born ex-actress and fashion model, Nico on vocals. His judgment was good: she had a light, sensual voice with a haunting quality to it.

Kicking off in New York, and touring the United States and Canada, the Velvet Underground caused howls of outrage and protest wherever they went. Sometimes they stunned their audiences into silence. Their music was relentless, pulsating, searingly dissonant, even brutally cacophonous; it clawed at the senses, a violent counter to the musical sunshine coming out of California.

The Velvets' first album, overseen by Warhol and with his famous banana sleeve design, can now be recognized as one of the most innovative and influential rock recordings of its period. No one before had spoken so frankly about drugs as they did in *Heroin* and *I'm Wait-*

Above: In the seventies, Reed was a key inspiration for the avant-garde. Despite that, he produced what some believe to be the worst rock record made!
Left: Lou, the rock and roll animal.

ing *For The Man* or dared to delve into subjects such as sado-masochism *(Venus In Furs)*. Not surprisingly, the album received little or no playings on radio and it soon disappeared. However, it is now regarded as one of the essential rock records.

But the failure had its effect. In 1967 Nico left and Warhol's attention was diverted to a new project. Even the critical press lost interest, which was unfortunate because the album released late that year, *White Heat, White Light* was as remarkable as its predecessor. It featured several less aggressive songs Reed had intended for Nico, but still offered nothing less than stark, uncompromising realism and revolutionary musical ideas. One track, the seventeen-minute *Sister Ray*, is a classic.

Disagreements and disillusionment led to John Cale's departure in 1969 to be replaced by the competent, but hardly comparable, Doug Yule. A third album released in March of that year, *The Velvet Underground*, was notable for the ballad *Pale Blue Eyes*. The whole recording was generally more placid, more restrained. The band had changed beyond recall and Reed knew it. In August 1970 he left, utterly disenchanted.

His last recording with the band shows the transition into a punchy rock and roll band with tracks like *Sweet Jane*. Reed has criticized

many aspects of *Loaded*, but it was a good album and a suitable swansong. By the time live recordings from Texas, San Francisco and New York had been released, the Velvets were more or less defunct.

Lou Reed went solo, and went to London to make his solo debut album. Despite a line-up including Rick Wakeman of Yes, *Lou Reed* was a poor production, but he was determined to produce something worthwhile in the UK. The opportunity came when David Bowie expressed a desire to produce for Reed.

Transformer appeared in 1972, and achieved reasonable success, especially among those unfamiliar with the Velvets' recordings – to them it was a novel and daring venture. Reed appeared with Bowie at London's Royal Festival Hall, complete with make up and a repertoire that was little more than self-parody. The album produced a hit single, however, *Walk on The Wild Side*. He followed its success with a UK tour.

He returned to the studio to make one of his most powerful but underrated statements. *Berlin*, a kind of operetta, is a harrowing and chilling experience, and divided the critics. Produced by Bob Ezrin (of Alice Cooper fame), it must have bewildered those who knew him only through *Transformer*, but seemed a logical sequel to anyone who had heard the Velvets.

His concert performances became variable despite the assistance of a superlative backing band: Dick Wagner and Steve Hunter (guitars), Prakash John (bass), and Whitey Glan (drums). They can be heard at their best in the rough-edged *Rock 'n' Roll Animal* a live concert

recording made in New York. Sadly the entire line-up quit shortly afterward to join Alice Cooper. The same concert yielded another live album in 1975, but the intervening studio album, *Sally Can't Dance*, was again a poor self-parody. In 1975 he released *Metal Machine Music*, a double album, each side 16.1 minutes long, consisting entirely of tape noise and electronic hiss punctuated by the occasional high-frequency spike. After numerous returns from record shops, an embarrassed RCA withdrew the album, and Lou Reed's career was at its nadir.

In 1976, he declared his intention to return to pure rock and roll, 'No more bullshit, dyed hair, faggot-junkie trip.' The result was *Coney Island Baby*, a good effort, but a critical flop. Unfortunately, he was to obtain only a luke-

warm response to the much better *Street Hassle* (1978) and *The Bells* (1979) albums, although they were highspots in art rock.

The eighties really only came alight musically for Reed with 1989's acclaimed *New York*. It was his biggest chart album for 15 years. In 1990 he reunited with Velvet Underground colleague John Cale for *Songs For Drella*, a tribute to recently deceased guru Andy Warhol, mining a similar theme in 1992 with *Magic And Loss*. The previous year had seen a one-off Velvets reunion in Paris, but despite this and a 1992 retrospective box set *Between Thought And Expression* Reed resolutely refused to look back.

The Velvet Underground were later to become the inspiration for many artists. Their initial impact was explosive and the shock waves are still being felt today.

Above and left: Seventies Lou Reed gigs were variable, but he retained a loyal British following. Here London fans try to get closer...

RECOMMENDED RECORDINGS
The Velvet Underground & Nico
White Light/White Heat
The Velvet Underground
1969 *(live)*
Loaded
(Lou Reed)
Transformer
Berlin
Rock 'n' Roll Animal
New York
Between Thought And Expression
(compilation)

GREAT BRITISH

QUEEN

With their unique blend of hard rock riffs, glam rock presentation and an undeniably self-mocking sense of humor, Queen established themselves over two decades as one of the world's undisputed supergroups. Their reign was brought to an abrupt end with the death of bisexual lead singer Freddie Mercury in November 1991, an early rock casualty of Aids, but their music will remain beloved by fans if almost universally reviled by the critics.

In 1970, hard rock was just beginning to emerge in the form of Eric Clapton's Cream and Jimi Hendrix: Mercury loved the power of rock, but dreamed of allying it with the Beach Boys' harmonies to create symphonic rock. His chosen vehicle was Smile, a London group formed by students Brian May (guitar) and Roger Taylor (drums). Bassist John Deacon completed the line-up in 1971, and the name change – a Mercury suggestion, naturally – was simultaneous.

Early in 1972, Queen were spotted by producer Roy Thomas Baker. The band's first album *Queen* and single *Keep Yourself Alive* were released the following year. Not that success was immediate: the single was rejected – five times – by the Radio 1 playlist panel. Instead of promoting the album, they disappeared to cut *Queen II* before touring Britain as special guests of Mott the Hoople.

In February 1974, the same month their first chart single *Seven Seas Of Rhye* reached No 10, *Queen II* reached No 5 and the band were soon bill-topping. But their first US concert tour ended abruptly when May contracted hepatitis and then a stomach ulcer: *Sheer Heart Attack*, their third LP, was recorded in no fewer than four studios.

When the single *Killer Queen* hit No 2 in October, it was the turning point. *Sheer Heart Attack* also made No 2, putting Queen on the map with a vengeance. Their second attempt at cracking North America in 1975 met the same fate as the first; this time Mercury contracted a throat virus.

Bohemian Rhapsody broke the three-minute barrier and established itself as one of rock's all-time classic singles. It also featured a ground-breaking video that cost under £5,000 and established Queen in the forefront of rock visuals. It came from *A Night At The Opera*, their first platinum disc. 1976 saw a free gig in London's Hyde Park for 150,000 fans, while their

eagerly awaited fifth album, *A Day At The Races*, clocked up half a million advance orders and not surprisingly reached No 1, the single, *Somebody To Love* No 2.

News Of The World, their annual album, hit the racks in October 1977, while *We Are The Champions* became their biggest-selling American single so far at No 4. The European leg of the 1978 tour was recorded for eventual release as the double album *Live Killers*; meanwhile, their next record, *Jazz*, was recorded in Switzerland and reached No 2.

In 1979, film-maker Dino de Laurentiis commissioned Queen to write the soundtrack to his next film, *Flash Gordon*. *Crazy Little Thing Called Love* – a song Freddie claimed he 'wrote in the bath' – topped the US charts, while on Boxing Day a Hammersmith Odeon concert was filmed and recorded as a fund-raiser for the people of war-torn Kampuchea. Freddie was now sporting his shortest haircut to date.

The Game hit the top of the album charts worldwide and included *Another One Bites The Dust*, their second American No 1. *Flash Gordon – The Original Soundtrack* was released in December: at this point it was calculated Queen had sold over 45,000,000 records worldwide.

Left: The great Freddie Mercury, the voice of Queen.
Top: Mercury and May, two of rock's finest talents.
Right: From left, May, Taylor, Mercury and Deacon.

Having conquered the western world, 1981 saw Queen embark on the first ever stadium tour of South America, playing to the world's biggest ever paying audience – 251,000 at Sao Paulo's Morumbi Stadium en route. *Queen's Greatest Hits* was released, and six years after *Bohemian Rhapsody*, they clocked up their second British No 1 single, *Under Pressure*, with guest vocalist David Bowie.

Hot Space appeared in 1982, but 1983 was reserved for solo projects. *The Works*, their 13th album, benefited from the break and spawned the No 2 hit single *Radio Ga Ga* and No 3 *I Want To Break Free*, promoted by a video of the band in drag which their US audience didn't appreciate.

Live Aid in 1985 was the biggest rock spectacle ever, and Queen were stars of the show. Mercury's long-playing solo debut *Mr Bad Guy* also appeared as he insisted 'It's probably brought us closer together and will enhance our careers. . . . Queen are gonna come back even bigger.' And they did. The band's 1986 album, *A Kind Of Magic* – music from the film *Highlander* – reached No 1 in the UK LP chart where it stayed for 13 straight weeks. It played a big part in Queen's total of 1,774,991 albums sold that year.

The European Magic tour played to over a million, including behind the Iron Curtain in Hungary where 80,000 people packed Budapest's Nep Stadium. After selling out Wembley, the outdoor Knebworth one-dayer in August was Queen's last ever UK concert.

In 1987 Mercury teamed up with Spanish opera star Montserrat Caballé for the album *Barcelona* and appeared on the soundtrack of Dave Clark's musical *Time*. In 1989 he announced he wouldn't be touring in future. 'I don't think a 42-year-old man should be running around in his leotard any more.'

The Miracle, which entered at No 1 in June, preceded by the No 3 single *I Want It All*. The British Phonographic Industry recognized their Outstanding Contribution to British Music with an award in early 1990, but Mercury's sickly appearance was noted. *Innuendo* entered the UK singles listings at No 1 in January 1991 – at six and a half minutes in length, the longest UK chart-topping single since *Rhapsody*. The album of the same name swiftly followed suit, but was overshadowed by the announcement on 23 November 1991 that the singer had been tested HIV positive and had Aids.

Mercury passed away the following day. Three months later, the audience at the Brits

Above: Few artists could get an audience eating out of their hand like Freddie Mercury, whose stage presence was unrivaled.
Right: The boys in action. There can never be another Queen.

awards ceremony honored Queen again when Brian May and Roger Taylor received an award for Best British Single (for *These Are The Days Of Our Lives*, which topped the charts in December 1991 as a fund-raiser for Aids charities, simultaneous with a second *Greatest Hits* package). Taylor (with his band The Cross) and May (with the 1992 hit single *Driven By You*) were already following solo careers: Deacon's plans were uncertain. Yet Queen had made their mark as master showmen of rock who found an amazingly wide audience and whose South American exploits effectively expanded the frontiers of the rock world.

RECOMMENDED RECORDINGS

Sheer Heart Attack
A Night At The Opera
Greatest Hits
Innuendo
Greatest Hits II

GENESIS

A long with groups like Yes and Emerson, Lake and Palmer, Genesis were pre-eminent in the progressive 'art rock' of the seventies. Originally formed as a kind of songwriters' co-operative, however, they placed less reliance on instrumental fireworks than their contemporaries, relying instead on lyrically ambitious recordings and highly theatrical stage presentations. Both, until his departure in 1975, centered around their gifted lead singer, Peter Gabriel.

Since his departure, the band has been fronted by their irrepressible and energetic drummer-turned-singer, Phil Collins. Ironically, and to the surprise of many, Collins has been able to sustain Genesis as a band while enjoying greater solo commercial success than either Gabriel or Steve Hackett.

Four aspiring songwriters met at Charterhouse Public School and formed a band, Garden Wall, to promote their work, (principally that of Peter Gabriel). Bringing in a fellow pupil, Anthony Phillips, they made a demonstration tape and took it along to producer/pop entrepreneur, Jonathan King, not least because he was an ex-Charterhouse student. King fixed a contract with Decca, and called the group Genesis despite a clash with a similarly titled American band. Luckily Genesis, USA, had little impact. Nor at first did the British equivalent, made up of Peter Gabriel (lead vocals; drums), Michael Rutherford (bass), Tony Banks (keyboards), Chris Stewart (drums) and Phillips on guitar.

Two singles, issued around 1968, disappeared without trace, and Stewart left, to be replaced by John Silver. Despite this, Decca allowed King to produce the first album, *From Genesis to Revelations*. But it was a muddled affair that did scant justice to the material (evident in its 1974 reissue as *In The Beginning*). Both producer and record company lost interest and the group, now split between art school and university, almost disintegrated.

Now Silver left, and John Mayhew took over on drums. Schoolfriend Richard McPhail became their manager and it was to his rented country cottage that the band retreated in October 1969 to work on fresh material. They produced sufficient songs for an album and the head of the adventurous Charisma label, Tony Stratton-Smith, signed them up in spring 1970. *Trespass* appeared in the October, to no great

acclaim, and both Phillips and Mayhew left for pastures new. Phil Collins joined as drummer and Steve Hackett was added on guitar in December.

With 1971's *Nursery Cryme*, they found their feet, and a following. It was an imaginative, fascinating album, making much use of the instrumental possibilities of the mellotron and, consequently, the beginnings of the sound which was to become unmistakeably Genesis. Tracks such as *Musical Box* and *Return Of The Giant Hogweed* remain favorites of Genesis fans to this day.

Foxtrot, issued 1972, took them into the 'big league' with remarkable cuts such as *Watcher Of The Skies* and the 23-minute epic, *Supper's Ready*. It drew large audiences for their 1972/73 winter tour, one which also saw the visual emphasis of the band concentrated on Peter Gabriel. His quasi-mystical vocals were enhanced by dramatic theatricals and he started wearing outrageous costumes and bizarre masks. 1973's successful live album is a good record of Genesis at this point of development.

Their favorite themes of myth, magic and fantasy were fully explored in the musically and lyrically remarkable *Selling England By The Pound* (1973) which produced a UK singles-chart breakthrough with *I Know What I Like*. This was the album which established them as leaders in British 'progressive rock,' a position reinforced by the pioneering and daring double 'concept album,' *Lamb Lies Down On Broadway* (1974). Written entirely by Gabriel, this saga of the fantastic adventures of a character known as Rael in contemporary New York attracted considerable attention in both Britain and America. On stage, Gabriel acted out the storyline as Rael in an extravagant presentation.

Then came rumors that Gabriel was tired of the constant touring and losing interest in what Genesis were doing. In June 1975 Gabriel stunned the rock world by announcing his departure. Few gave much for Genesis' chances of survival without him, especially when hundreds of auditions failed to find a suitable replacement. Eventually Collins took the lead vocal limelight, with surprising skill and confidence. Their next album, *A Trick of the Tail*, met with great critical approval and commercial success. It was followed in 1976 by a two-month American tour (with ex-Yes and King Crimson drummer, Bill Bruford, taking over from Collins).

Within the year, the equally excellent *Wind and Wuthering* had been released. Recorded in Holland, and giving Genesis a US singles chart entry with *Your Own Special Way*, this scotched the remaining persistent rumors of a break-up.

Chester Thompson (ex-Mothers of Invention) played drums as well as Bruford on a 45-city American tour, followed by concerts in Brazil and Paris, and three sell-out dates at London's Earls Court. The Paris performances were recorded for the double live album *Seconds Out* (1977).

Far left, top: Founder-member, Michael Rutherford demonstrates the technique of the twin-necked Rickenbacker.
Top left: From left, Rutherford, Banks, Gabriel and Collins, then drums, now vocals.
Left: Peter Gabriel takes flight; with each tour, the theatricals became ever more spectacular.

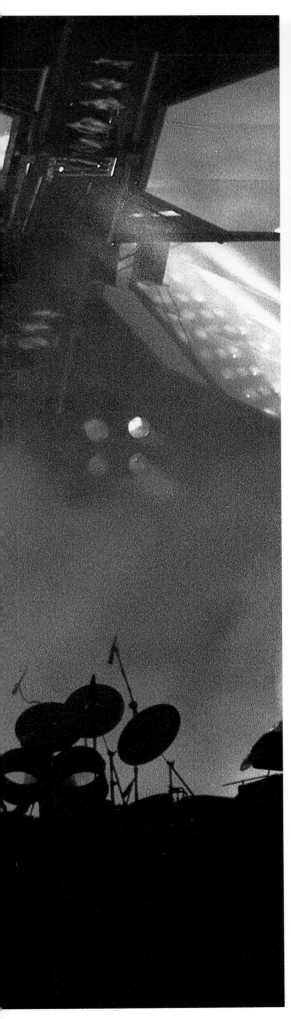

Above: Phil Collins on vocals and tambourine. in concert in 1982.
Left: One of Genesis' spectacular lightshows, at London's Wembley arena.
Right: Michael Rutherford plays a moody chord.

Following Hackett's decision to go solo in the summer of 1977, 'the end is nigh' stories abounded once again. But the remaining trio, Banks, Rutherford and Collins, assisted by Chester Thompson and US guitarist, Daryl Stuermer, defied the doom-mongerers with *And Then There Were Three*. This was a much more commercial album than any previous efforts, with eleven good tracks; one of them became the band's biggest-selling single, *Follow Me, Follow You* (a UK No 7 and US No 23).

As the 'new wave' movement grew in the late seventies, Genesis wisely took a breather to work on solo projects. *Duke* (1980) was the band's next release, and their least grandiose recording to date with the emphasis on percussive rhythms and strong melody.

1981's *Abacab*, the group's twelfth album, was solid, if not outstanding, and received mixed reviews. *Three Sides Live* was the group's only LP of 1982, albeit a double, containing, as the name implies, concert performances of tracks from *Duke* and *Abacab*.

1984's simply-titled *Genesis* (their third consecutive UK No 1 album) was followed by much solo work which saw Collins establish himself as a singer-songwriter, scoring massive transatlantic hit albums with *Face Value, Hello I Must Be Going, No Jacket Required* and *But Seriously*, plus a live LP (all but the second hit the top in Britain). He also appeared in the film *Buster* (1988), from which the UK chart-topping *Groovy Kind Of Love* was taken. Rutherford headed transatlantic hitmakers Mike and the Mechanics, with Paul Carrack.

Further group releases comprised 1986's *Invisible Touch* (UK/US top three with five US top-five singles including their debut chart-topper, *Invisible Touch*) and 1991's *We Can't Dance* (No 2 UK/7 US). It seemed Genesis would survive as a very occasional and profitable threesome.

RECOMMENDED RECORDINGS

Nursery Cryme
Foxtrot
Genesis Live *(live)*
Selling England By The Pound
The Lamb Lies Down On Broadway
(double)
A Trick Of the Tail
Wind And Wuthering
Seconds Out *(live/double)*
. . . And Then There Were Three . . .
Abacab
Genesis
(Phil Collins solo)
Face Value
Hello, I Must Be Going
No Jacket Required
But Seriously

ROXY MUSIC

Shifting effortlessly through a variety of styles during the seventies, from high-camp glitter rock to mellow, romantic crooning, Roxy Music were never less than highly sophisticated, and widely influential. At its best, their music took a fresh and fascinating approach to rock, as did their presentation. It is a band of strong individual personalities, dominant among them lead vocalist, lyricist, and founder-member, Bryan Ferry – possessor of one of rock's most distinctive-ever voices and personalities.

Miner's son, Ferry, was born in Washington, County Durham, in September 1945 and developed an early interest in music. By 1964, he was playing in a couple of local groups – Banshees and Gas Board. Graduating from Newcastle University in 1968 with a degree in fine arts, he worked as a teacher but continued to nurture musical ambitions.

Learning music, playing and composing in his spare time, Ferry finally decided to take up music full-time in 1970. He and Simpson decided to form a band and, seeking something different from the traditional guitars, bass and drums, advertised for a reeds player in the local press. As a result, saxophonist and oboist, Andy Mackay, joined them in January 1971 and also introduced synthesizer man, Brian Eno. With Dexter Lloyd on drums and Roger Bunn on guitar, the first Roxy Music was completed, but it was short-lived. Lloyd soon left and was replaced by Paul Thompson in June 1971. Guitarist, Phil Manzanera was also keen to join but, when Ferry recruited David O'List, he had to be content with a role as sound mixer. Manzanera's chance came when both O'List and Bunn departed in rapid succession.

Record companies were wary at first of the band's very different, seamlessly textured sound and cool image, but Island's Chris Blackwell decided to take a chance and was pleasantly surprised when the first album, *Roxy Music*, produced by ex-King Crimson vocalist, Pete Sinfield, was a critical and commercial success. Encouraged by this, Ferry then suggested the bold move of issuing a single but not including it, as was accepted practice, on a subsequent LP. A first UK tour in August 1972 and the rise of *Virginia Plain* to No 4 won them wide popularity and aroused much interest.

Sadly, founder-member Graham Simpson was unable to enjoy the accolades. He had suffered a nervous breakdown prior to the

recording of *Virginia Plain* and been replaced by Rik Kenton. However, it was but the beginning of the band's problems in finding a permanent bass player. John Porter, Sal Maida, Johnny Gustafson, Rick Wills and John Wetton were all to play on tours and albums over the coming years. Porter was around long enough to record the outstanding, if idiosyncratic, *For Your Pleasure* album in January and February 1973. Produced by Chris Thomas, it was notable for entertaining tracks such as *Do The Strand* and for Eno's avant-garde use of the synthesizer. The mood of vague decadence tinged with romance and nostalgia was greatly induced by Ferry's lyrics.

Eno's work was too avant-garde, as it was to turn out, for Ferry, who had radically different ideas about the way Roxy Music should develop. After touring America in late 1972 and Europe in spring 1973 Ferry and Eno argued after a concert in Newcastle. Eno left for a solo career that, if not commercially successful, has been of great musical importance.

Eddie Jobson replaced him, a violinist as well as keyboard player from Curved Air, whose melodic gifts were to be a considerable asset, especially as he quickly established a rapport with Mackay.

Returning to live performance in autumn 1973, Ferry played the ultra-cool image to the full, with a short, well-groomed hairstyle and white tuxedo. He had also decided to attempt a parallel solo career, beginning with an album of personal favorites entitled *These Foolish Things*. One, a cover of Dylan's *A Hard Rain's Gonna Fall* reached No 10 in the UK charts during 1973, a year that also saw singles success for the band as a whole with *Pyjamarama* (also a No 10), and *Street Life* from the album *Stranded*, which went to No 9. The album, an expert production by Chris Thomas (who also played bass on the hit single!) was more refined and less experimental than previous efforts and,

Above and right: Lead vocalist, Bryan Ferry, has attempted to combine a solo career with that in the group, but with variable critical success in the former.

with the aid of nationwide live gigs, made No 1 in the British album chart. Tours of the US between 1974 and 1976 helped establish the band there, as did two fine albums, *Country Life* and what is often regarded as Roxy Music's masterpiece, *Siren*. A single cut from the latter, *Love Is The Drug*, made No 30 in America, and No 2 in Britain in 1975.

Ferry had also enjoyed his solo successes during the period: a stylish remake of the sixties hit, *The In Crowd* and the great standard, *Smoke Gets In Your Eyes*, both scoring in 1974. His second solo album, *Another Time, Another Place*, relied on original material. It was followed in 1976 by a curious, and ironically titled, compilation called *Let's Stick Together*. Mainly intended for the American market, it included humorless solo efforts and reworkings of Roxy Music material, but to no great effect, although the title track became a UK No 4.

Unable to reconcile his two, by now very different, careers as soloist and lead vocalist, Ferry elected to concentrate on the former and Roxy Music were to all intents and purposes defunct after June 1976, with some bad feeling between Ferry and Manzanera.

The same year Ferry's solo EP, imaginatively called *Extended Play*, reached No 7, while a successful live LP *Viva* was issued of recordings made during concerts in the UK. (Roxy Music were one of the first bands to make a point of recording all their live performances.) A *Greatest Hits* compilation issued in 1977 contrasted strongly with Ferry's unimpressive, disco-oriented, *In Your Mind*, of the same year. He had two more hit singles, though: *This Is Tomorrow* (No 9) and *Tokyo Joe* (No 15) which indicated a faithful following.

Then, just when it seemed his solo venture would lose momentum, Ferry produced his best album to date, *The Bride Stripped Bare*. In it he reverted to an emotional and creative honesty that had been subdued since the years of Roxy Music and cast aside his slick image. In the same year, 1978, he approached Mackay, Manzanera and Thompson to re-form the band, enlisting ex-Vibrator, Gary Tibbs, as yet another bassist, and ex-Ace, Paul Carrack, on keyboards.

Reunited as Roxy Music, they recorded *Manifesto* for release in 1979 and immediately returned to the UK singles charts with two cuts from the album, *Dance Away* (No 2) and *Angel Eyes* (No 4). They toured a great deal, including America, in spring 1979 (but with little reward in terms of record sales), before producing 1980's *Flesh And Blood*, an album in which they reached new heights both in quality of material and the sound they created.

Hit singles in 1980 came with *Over You, Oh Yeah (On The Radio)* (both No 5), and *The Same Old Scene* (No 12). In 1981, in a moving tribute to the recently murdered John Lennon, they recorded his song *Jealous Guy* and obtained a first UK No 1.

Now it was the turn of Paul Thompson to leave and top session players were brought in to help record *Avalon*, another impressive, polished and highly professional piece of work. It was issued in 1982 to a mixed reception, the title track making No 13 in the UK (following the success of another classic track, *More Than This* (No 6) earlier in the year).

A number of compilations (notably 1986's UK chart-topping *Street Life*) and a couple of lack luster live LPs were the last heard from Roxy in the eighties. Manzanera and Mackay formed a short-lived soundalike group, the Explorers, and Ferry continued slowly on his solo way with *Boys And Girls* (1985) and *Bête Noire* (1987).

Roxy Music had proved one of the most influential groups of the seventies before metamorphosing into a hip easy listening outfit in the eighties. Since Ferry had previously reunited with his partners when his solo career seemed to be faltering, a nineties re-formation remained a possibility.

RECOMMENDED RECORDINGS
Roxy Music*
For Your Pleasure*
Stranded*
Country Life*
Siren*
Viva *(live)*
Greatest Hits
Manifesto*
Flesh And Blood*
Avalon
(*also available in seven-disc boxed set)
(Bryan Ferry solo)
These Foolish Things
Boys And Girls
Bête Noire

Top left: Founder-member, and brilliant saxophonist, Andy Mackay takes center-stage in a UK TV recording.
Left: Roxy Music on stage, one of the most stylish and imaginative bands to emerge in the UK during the seventies.
Right: Bryan Ferry takes a turn on keyboards.

CLIFF RICHARD

*A*t an age when many rock stars would contemplate retirement or a comfortable, easy living on the cabaret circuit, the evergreen Cliff maintains and even increases his status as a great live performer and recording artist. Britain's first rock superstar effortlessly became an accomplished and admired family entertainer. A recent improvement in the quality of his material now means, after a lean spell in the seventies, Cliff can once again expect to make the charts with regularity and his latest albums are every bit as good as (and often better than) those he made twenty or more years ago. Cliff Richard OBE is Britain's greatest rock-and-roll survivor.

Cliff was born Harry Rodger Webb in Lucknow, India in October 1940. Returning to the UK in 1948, the family went to live in Cheshunt, Hertfordshire, and, after schooling, Harry went to work as a clerk. He discovered rock and roll, like just about everyone else in Britain, through the records of Bill Haley and Elvis Presley and played in skiffle groups before forming a band of his own with friends, The Drifters. They were resident at Butlin's holiday camp in Clacton in 1958, and then impressed agent, George Canjou, with a performance at the Shepherd's Bush Odeon in London. Cliff was the best of the many Presley imitators he'd noted and a recording contract with EMI's Columbia label followed in August. On tour, they were billed as Cliff Richard and The Drifters. Ian Samwell, one of the backing group's guitarists, penned the first hit single, *Move It*, still one of the best things Cliff has ever recorded. It made No 2 that year. Recorded with only one member of The Drifters (the rest were session men) it can justly claim to be Britain's first true rock-and-roll record.

Booked as a support act to the Kalin Twins on a national tour, Cliff made some important changes to his backing band. Samwell and Terry Smart (drums) were retained, but the others were replaced by two guitarists from Newcastle – Brian Marvin (known as Hank B.) and Bruce Welch.

Also on the bill were the Most Brothers and they included a talented guitarist and drummer: Jet Harris and Tony Meehan. After playing with Cliff during the tour, they joined his backing band to replace Samwell and Smart.

They had three more rock singles in the UK chart: *High Class Baby* (No 7); *Livin' Lovin' Doll* (No 20) and *Mean Streak/Never Mind* (No 10).

Then top songwriter, Lionel Bart, came up with the catchy pop number that was to give Cliff his first No 1; *Living Doll* made the top in July 1959 (and No 30 in the USA). Its success, and that of *Travellin' Light* (another No 1 later that year) were aided by regular appearances on the TV pop show *Oh Boy*, nationwide tours, and Cliff's film debut in *Serious Charge* where he sang *Living Doll*.

By 1960, they were Britain's first rock superstars, so much so that a change of name was needed to avoid confusion with the American vocal group, The Drifters. It was Jet Harris who came up with the new name – they were, after all, very much in Cliff's shadow. But that situation was to change. The same year, the Shadows recorded a Jerry Lordan instrumental called *Apache*, and had a No 1 in their own right. With it, Hank Marvin set the style for all aspiring guitarists.

In the early sixties both Cliff and The Shadows appeared, Presley-fashion, in films. The title songs from *The Young Ones* (1962) and *Summer Holiday* (1963) contributed to the eight No 1 hits secured in Britain by 1968 (he had registered no less than 43 hits in all by that date).

Above: Cliff and Norrie Paramor collect one of his first gold discs.
Right: Rock's great survivor.

Between 1960 and 1965, every one of his single releases made the top ten, and memorable No 1s were *Please Don't Tease* (1960), *Bachelor Boy* (1962), and *The Minute You're Gone* (1965).

The Shadows had instrumental success with 24 hits in eight years, including four No 1s in addition to *Apache*: 1961's *Kon Tiki*; the wistful *Wonderful Land* of 1962; *Dance On* (1963); and, their last chart-topper, 1963's *Foot Tapper*.

During 1962 Jet Harris and Tony Meehan set off on a career as a duo. Meehan was replaced by Brian Bennett on drums, but Bruce 'Licorice' Locking's tenure on bass was brief, and John Rostill took his place.

Although Cliff's popularity withstood the coming of Merseybeat and British rhythm and blues, he could never achieve comparable success in the United States. By the mid-sixties his transformation from leather-and-sideburns rocker into clean-cut, clean-living entertainer was well under way, especially, following his much-publicized conversion to Christianity.

Far left: The best of the British Elvis imitators.
Left and above: The sixties college boy look,
and the lean rocker of 1983.
Overleaf: Cliff in concert, ever more energetic
and polished, and always great entertainment.

The years of progressive rock left him behind but, thanks to a TV series of his own (which was responsible for introducing Olivia Newton-John to the world at large) he remained a top attraction, representing the UK twice in the Eurovision Song Contest. His 1968 entry, *Congratulations*, went to No 1. That year The Shadows decided to disband, although they occasionally reunited for special performances and to back Cliff. Marvin and Welch got together with Australian John Farrar, in a threesome which enjoyed some success in the early seventies, but all three soon became involved in other projects, Welch producing some of the finest of Cliff's later albums. In 1977, EMI released the generous compilation album, *Twenty Golden Greats*, and it shot to the top of the UK album chart. The Shadows re-formed to capitalize on the success and played a sell-out tour! Surprise hit singles followed for them in 1978 and 1979 with *Don't Cry For Me Argentina* and *Theme From the Deer Hunter (Cavatina)*.

Although all his singles releases made the top twenty during the early seventies, it was a 1976 hit that truly re-established Cliff as a force in rock music: the poignant *Miss You Nights* made No 15 and was followed the same year by the raw, up-tempo, *Devil Woman* which made No 9 in the UK and gave him his first, long-awaited American top-ten entry (No 6). The album *I'm Nearly Famous* was a rousing return to good-time rock and roll, and a superb production by Bruce Welch. The follow-up LP, *Every Face Tells A Story*, showed the same qualities and suddenly Cliff Richard was a name you could mention again in fashionable rock circles. He became the first Western rock-and-roll performer to tour the Soviet Union.

40 Golden Greats, released in 1977, was a predictably huge seller, topping the UK album charts, and the single *My Kinda Life* reached No 14. Celebrating twenty years at the top in 1978, Cliff released his fortieth album, the excellent *Green Light* and reunited with The Shadows for an anniversary concert at the London Palladium. 1979 saw another fine LP, *Rock 'N' Roll Juvenile* and his tenth British No 1, *We Don't Talk Anymore* (US No 7).

In the New Years Honours List of 1980, he was awarded an OBE, and his undying popularity was evident from three weeks of sell-out concerts at the Apollo Theatre in London. Simultaneously, *Carrie* was rising to No 4, while *Dreamin'* added to his American following, reaching No 7 there (UK No 5). A duet single with Olivia Newton-John was less successful, *Suddenly* (from the film *Xanadu*) making No 15 in Britain and No 20 across the Atlantic.

In 1981, the Americans finally took Cliff to their hearts on a sell-out coast-to-coast tour, equaled by a British tour later in the year. Singles success came with *Wired For Sound* going to No 4 (title track from another well-constructed album), and *Daddy's Home* (No 2). Two more top-twenty entries came in 1982.

By 1983 Cliff had enjoyed 25 years at the top of his profession, his still-youthful good looks a tribute to the virtues of clean living! This broad-based family appeal shows no sign of diminishing and there is no reason why he shouldn't still add to those 80-odd hit singles and 40-odd albums. His latest LPs, *So Far So Good, Dressed For The Occasion* and *Silver* show no flagging of inspiration or polished musicianship. *True Love Ways* (No 8) and a duet with Phil Everly, *She Means Nothing To Me*, (No 9) added to

those hit singles during 1983, and he's one of the best live performers around.

The eighties saw duets with Sarah Brightman, Elton John and Janet Jackson, an appearance in the musical *Time*, a remake of *Living Doll* with alternative comedians the Young Ones (a 1986 No 1 in Britain 27 years after the original), his 100th single release and, late in the decade, some of his most popular LPs ever. Three Christmas chart-topping singles from 1988-90 with *Mistletoe And Wine, Do They Know It's Christmas?* (Band Aid) and *Saviour's Day* made him even more of an institution. *The Event*, a double LP of a live show celebrating his 30th year in showbiz, was yet another big seller. We haven't seen the last of Cliff.

RECOMMENDED RECORDINGS

(Cliff Richard)
Cliff's Hit Album (compilation)
The Young Ones
Summer Holiday
40 Golden Greats (compilation)
I'm Nearly Famous
Every Face Tells A Story
Green Light
Rock 'N' Roll Juvenile
I'm No Hero
Wired For Sound
Dressed For The Occasion
So Far . . . So Good
Silver
(The Shadows)
20 Golden Greats (compilation)
Rockin' With Curly Leads
Specs Appeal

STATUS QUO

S tatus Quo are something of a phenomenon (and anachronism) in British rock music. For many years they've defied the trends, and the critics, retaining a passionately loyal following and achieving steady commercial success. To many, their music is trite, tediously repetitive, and utterly characterless: rock dinosaurs who haven't had an original thought for a decade. Their flag-waving fans, however, disagree. They regard their crashing, relentless twelve-bar boogie as quite the most exciting and entertaining thing pop music has to offer, and prove it by putting almost every one of their albums into the British top five. The critics, they say, are snobs and poseurs.

Simple music for simple minds; or good, earthy, working-class heavy metal? Whatever, any band that can claim the heir to the throne of England as a fan (non-headbanging variety) can't be all bad.

Above: Guitarist, Rick Parfitt and behind him the band's co-founder, Francis Rossi.

Right: Francis Rossi – rocking all over the world.
Below: Lancaster admires Rossi's flying mane!

Francis Rossi, son of an ice-cream vendor, and Alan Lancaster met at school in south London and formed a band at the age of twelve in 1962. They called themselves The Scorpions, with Rossi on guitar and Lancaster on bass. With two more friends on organ and drums, they later became the Spectres. In September of that year they met up with drummer John Coghlan who was rehearsing with a band of his own in a room next door to them. There was mutual appreciation, and due agreement to form a group from members of both outfits. In April 1965, Roy Lynes joined on keyboards.

Turning professional in 1966, they cut three long-forgotten singles for Pye before changing the name of the band to Traffic and then, to avoid a clash with Stevie Winwood and Dave Mason's group of the same name, to Traffic Jam. Another single made little impression on British record buyers and they were forced to do gigs around the coastal holiday camps during the summer and play support to visiting American performers.

In November 1967 Rick Parfitt joined Rossi (who called himself Mike) on guitar and vocals, and in the August they changed the name of the band to Status Quo. The breakthrough came in early 1968 with a bit of Rossi-penned psychedelia entitled *Pictures of Matchstick Men* (much wah-wah, fuzz and phased vocals and their only US hit, a No 12). It was an international top-ten hit, and the follow up, *Ice In The Sun,* if not of quite the same standard, was

STATUS QUO

also successful.

But it was short-lived success: the inspiration dried up. The band took time out to rethink their futures and emerged in 1970, minus Roy Lynes, as a straight twelve-bar boogie outfit, unashamedly musically unambitious with no pretensions to profundity. They scored an immediate hit with *Down the Dustpipe*. They took their brand of high-voltage pop around the club and college circuit, culminating in a fine performance at the 1972 Reading Festival.

Moving to the Vertigo label, 1973 saw the Quo's first LP success with *Piledriver*, which aptly summed up their style! It was followed by three hit singles: *Paper Plane, Mean Girl* and the rollicking *Caroline*. But the basic jaunty, uncomplicated formula was applied to all three and, despite the withering reprobation of rock critics, their 1974 recordings made the top of the UK album chart with *Quo* and *On The Level* and the singles chart with *Down Down*. Between 1974 and 1979, Andy Brown joined them off-and-on to add keyboards to the line-up. 1976 saw hit singles with *Rain* and *Mystery Song* and another No 1 album, *Blue For You*.

There is no disputing that their resurgence in the late seventies and early eighties was largely due to the general popularity of heavy metal, but a run of eight successive albums in the UK top five is no mean achievement. *Something 'bout You Baby I Like* and *What You're Proposing* also hit the singles charts.

The eighties saw great changes. Pete Kirchner took over the drum stool in 1982, while two years later the group split completely, reforming in '85 for Live Aid. But when they returned in earnest it was without Alan Lancaster.

Parfitt, Rossi and Brown continued with a new rhythm section of Jeff Rich (drums) and 'Rhino' Edwards (bass) from the Climax Blues Band, and celebrated their quarter-century in the business in 1990 with the single *Anniversary Waltz* and platinum compilation *Rocking All Over The Years*.

In 1991 they dressed in tuxedos for the BPI's Outstanding Contribution to British Music award, while 1992 saw them enter the *Guinness Book of Records* for playing four gigs across Britain on a single day to tie in with their aptly titled LP *Rock Till You Drop*. British rock without Status Quo seemed unthinkable.

RECOMMENDED RECORDINGS	
Piledriver	
Rockin' All Over The World	
Twelve Gold Bars	
On The Level	
Never Too Late	

Above: Alan Lancaster was a Quo founder member and gave his all.
Right: Rossi's hair rises to the occasion in another burst of 12-bar boogie.
Below: Parfitt and Lancaster enjoy a fast-fingered jam.

DURAN DURAN

*A*t one time, Duran Duran seemed the band most likely to survive teen-idol status and the new romantic cult and broaden both their musical base and their audience appeal. They produced above-average, bright and entertaining material, looked stunning and enjoyed good recordings. They were also forerunners in producing successful pop videos.

Birmingham was the band's starting-off point in 1978, specifically the fashionable haunt of the new romantics, the Rum Runner Club, owned by the Berrow brothers who eventually came to manage the band. Sixteen-year-old Nick Rhodes (synthesizer), and eighteen-year-old John Taylor (then guitar, now bass) were the founders, taking the name Duran Duran from the villain in the film *Barbarella*. Steve Duffy joined them on vocals and Simon Colley on bass. Duffy was soon replaced by vocalist Andy Wicket and the band was augmented by Roger Taylor (drums). Andy Taylor was recruited on guitar after answering an advertisement in *Melody Maker*, enabling John to move to bass. The sudden departure of Andy Wicket then necessitated a search for a new lead vocalist and Simon Le Bon was chosen.

Duran Duran appeared at the 1980 Edinburgh festival and then supported a Hazel O'Connor tour. The same year EMI signed them up and issued a first single, *Planet Earth*, early in 1981. It was an auspicious debut, reaching No 12 in the UK and No 1 in Australia, and was followed by a tour in March 1981. The band added three more hit singles in the same year, *Careless Memories, Girls On Film* (No 5) and *My Own Way* (No 14). A second UK tour took place in the autumn of 1981.

Their career took off in the United States in 1982, where new romanticism was just becoming the vogue, with *Hungry Like The Wolf*. It made No 3 in America and No 5 in the UK, their following in the US undoubtedly helped by showings of their videos on American TV.

Although the follow-up did little in the US, *Save A Prayer* took them to No 2, their highest placing yet in Britain. In 1981 a debut album, *Duran Duran*, which included their first three single hits, predictably made the charts, as did *Rio* whose title track made No 9 in the UK and No 14 in the US. *Rio* also included the hit singles, *My Own Way* and *Hungry Like The Wolf*.

A first world tour began in Australia during April 1982, and lasted eight months. Another best-selling, if not so musically inspired, album

followed in 1983, *Seven And The Ragged Tiger*. The band finally hit the UK No 1 spot in March 1983 with *Is There Something I Should Know?* – completing a sequence of eight consecutive hit singles, all their own original compositions. The ninth, *Union Of The Snake*, enjoyed similar success toward the end of 1983, as did an eleven-track videotape album.

In 1985 the band went their separate ways: Andy Taylor and John Taylor produced a record with Tony Thompson on drums and Robert Palmer singing under the name Power Station. It produced hits in Britain and the US, including Marc Bolan's classic, *Get It On*. The rest of the band – Le Bon, Rhodes and Taylor – continued into the nineties under the name

Top: Duran Duran launching another of their highly professional videos.
Right: Lead singer, Simon le Bon.
Above: From left, Andy Taylor, Roger Taylor, John Taylor, Simon le Bon and Nick Rhodes.

Arcadia. Though no longer chart fixtures, they scored US top-five singles with *Notorious* (1987) and *I Don't Want Your Love* (1988), and UK top ten hits with the single *All She Wants Is* (1989) and LP *Liberty*.

RECOMMENDED RECORDINGS
Rio
Decade *(compilation)*

EURYTH-MICS

The unlikely combination of bearded, unkempt musician David A Stewart and close-cropped, highly visual vocalist Annie Lennox, otherwise known as Eurythmics, turned in some of the eighties' classic chart singles. Stewart (earlier in folk-rockers Longdancer) and waitress Lennox met at the height of punk in 1977, and out of their personal relationship came The Tourists, who made three albums and had a big UK hit with a cover of Dusty Springfield's I Only Want To Be With You. *It wouldn't be long before the couple would become one of the most distinctive and respected partnerships in rock music, whose technical skill and mastery of lyrics have earned them global success.*

Continuing as a duo after the Tourists' 1980 split, they took a new name (from a form of dance-mime fusion) and moved quickly from traditional guitar-based sounds into more experimental synthesized pop of their debut *In The Garden* (1981) and the more assured *Sweet Dreams (Are Made Of This)* (1982) which spawned *Love Is A Stranger* and a US chart-topping title track. As the love affair ended, the musical relationship flowered: Lennox's androgynous image worked well in the fast-arriving video age, notably her cross-dressing in *Who's That Girl?* from 1983's UK chart-topping *Touch*.

Their meteoric rise slowed somewhat as the *Touch Dance* remix album failed to sell and their soundtrack for *1984* was rejected by the film-makers (a compromise was eventually reached). But 1985's *There Must Be An Angel* was their first UK No 1 from the *Be Yourself Tonight* album, which also included a torrid duet between Lennox and soul diva Aretha Franklin, *Sisters Are Doing It For Themselves*.

Sales started falling with the less inspired albums *Revenge* and *Savage*, but 1989's *We Two Are One* deservedly put them back on top of the British album chart. A *Greatest Hits* collection repeated that feat for much of 1991 and went multi-platinum, but by then Lennox – married and with a child – was recording her solo debut and Stewart was a much in-demand producer working with Tom Petty, Dylan, Geldof and more. He also had an instrumental film hit with Dutch saxophonist Candy Dulfer, *Lily Was Here*, and cut two solo albums as the Spiritual Cowboys.

Now domiciled in the States with wife Siobhan Fahey (ex-Bananarama, and now of Shakespears Sister), Stewart suggested in 1992 that the Eurythmics teaming was over for good – and if so this would be a significant loss to British pop.

Above: Few artists can bring as much intensity to a performance as Annie Lennox.
Right: A trained singer, Annie is a talent in her own right, but her partnership with Dave Stewart produced one of the most accomplished acts in rock.

RECOMMENDED RECORDINGS
Sweet Dreams (Are Made Of This)
Be Yourself Tonight
We Two Are One
Greatest Hits

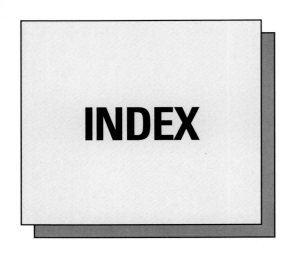

INDEX

CREDITS

The publisher would like to thank Jane Alexander, the editor, Adrian Hodgkins, the designer, P Murphy for preparing the index and David Redfern for his help in supplying and choosing most of the illustrations.

DR refers to David Redfern Photography throughout.

David Redfern Photography pp 6-7, 20, 21, 23, 24, 25, 30, 31 (top), 32 (all three), 36, 39 (both), 42, 44 (top and left), 45 (top left and right), 46, 47 (all three), 48 (below), 49, 52-53, 56-57, 58, 59 (all three), 60, 64, 65, 67 (all three), 68, 69 (top), 75 (left), 78, 79, 81 (right), 82 (top left), 86 (both), 88 (top), 92, 93, 100, 101, 102-103, 104 (top), 110-111 (all five), 119 (top), 121 (top), 126 (below), 127 (both), 128 (all three), 129, 132, 133, 134 (right), 135, 136 (both), 137, 138, 139 (all three), 141 (top), 142 (right), 143, 144, 146 (below), 149 (both), 150, 151 (both), 152 (all three), 153, 160, 161, 162, 163, 164, 165, 167, 170, 171 (both), 172-173, 176 (both), 181, 185 (both), 186 (left), 189 (both), 194-195, 199, 200 (both), 201, 203 (top), 204, 205, 206 (top), 208, 209, 210, 211 (both), 212 (top), 213, 221
DR, photo Richard Aaron pp 27, 54 (right), 69 (below right), 70, 74 (bottom), 75 (bottom right), 81 (top and below left), 83, 89, 90, 91 (both), 116-117 (all three), 118 (top), 119 (below), 130
DR, photo Cyrus Andrews pp 22, 40, 54 (left), 72, 73 (below), 80, 140, 142 (top left), 166 (top), 183, 186-187, 188
DR, photo Joel Axelrad p 37
DR, photo Joel Axelrad/Retna pp 74 (top), 75 (top right)
DR, photo James Barrow p 73 (top)
DR, photo Keith Bernstein pp 109 (right), 114 (both), 203 (below)
DR, photo Garry Brandon p 71 (top)
DR, photo Joel Brodsky p 62
DR, photo Mike Cameron, p 71 (bottom)
DR, photo Fin Costello p 16 (top)
DR, photo Peter Cronin pp 44 (top), 120 (top and right), 141 (below right)
DR, photo David Ellis pp 14, 38 (below), 43 (right), 66, 87, 88 (below), 104 (below), 105 (top), 134 (left), 169, 177, 192, 193, 207, 214 (both), 215
DR, photo Collin Fuller p 105 (top)
DR, photo Suzi Gibbons pp 131 (top left & right), 196, 197 (bottom), 198
DR, photo Mick Hutson pp 16 (bottom), 17, 28 (left), 131 (bottom left)
DR, photo Bob King pp 197 (top), 220
DR, photo Rafael Macia pp 45, 184
DR, photo Stephen Morley pp 10, 11, 19, 31 (below), 33, 41, 43 (left), 55 (top), 69 (below left), 106-107, 108 (both), 109 (left), 114, 121 (bottom two), 132, 191 (right)
DR, photo Mike Prior pp 55 (top), 77 (center right), 94-95 (all four), 96-97 (all three), 125, 206 (below), 216 (both), 217
DR, photo Andrew Putler pp 26, 82 (cover and right), 98-99 (all three), 122-123, 124, 126 (top), 166 (below), 168 (left), 212 (below)
DR, photo Max Redfern pp 119 (top), 202
DR, photo Rob Verhorst pp 28 (right), 29
AP Worldwide pp 8-9 (all three), 50, 51, 63 (below), 148 (bottom), 157 (top right), 159 (below), 218 (below)
CBS pp 18, 19, 63 (top)
Decca International p 177-178
EMI p 61
Epic p 13
London Features International pp 15, 112 (top, Scott Downie), 112 (bottom, Neal Preston), 113 (Ken Regan)
Michael Ochs Archive pp 34 (both), 35, 148 (top two), 154-155, 156-157 (main pic), 158 (both), 159 (top), 178, 179, 180
Proteus Publishing p 182 (both)
RCA p 190
Retna, photo M Rutland p 84-85 (below)
Retna, photo K Taback p 85 (top right)
Retna, photo Rocky Widner p 77 (top left)
Retna, photo Richard Young p 84 (top)
SKR Photo/LFI p 145, 146
SKR/Retna pp 146 (top), 147 (top)
Stiff Records p 120 (left)
Tamla Motown p 12